Reliability in Pragmatics

OXFORD STUDIES IN SEMANTICS AND PRAGMATICS

GENERAL EDITORS: Chris Barker, *New York University*, and Chris Kennedy, *University of Chicago*

PUBLISHED

IN PREPARATION

Reliability in Pragmatics

ERIC McCREADY

OXFORD
UNIVERSITY PRESS

UNIVERSITY PRESS

Great Clarendon Street, Oxford, OX2 6DP,
United Kingdom

Oxford University Press is a department of the University of Oxford.
It furthers the University's objective of excellence in research, scholarship,
and education by publishing worldwide. Oxford is a registered trade mark of
Oxford University Press in the UK and in certain other countries

First Edition published in 2015
Impression: 1

Published in the United States of America by Oxford University Press
198 Madison Avenue, New York, NY 10016, United States of America

British Library Cataloguing in Publication Data
Data available

Library of Congress Control Number: 2014938177

ISBN 978-0-19-870283-2 (Hbk)
ISBN 978-0-19-870284-9 (Pbk)

Printed and bound by
CPI Group (UK) Ltd, Croydon, CR0 4YY

Contents

General Preface

Oxford Studies in Semantics and Pragmatics publishes original research on meaning in natural language within contemporary semantics and pragmatics. Authors present their work in the context of past and present lines of inquiry and in a manner accessible both to scholars whose core areas of expertise are in linguistic semantics and pragmatics, and to researchers in related and allied fields such as syntax, lexicology, philosophy, and cognitive science. The series emphasizes rigorous theoretical analysis grounded in detailed empirical investigation of particular languages.

This is a companion series to *Oxford Surveys in Semantics and Pragmatics*. The *Surveys* series provides critical overviews of the major approaches to core semantic and pragmatic phenomena, a discussion of their relative value, and an assessment of the degree of consensus that exists about any one of them. The *Studies* series equally seeks to put empirical complexity and theoretical debate into comprehensible perspective, but with a narrower focus and correspondingly greater depth. In both series, authors develop and defend the approach and line of argument which they find most convincing and productive.

This book is about the reliability of what we say to one another. Starting from first principles of cooperative behavior, McCready develops a pragmatic model of communication in which we track each other's accuracy across multiple encounters. On this view, explicitly withholding full endorsement of one's own assertions (that is, various forms of hedging) can serve to protect one's reputation for reliability. McCready goes on to apply this general pragmatic view to the semantics of evidential marking, that is, the ways in which some languages grammatically encode the source of the evidence supporting the content of an utterance. This leads to an innovative formal model of dynamic update on which we each maintain multiple pictures of how the world might be, one for each potentially fallible source of information. Evidentiality marking helps us manage these alternatives, in particular, contributing to preferences for guiding belief acquisition when the individual pictures don't agree. Though the discussions are theoretically sophisticated, technically explicit, and fully precise, the writing throughout is both clear and clear-headed, emphasizing insight and approachability. The end result is a comprehensive synthesis of the pragmatic and semantic aspects of our need to explicitly negotiate the reliability of our words.

Preface

The idea for this book started with a packet of KitKats. These particular KitKats, sold at some convenience store somewhere in Tokyo, were green tea flavored (I didn't buy them, so I don't know if this refers to the chocolate or to the cookie part, or both). The packet depicted a whirlpool of green tea receding into the depths of the box, with some green KitKats suspended above the liquid. There was an inscription: "This picture is an image," meaning that the image on the packet was not a direct representation of the contents. Well, perhaps not. I imagined an irate consumer who expected to be sucked down into green tea world on ripping off the foil. Surely there could be no such person. But what then was the point of the disclaimer? And . . . what could possibly be the point of disclaimers in general? How could they work? After all, they essentially indicate that the producer isn't willing to take responsibility for what the advertisement says. How could such a thing assist in advertising? Wouldn't it just cause everyone to ignore what was being said? And if not, why not? The linguistic connection to hedging is obvious, and many of the questions there are the same. The first part of the book arose directly from this puzzlement, together with a fortuitous invitation to speak at Szklarska Poreba, which gave me an opportunity to start exploring the idea. I eventually noticed that the mechanisms invoked there related closely to other issues I had been worrying about in the context of how to process evidentially marked sentences; this led to the work reported on in the second part of the book. Drawing the connections out and mapping the territory they define has been enjoyable; I hope that the book successfully makes the case that the boundaries the project sets are natural and yield a non-gerrymandered analytical domain. The book itself has been a pleasure to write, at least most of the time. In general the whole project of exploring this literature has been enjoyable. I thank the series editors and Oxford University Press for giving the opportunity, and John Davey and Julia Steer for making the editorial process painless (at least from my side).

I also want to thank, for advice and/or comments: several anonymous reviewers (especially the two reviewers for OUP, who provided extensive and useful comments), Nicholas Asher, Patrick Caudal, David Etlin, Michael Franke, Hans-Martin Gärtner, Jonathan Ginzberg, Daniel

Gutzmann, Makoto Kanazawa, Magda Kaufmann, Chris Kennedy, Chungmin Lee, Toshiyuki Miyake, Midori Morita, Anna Pilikova, Jason Quinley, Stephanie Solt, Yasutada Sudo, Chris Tancredi, Shigeo Tonoike, Linton Wang, Stephen Wechsler, Gregoire Winterstein, Henk Zeevat, Ede Zimmermann, Malte Zimmermann, audiences at Szklarska Poreba 11, National Chung Cheng University, NII, University of Chicago, University of Frankfurt, University of Paris 7, anyone not mentioned here but thanked elsewhere in the book, and anyone else I have forgotten. Thanks also to Aoyama Gakuin University for giving me leave in 2011–2012 to work on the book (also, the final part of the preparation process was partially funded by JSPS Kiban C Grant #25370441). Thanks most of all to Midori, Kai, Colin, and Tyler for putting up with the time I took away from our lives together to write this book. And thanks to you, the reader, for putting some of your own time into reading it.

The book is dedicated to Norry Ogata. Before he passed away, we planned to work out some of the issues addressed in chapter 7 together. Though the realization here is not precisely the one he championed in our discussions on the topic, I guess he would have liked the way I have done things. I am not the only one to be sad that he is not around to see this work.

How dangerous credible voices are, authoritative voices, voices that never lie, as if waiting for the day when the time has come and it is really worth the trouble, and then effortlessly they persuade us of the most far-fetched or poisonous things.

Javier Marías, Dark Back of Time

1

Introduction

This book is concerned with two sets of phenomena. The first relate to cooperation and cooperativity in linguistic practice. The second involve evidence and its natural language expression, evidentiality. I will argue that, from a certain perspective, these phenomena are closely related at a deep level.

This relationship might not be obvious at first glance. What could cooperation and evidentiality have in common? The first is pragmatic, the second semantic, or so the story usually goes. But both have a key common feature. Our behavior with respect to a speaker will differ depending on whether we take her to be cooperative. Similarly, our behavior with respect to an evidence source will differ depending on whether we take it to be reliable in the information it transmits. Both of these judgements are mediated by past experience of reliability: reliability qua conversational participant in the first case, and reliability qua information source in the second. This process of judging reliability, and its linguistic consequences, are the focus of this book.

1.1 Cooperation

Pragmatic tools are by now indispensable in the toolkit of the formal linguist interested in meaning. They are, of course, used in the analysis of core pragmatic phenomena like conversational implicature and speech acts, but also much more generally; for example, assertability has been used as a component of explanations of the ungrammaticality of certain kinds of trivial sentences (Gajewski 2002). Here, the notion of a reasonable discourse move plays a key role, and, behind it, the notion of cooperativity, as it is taken for granted that cooperative speakers will not attempt certain kinds of conversational moves.

The use of the notion of cooperation in pragmatics can of course be traced back to Grice (1975). Here is a familiar quotation from this fount of the modern view of pragmatics:

Make your conversational contribution such as is required, at the stage at which it occurs, by the accepted purpose or direction of the talk exchange in which you are engaged.

This is the *Cooperative Principle*. One might wonder about the extent to which this principle is justified. Do all people follow it? Some have called its universality into question, such as Ochs (Keenan) (1976), who discusses what she views as a consistent violation of Gricean Quantity by speakers of Malagasy. This conclusion is criticized, in my view convincingly, by Prince (1982). But one may still wonder whether the assumption of cooperativity fails under some circumstances, and, if so, what unifying features those circumstances might have. Still more generally, what justifies assuming cooperativity in the first place, under any circumstances at all? Communication is usually thought of as a mostly cooperative activity. My goal is to pass along to you a piece of information that I take to be true; your goal is to recover the information I intend to pass along. The benefits of doing so are obvious, at least for the hearer. The cooperative nature of this activity is reflected in standard models of convention in communication, both human and animal. The most common model here is that of a signaling game (e.g. Lewis 1969; van Rooij 2004). Here the basic idea is that the goal of speakers and hearers is to coordinate on signals for describing the world; the goal of both individuals involved is for all participants in the game to have true knowledge of the facts. Indeed, this does cover much of communicative activity, and certainly it is a useful model when thinking about how signals might evolve (Skyrms 1996).

Things are not always so clear-cut. A speaker may intend to deceive. Lying is always an option, even if there are consequences as clearly defined as one might find in a court of law. We often find signals sent with deceitful intent. This situation also arises with animals: species as disparate as vervet monkeys and mantis shrimp produce signals with "nonfactual" meanings (Krebs and Davies 1993). It is clear that such behavior comes with penalties if repeated or performed for malicious reasons (i.e. for reasons not intended to produce benefit for a given social group of which the communicator is a member). For example, it has been shown via experimental studies that vervet monkeys eventually stop responding when a signal is produced (via recorded stimuli) in the absence of the proper trigger (Cheney and Seyfarth 1990). The same observation is reflected in the story of "the boy who cried wolf": eventually, the boy's signals were disregarded, with negative consequences for the communicator. In more normal situations, we also find cases like attempts to mislead the police and communication taking place in various other kinds of settings where full cooperation is not expected (see Asher and Lascarides 2013). Given all this, what can we say in general about cooperativity? The aim of chapter 2 is to introduce analyses set within game theory which allow the derivation of cooperative behavior. The basic idea here is that, supposing that agents aim to maximize their personal benefit, it is rational to behave in a cooperative way given the assumptions of a continuing interaction, a means for the agents to monitor each other's behavior, and a way to punish agents who aren't cooperative in the requisite way. I will present (versions of) these analyses together with the basic game theory required to understand how they work. We will see that, indeed, cooperativity can be put on a rational basis in a very general way.

But there are contexts in which the situation is more complex. Suppose that you explicitly tell me that what you say is, or might be, false. What could be your motivation for this action, given that your expressed lack of confidence would be expected to reduce the probability that I accept your statement? It doesn't seem obvious that I should then believe what you say, especially if it is obvious that our interests do not coincide. One might be tempted to answer: you shouldn't. By choosing to trust in such situations you open yourself to a good deal of (possibly) unnecessary risk. But, in fact, this lack of trust is not always what we find in human behavior. Chapter 3 aims to understand why it appears rational to come to believe (at least to some extent) content which is asserted but at the same time hedged, in that the speaker explicitly indicates that she lacks complete confidence in her assertion, or even finds its content quite likely to be false. These phenomena turn out to fit naturally into the picture of cooperation presented in chapter 2; in this setting, hedges can be seen as grammatical mechanisms for protecting reputations. By using such protection, a speaker can (try to) ensure that honest mistakes don't destroy the possibility of future trust and cooperation. To this end, I develop a simple model of reputations and how they can be computed from histories of speaker behavior, and proceed to apply it to hedges.

Chapter 3 focuses on hedges that are oriented to truth. Such hedges shield the speaker from blame if it turns out that her assertion fails to represent the facts correctly. These are the sort of thing we usually imagine when the topic of hedging arises. Chapter 4 argues that natural language makes other kinds of hedges available, focusing on the case of so-called biscuit conditionals. Biscuit conditionals have the form of conditionals, but assert their consequents (according to most scholars). Most research on such conditionals has attempted to unify them with other, more familiar, conditional types such as indicative conditionals which indicate the usual kind of conditional dependence between antecedent and consequent. But biscuit conditionals admit paraphrases as hedged assertions, given the right kind of hedge. Truth-oriented hedging can be viewed as hedging over implicatures of truth arising from Gricean Quality. If it is possible to hedge other kinds of implicatures, a natural account of biscuit conditionals arises which treats them as hedges of a special kind. Chapter 4 is devoted to spelling out this idea and considering the effect of hedging other kinds of not clearly truth-conditional content, specifically expressive content and assertions performed with epistemic modals.

The semantically inclined reader might wonder how all this can be achieved. Hedges have the form of ordinary clauses; there is no special grammatical construction or lexical item that invariably indicates a hedge. How then can one derive hedged interpretations (without stipulation)? Chapter 5 proposes an approach to the compositional (or semi-compositional) interpretation of hedges. This approach has two essential ingredients. It begins with the observation that there is no way to interpret a hedged assertion of the form $\varphi \wedge \Diamond \neg \varphi$ in a way consistent with standard assumptions about norms of assertion; in short, a claim like this one is Moore-paradoxical and will result in infelicity in the absence of some change in interpretation. I argue that the parenthetical nature of the hedge and its consequent interpretation as a nonasserted conventional implicature allows just such a change: the problematic clause can be reanalyzed as a hedge. Chapter 5 spells this idea out, together with a new picture of the process of information transfer between speech acts and linguistic content.

1.2 Evidentiality

The first part of the book is concerned with cooperativity. As described above, it turns out that there are grammatical phenomena relating to cooperation. This observation provides a new illustration of the close relationship between the conventional information given by semantic content and the reasoning and judgements about speaker behavior in their use of language characteristic of pragmatics.[1] The particular analysis in this first part involves inductive reasoning about interactional histories. The second part of this book is concerned with an interestingly similar set of facts relating to a set of grammatical phenomena which exhibit very similar patterns of reasoning. These are the evidentials: roughly, expressions which indicate a speaker's source of justification for the speech act being made. There, I argue that there are close parallels between judgements about cooperativity and judgements about the reliability of justification which show themselves in linguistic behavior.

The relation between the meaning and use of evidentials and the notion of evidence itself is complex and difficult. Chapter 6 is concerned largely with some essential facts about evidentials and evidence. It provides an (opinionated) overview of some aspects of the space of evidential constructions and meanings as they are currently understood in formal semantics and pragmatics. My main aim in this chapter is to summarize some results in the theory of evidentials, and also to indicate some unresolved problems which I will address in the rest of the book.

How do evidentials relate to the sources of evidence which they mark? This relationship is usually taken for granted in the literature: use of an evidential marking e-type evidence indicates that the speaker has information acquired from an e-type evidence source. This is enough for the semantic analysis of these constructions. But what about their pragmatics? People often have information coming from multiple sources; which evidential should they use? And how does the presence of evidential marking relate to the likelihood agents assign to the truth of a particular utterance? Pretty clearly, the relation is not fully transparent: one can have experience with how people use evidential sentences, and with how people use evidence, with (in principle) quite different results. Still, I argue, although these two kinds of experience are of quite different characters, they nonetheless behave similarly with respect to the kind of induction assumed in my discussion of cooperativity.

Chapter 7 presents the formal core of a theory of the pragmatics of evidentials, and of evidence-based information acquisition. The theory includes two key elements. The first is a multi tiered system of

---

[1] These observations relate, I think, in interesting ways to current discussions of how implicatures are generated. I won't here explicitly enter into the debate between those who believe that implicatures are grammatical in nature and those who believe they come from pragmatic reasoning (though the theoretical positions I have taken in this book probably betray my inclinations).

dynamic update which, to my knowledge, does not have a precedent in linguistic applications. In this system, global belief states consist of possibly many substates, each of which is updated dynamically by information acquired via a particular evidence source; updates themselves are carried out using the notion of preference upgrade. These substates—evidential selves, as it were, if one takes seriously the idea of individuals as conglomerates—are then combined using techniques from belief aggregation, where a priority ordering on the substates privileges this evidence source over that in case of conflict. This ordering is, by hypothesis, derived from the reliability of the evidence sources that comprise it, by way of the probability that information coming from that source is true. The resulting system is shown to be able to handle a number of potentially puzzling cases of the use of evidentials, and of evidence, given certain principles of evidential usage.

Some problems remain after this presentation of the core theory. One telling issue can be seen by considering the notion of "best possible grounds" for a belief, which has been applied in the analysis of direct evidentials. Ordinarily, perceptual evidence is best in this context, for perception is in general the most reliable of our information sources (a claim argued for extensively in the epistemological literature). The best possible grounds for a proposition can vary depending on the circumstances of evaluation: for example, given that a particular individual is consistently and extraordinarily reliable as a testifier, the probability of a particular piece of his testimony being accurate will slowly rise, even to the point where it can overshadow certain kinds of perceptual evidence (though perhaps for only a limited domain). This change in perceived reliability can lead to a new ranking of information sources, and consequently to shifts in what counts as the best possible grounds for a particular claim. But the system of chapter 7 has no direct way to model these changes. Chapter 8 rectifies this situation by allowing changes in probabilities due to conditionalization. In general, the content of interactional histories will change the perceived reliability of testimonial agents; something similar can be said for evidence sources in general, a topic also explored in this chapter.

The book concludes with chapter 10, a brief summary of the book's contents and a speculation or two for the future. Before that, though, chapter 9 brings the two strands of the book together with an explicit consideration of testimonial evidence. There, I begin by situating the theory developed in this book within philosophical theories of testimony; it turns out to be (by my diagnosis) a "hybrid" theory with both reductionist and anti-reductionist elements. I compare it to some views in the philosophical literature and show that it satisfies a number of criteria that have been proposed for a proper theory of testimony. I then turn to a kind of paradox of testimony. Certain nonreductionist views of testimony, including my own, which supports the idea by the utility of cooperative behavior, suppose that testimony should be believed in the absence of reasons not to do so. The same should, perhaps, hold for hearsay evidentials. But another strand of work on hearsay evidentials leads us to believe that they implicate that the speaker has relatively little confidence in the evidential prejacent. What then should be believed? This dilemma proves to have an extremely simple resolution in my theory, once it is observed that information coming from testimonial agents can also be associated with distinct information sources. This observation necessitates distinguishing two different kinds of substates. After spelling out the required complications, I finally turn to a consideration of the content of hedged assertions and the degree of belief they should inspire; the claim is that a natural model is available of update with hedged content within this system that captures, simultaneously, the binary quality of hedging together with the continuous feel of the beliefs hedged content can inspire. This second part of the book thus deepens the views of the first, and brings out some deep connections between hedging and evidentiality.

The first half of the book takes its primary formal inspiration from the theory of repeated games. An important feature of the second half of the book is its heavy use of techniques from formal epistemology and the philosophical literature on testimony, itself epistemological in quality. In general, there seems to be surprisingly little interaction between epistemologists and researchers in formal semantics and pragmatics, especially given the extensive contacts between linguists and philosophers of language (and related areas). Formal epistemologists have developed many tools that would be of obvious utility for linguists; linguists have extensive empirical linguistic data that would likely be useful testing grounds for epistemological hypotheses. The study of evidentials seems to be an obvious overlap where joint work would be productive. One of my hopes for this book is that it will stimulate at least a bit of such traffic. Consequently, I have tried to write it in such a way that its content is accessible (and of interest) to both linguists and philosophers.

1.3 Reliability

The book thus comprises two parts, each with a quite different focus. But, as the preceding summary of the flow of the discussion has shown, there is considerable overlap in the two parts from a formal perspective. Cooperativity is concerned (on my view) with maximizing utility in repeated games, and can be seen as arising from evolutionary considerations; evidentiality is concerned more directly with the reliability of information and how it interacts with belief acquisition, so the appropriate tools are those of dynamic semantics. These are significant differences, and the superficial forms of the theories needed to understand the phenomena are quite different, as the reader will see. But, at a core level, there is a deep similarity in the ways in which judgements about cooperativity and reliability are made.

At the heart of this book is the model of interactional histories which I use in making judgements about reliability and cooperativity. This model is simple. According to it, agents keep records of their experience with information sources of various kinds, including other conversational agents. These records, which I call histories, are simply sequences of elements of the form

$$\langle \varphi, v, \mathcal{P} \rangle$$

where the element φ is the content acquired from the source, the second element indicates the truth or otherwise of φ (and thus can be identified with one of the three options T, F, and ?), and $\mathcal{P}$ is a set of properties which are relevant with respect to the particular interaction. I will often use the projection functions π_1, π_2, and π_3 to pick out elements of these tuples in the sequel.

Given their first elements, histories of this kind are restricted to interactions involving the acquisition of propositional content, and as such are a special case of a more general phenomenon. They contain all the information necessary to perform quite sophisticated reasoning about information sources, even down to particular occasions of use or contents. This kind of reasoning is quite general, and something I take to be a key element of how linguistic communication works: we must judge the reliability of our interlocutors, and of the information we acquire and pass on. As already discussed in brief, there are often grammatical reflexes of these processes, such as evidentiality, one focus of this book. We know that world knowledge plays a deep and essential role in pragmatics: in essence, information about interactional histories is one important, yet little discussed, kind of world knowledge.

The precise kinds of reasoning performed with this world knowledge are up for debate. In this book, I use what amounts to the simplest possibility: induction over histories. Given a certain proportion within a history (or a restriction of a history) of information acquisition events with a particular property, a probability of the next event having that property can be recovered: this probability, when taken with respect to truth, is the reliability of that source. Plainly, this method for judging reliability is simple; likely it is too simple to have genuine psychological reality. Since my goal is the understanding of how linguistic behavior interacts with reputation and reliability, the actual mechanisms of inductive inference are something I cannot pursue in this book. Still, I think my main results will carry over even if the particular decision method is changed.

The structure of the book means that the reader interested in both cooperativity and evidentiality can read straight through. But the reader interested in only one or the other topic must be a bit more selective. If the reader is not concerned with evidentiality, life is easy: the second part of the book can mostly be ignored, though chapter 9 will be of interest due to its focus on testimony and hedging; since that chapter assumes the content of chapters 7 and 8, they must be read first. But at least some of chapter 9 will be accessible without doing so, and most of it will be understandable even after just a skimming of the other chapters. The reader interested in evidentials only should read chapter 3, as it introduces the history models, but then can in principle go directly to the second part of the book. Still, the book is developed mostly in a linear way, and the later chapters refine and extend the earlier ones substantially. In the latter half, only chapter 6 has no direct connection with the first part of the book. To avoid confusion and to make reference somewhat more convenient I have assembled the full and final theoretical framework into a technical appendix. I hope that the book is relatively self-contained, though of necessity acquaintance with current work in semantics and pragmatics is presupposed, and also the mathematical sophistication needed to read that literature, though not, I think (or hope), more.

Part I
Reputation and Cooperation

2

Cooperation

The first part of this book is about cooperation in communication. Standardly, cooperation is viewed from a Gricean perspective within formal linguistics. The aim of this chapter is to show one way in which Gricean cooperation can be justified, which allows later connection to grammatical phenomena which facilitate judgements about cooperativity. Like many others (some of whom will be discussed presently), I will be using game theory to carry out this project; unlike most others, I will primarily focus on games that are repeated many times, as the key notion I will be working with is *reputation*, as an indirect means of increasing the utility of communicative interaction.[1] Cooperation is a very broad notion and a single book cannot do justice to all its aspects (much less half a book). Consequently, I will narrow the focus to a pair of questions and their ramifications. First, from the perspective of a hearer, when is it reasonable to trust the information proffered to us by our interlocutors? Second, from the speaker's side, how can one increase the likelihood of such trust, and what mechanisms does one have available to safeguard any trust that might already exist? I will claim (in line with the work on testimony discussed in chapter 9) that trust is an initial normative assumption, but one that can be overridden by sufficient bad behavior; as we will see in the next chapter, there exist linguistic mechanisms—namely hedges—for avoiding the consequences that can arise from apparent uncooperativity. In this chapter, I will lay the groundwork for the main analysis. My analysis of communicative cooperation will be based on repeated games; it is thus necessary to ensure that the reader is familiar with the basic tools of game theory. This chapter will carry out this task in the context of discussing existing derivations of cooperativity in the literature. It is my hope that at least some parts of the discussion will be novel to a range of readers; ideally, even the reader familiar with game theory will find something of interest in the chapter. For those who are familiar with (repeated) games and

---

[1] As will become clear, I mean "utility" here in both its technical and non technical senses.

with Gricean notions of cooperativity, and further are unwilling to take the chance of boredom, it is probably safe to skip ahead to the next chapter. The discussion here will be structured as follows. I will first show in section 2.1 that it is not always rational to cooperate given that agents sometimes have conflicting desires. This section will introduce the basic notions of game theory. The following section (2.2) considers explanations of cooperation and altruistic behavior that have been offered within theoretical biology. Here I will introduce repeated games and show their efficacy in ensuring cooperative behavior. The final part of the chapter (2.3) introduces signaling games and cooperation in the particular context of linguistic communication. Throughout, I will be examining the notion of Gricean cooperativity and attempting to relate it, a normative principle, to the game-theoretic models discussed, which do not directly make provisions for normativity.

2.1 Is cooperation rational?

What is it to be cooperative? This question is complex and domain-specific. Cooperative communication might be characterized as performance of communicative acts that are truthful and provide information that is of use to the hearer, as with Gricean theory; cooperation in community life might involve active participation in group projects without excessive complaint. Abstracting away from the details of particular scenarios, we can say that cooperative behavior involves working to realize the goals of the other agents in the scenario as well as one's own, or at the very least not working against them. In the context of game theory, this amounts to assisting others to maximize their utility functions.

Game theory assumes the existence of an abstract notion of utility, understood as a measure of the benefit an agent derives from a given action or scenario.[2] It is assumed that the sole goal of agents is to maximize their utilities, meaning that the higher the utility of a situation is for an agent, the more the agent prefers the situation. (I will also use the term *payoff* for the utility of particular outcomes.) The usual decision-theoretic case is one in which only one agent's choices affect the outcome. For instance, suppose that I am offered a choice of beer, wine, or coffee, and my preferences over those drinks are ordered $m > b >$

---

[2] This idea plays an essential role in decision theory as well. See Jeffrey (1983) for extensive discussion.

$w > c$ ($m =$ a martini). This preference ordering can be represented by the following matrix. Here, the numbers indicate the preferences of the agent. The particular numbers chosen are not important; what matters is the relation between them.[3]

m	4
b	3
w	2
c	1

Given that my aim is to maximize my utilities, I should choose to have a martini; but since this is not an available option, my best choice is to have a beer, as beer is payoff-maximal within the choice set. As this example makes clear, the best choice depends on the facts; as is philosophically standard, action is dependent on belief.

Suppose now that another agent enters the picture, one with influence over the space of possibilities, and consequently over the payoffs. For instance, suppose that Adam has invited Bella to his house this afternoon.[4] Bella must decide what to take as a snack: her choices are (say) cake or pretzels. Adam is known to only serve beer or coffee to his guests and not to prepare more than one option. What then should Bella take? Suppose her preferences are represented by the following utility matrix:

	beer	coffee
cake	−2	2
pretzels	3	−1

As will be clear to the reader, not much can be said about Bella's optimal choice here without further information. Given the structure of her preferences, she would of course prefer to be in the situation where either she brings pretzels and Adam provides beer, or she brings cake and Adam provides coffee. But she cannot choose between these situations, only whether to bring cake or pretzels. Her optimal choice depends on whether she thinks Adam is more likely to have prepared beer or coffee. We therefore must add a representation of judgements about likelihood to the model. This is straightforwardly done via probability

---

[3] In fact, the precise utilities do not affect the outcomes of decisions or games under addition of any positive constant. (The technical term is "invariance under positive affine transformations." See e.g. Myerson 1991 for details.)

[4] The following is a modified version of an example of Jeffrey's.

functions. We can use subjective probabilities here, and so think of probability functions as mapping pairs of agents and propositions to real numbers in the interval [0,1]; we also require them to satisfy the usual postulates in (2.1). (2.1a) states that the probability of a tautology is 1, (2.1b) disallows negative probabilities and probabilities larger than 100%, and (2.1c) says that probability is additive for independent propositions.

(2.1) $\mathcal{P}$ satisfies:

      a. $\mathcal{P}(W) = 1$

      b. $0 \leq \mathcal{P}(\varphi) \leq 1$ for all φ

      c. If $\varphi \cap \psi = \varnothing$, then $\mathcal{P}(\varphi) + \mathcal{P}(\psi) = \mathcal{P}(\varphi \vee \psi)$

Let us suppose that Bella has no information whatever about what Adam is likely to do, and so assigns both *beer* and *coffee* a probability of 0.5. This means that the *expected utility* of bringing cake is 0 for her: there is 50% chance of beer and a 50% chance of coffee, with utilities of −2 and 2 respectively; multiplying the utility of each outcome by its probability yields an overall expected gain of 0. For the other case, we have $0.5 \times 3 + 0.5 \times -1 = 1$, so the expected gain of bringing pretzels is 1, meaning that it is the better option. This example illustrates one of the fundamental notions at work in game theory, that of expected utility: this is arrived at by computing the expected utility gain of some option based on the likelihood of all possible outcomes that it could play a role in. More formally, we have the following definition of expected utility for agent a, choice c, and world w:

$$EU_a(c) = \sum_w U_a(c, w)P(w).$$

In this example, Bella had no information at all about what Adam might be expected to do. But presumably Adam also has preferences about what he eats and drinks, which also ought to form part of the model. If Bella knows something about these preferences, she can use them to predict Adam's behavior, and modify her behavior accordingly in order to maximize her utilities. This is the leading idea of game theory. Let us suppose that information is available about Adam's preferences as well as Bella's. In the following matrix, each cell contains a tuple of two utilities, one for each agent; as is standard in game theory, the first numeral represents the row player's utilities and the second numeral the column player's. Thus, according to this representation, Adam and Bella have the same preferences, but Adam's are a bit stronger with respect to beer with cake; also, he likes the coffee and cake combination less than Bella does.

	beer	*coffee*
cake	−2, −3	2, 1
pretzels	3, 3	−1, −1

If the information in this matrix is common knowledge of both players, what is the outcome going to be? Let's first suppose that Adam is reasoning about Bella's likely actions.[5] In the absence of any information about Bella's choices, he is indifferent between preparing beer and coffee (since $0.5 \times -3 + 0.5 \times 3 = 0$ and $0.5 \times 1 + 0.5 \times -1 = 0$). However, given that Bella brings pretzels, he would prefer to prepare beer, and given that she brings cake, he would prefer to provide coffee. Adam's choices thus depend on Bella's, and Bella's in turn on Adam's: this is precisely the sort of situation game theory is designed to help understand.

As the reader will have observed, intuitively the best situation for both individuals is one in which Adam provides beer and Bella pretzels. But this outcome is not guaranteed by the standard method of strategy choice in game theory, which involves the notion of *Nash equilibrium*. A Nash equilibrium is a situation in which each player uses their optimal strategy given the strategies of the other players; this situation can be understood as one in which no player has a utility-based incentive to unilaterally change their move. In the present context, it is obvious that there are two Nash equilibria: the first is the beer-pretzels one, but the situation in which Bella brings cake and Adam makes coffee is also an equilibrium, for, given that Bella brings cake, Adam prefers to make coffee, and given that there is coffee, Bella prefers to bring cake. To choose between these equilibria, a refinement of the selection mechanism is needed: in linguistic applications, most researchers have made use of models that prefer *Pareto-efficient* equilibria (e.g. Parikh 2001; Benz et al. 2006b; Parikh 2010), which are those which each player prefers to other available equilibria.[6] In the above game, the Pareto-efficient equilibrium is *beer-pretzels*, for here the payoffs are (3,3), as opposed to the *coffee-cake* equilibrium, where the payoffs are only (2,1).

---

[5] As is well known, the discussion in the main text could be rephrased in terms of pure maximization of functions, with all anthropomorphism eliminated, since game theory is ultimately a purely mathematical theory; still, I will talk in terms of individual reasoning and decision as it is more intuitive, as is also standard in many introductory texts.

[6] This is the strong version; weakly Pareto-efficient equilibria are those which are better than others for at least one player, while not making any other player worse off. See Hammes (2008) for details.

In the above game, as we saw, both Nash equilibria yielded beneficial outcomes for each player (as shown by the availability of positive payoffs for each of them). But this is not always the case. Indeed, the Nash solution concept does not always even yield the outcome which is least negative. The standard example of this situation is the Prisoner's Dilemma, which can be exemplified by the following game.

	c	d
c	$-2, -2$	$-10, 0$
d	$0, -10,$	$-8, -8$

The usual story told to illustrate this game involves two people involved in a crime. They are picked up by the police, who have no conclusive proof of their guilt, but can convict them on a minor charge (for a brief stint in jail, -2). They separately offer each criminal clemency on the small charge (a final utility of 0) in exchange for testifying against the other criminal in the big case, who will then take the full brunt of the law (penalty: -10). The only catch is that if the other criminal also testifies, both go to jail for a relatively long time (for a utility of -8). The choice is to cooperate with the other criminal ("c") or defect ("d"). What is the optimal action?

Intuitively, on the basis of human social norms, each criminal should cooperate with each other and stay quiet. But this is not the prediction of game theory. Take the perspective of one of the criminals (say, the row player) and suppose that we are in the cell (c, c). Then the other criminal is playing c; but, clearly, if that is so then our criminal has every incentive to change his move, for doing so will change his outcome from utility -2 to utility 0. We are then in cell (d, c). But here the column player can improve her outcome by moving from c to d, which will result in a change from -10 to -8. The column player's reasoning is entirely similar; the sole Nash equilibrium of the game is consequently (d,d), in which each player receives a suboptimal outcome.

On an intuitive level, neither agent in this equilibrium plays a cooperative action. Let us characterize cooperativity slightly more explicitly: suppose that an action is cooperative iff that action does not harm the other game players. This is just to say that the action must lead to a Pareto-efficient equilibrium. This definition is weak, but it will do for a start. From the Prisoner's Dilemma, it becomes clear that cooperative behavior is not guaranteed by game theory in any sense, and so neither are Pareto-efficient results. For cooperative behavior (in the sense I have defined it here) to arise in a simple game like those we have seen so far, the incentives of the players must be aligned in the proper way; in particular, the action selected in equilibrium is required to be beneficial for each player. Thus, cooperative behavior depends purely on game structure. There is something unwelcome about this result, especially in the communicative contexts which are our concern here.

As already mentioned in section 1.1, the usual picture of cooperation in pragmatics comes from the work of Grice (1975), which I will briefly review. Grice proposes that individuals engaged in communication are normatively required to act in a cooperative manner, understood via his Cooperative Principle. This principle is usually broken down into four maxims, the Maxims of Quality, Quantity, Relevance, and Manner, though it is not universally accepted that this set of maxims is either necessary or sufficient (cf. e.g. Sperber and Wilson 1986; Levinson 2000). These maxims can be roughly paraphrased as follows.

(2.2)   a. **Quality.** Be truthful: do not say things that you believe to be false or that lack an evidential basis.

   b. **Quantity.** Give the proper amount of information: do not be under- or over-informative.

   c. **Relevance.** Be relevant: do not speak off topic.

   d. **Manner.** Be clear: avoid obscurity, unresolvable ambiguity, and chaotic speech.

These maxims can be articulated further, but I will make use only of the four above here. What is the status of the Cooperative Principle, and by extension the maxims that derive from it? The preceding discussion shows, from a game-theoretic perspective, that cooperation cannot be guaranteed in the general case from the perspective of utility maximization and, by extension, on the basis of rational considerations. More is needed: assumptions about game structure, payoffs, or some other means of ensuring that cooperativity is a rational outcome. The upshot is that cooperativity cannot be viewed as a general normative principle, but instead that it is a purely contingent matter, at least for the whole spectrum of human behavior.

Several avenues present themselves for a justification of the Cooperative Principle. One way looks to evolution for reasons cooperativity might arise. Here, the crucial issue involves how interaction between organisms works. This problem, under the rubric of the evolution of altruism, has received a great deal of attention in evolutionary biology, where a number of solutions to this problem have been proposed;

I turn to these in the next section. The results of this investigation can be applied to the specific case of communication. I will argue that the combination of evolutionary considerations and certain aspects of the communicative process yields a justification of cooperation. The key notion here is one of *reputation*; it turns out that the existence of reputations, along with a mechanism for punishing those with bad reputations, results in cooperative behavior arising.

2.2 Cooperation, evolution, and reputation

Evolutionary theory takes selection of species or individuals to take place through a process of survival of the fittest. The implication is that individuals behave as fitness maximizers; in terms of standard mathematical models of behavior, they attempt to find the maximal possible value for a utility function in a game that describes the interaction they face (McElreath and Boyd 2007). In game-theoretic terms, the expectation is that the behavior of the individual organisms in the interaction forms a Nash equilibrium. In general, these equilibria are of a special type, because the games they are associated with are set in *evolutionary game theory* (Gintis 2000a). Evolutionary game theory effectively deals in repeated games, with utilities correlating directly with fitness; the proportion of agents which play successful strategies (in comparison to the other players) increases, while the proportion of agents playing low-utility strategies (with respect to the majority) decreases. Equilibria then consist of so-called evolutionarily stable strategies, which are strategies which cannot be destabilized even given fluctuation in the strategy proportions played in the general population. In a game where all agents have correlated utility functions, the evolutionarily stable strategies will be ones which cause all agents to benefit, and cooperation will result.

However, it is rarely the case that maximizing one's own fitness implies maximizing the fitness of others. In ecological settings, organisms face competition for resources: if there is only one deer to eat, the wolf who gets the most meat is likely to live longer. As this example shows, in nature one often finds prisoner's dilemma situations in which unilateral noncooperation leads to higher fitness for the noncooperating individual. Thus cooperation cannot be expected to arise in the general case, but rather to come about only under specialized circumstances (Sober and Wilson 1999). Still, it may remain the case that universal noncooperation leads to lowered fitness for all, as in Skyrms's (2004) example of the Stag Hunt, or the Tragedy of the Commons. In the

Stag Hunt (originally an example of Rousseau's), for instance, a group of hunters must decide what to hunt: if they hunt rabbits, each is guaranteed to catch something, but not much; but if they hunt stag, they can all get a larger quantity of meat (corresponding to a utility larger than that of catching a rabbit), if all join the hunt, but otherwise nothing. Thus there is incentive to hunt stag only if all others also do so; but if there is worry that another player might hunt rabbits, there is reason to hunt rabbits as well, though given the right action by all players cooperation in the stag hunt is optimal. In general, instances of cooperation are not difficult to find in nature: parents supporting their offspring without expectation of reciprocation, the societies of eusocial insects, pack behavior, and even more or less purely altruistic behavior.

Cooperation is thus quite widespread. How can it be explained? There are several competing approaches, of which we will examine three: the theory of inclusive fitness, the theory of group selection, and the theory of repeated interaction. Ultimately, repeated interaction will be the crucial ingredient of the analysis of hedging that is the purpose of the first part of this book.

Up to now, I have talked as if evolution operates at the level of individual organisms which compete for resources and play various strategies against each other. Those organisms playing the best strategy eventually come to dominate the population. But what if evolution does not select organisms at all? This question is at the root of the first two theories we will consider.[7]

Some theories of evolution have it that selection takes place at the level of genes rather than at the level of individuals, so that individual selection only matters in the sense that this or that gene gains a selectional advantage. On this view, cooperation is predicted when genes are shared between individuals, because helping another individual with whom one shares genes means increasing the fitness of (the relevant part of) one's own set of genes (e.g. Hamilton 1963, 1964; Maynard Smith 1964). Implementing this idea game-theoretically can in principle be done in (at least) two ways: by understanding utilities to be computed for genes directly, or by computing the utility of cooperative action as a function of the degree to which individuals are related at the genetic level. The former method is not fully compatible with game theory in the sense of predicting (or indicating) the optimal actions of agents. Since genes are not actors in games, "their" utilities are not very relevant to

---

[7] The complex of issues surrounding this question is addressed in detail by Okasha (2006).

action choice. The second option is therefore to be preferred. Suppose that the utility of my actions is computed as the sum of my utilities and your utilities multiplied by the degree of our genetic relationship, so $(U_a + U_b) \times Rel(a, b)$, for $Rel(a, b)$ the percent of genetic material shared by a and b. Cooperative behavior is then expected to the degree that genes are shared. But, plainly, this is a special case with respect to the general theory of cooperative behavior. It is not obvious how to apply it to the general case of cooperation between individuals that may or may not be genetically related, or to our central problem here, the case of truthful communication.

A second way of deriving cooperative behavior has more obvious relevance for the (normative) facts about human communication encapsulated in Grice's Maxims. As just stated, there is debate in evolutionary theory about the level at which selection applies. We have seen that it can be viewed as selecting for individuals or for genes, but other possibilities remain, for example groups of individuals. The theory of group selection was widely rejected for many years (Sober and Wilson 1999), but has recently been enjoying a resurgence (see discussion in Okasha 2006). Here, the units of selection to which evolutionary mechanisms apply are groups, which means that group-level traits can be directly selected for. One such trait is cooperation. With this change in levels of selection, it becomes theoretically possible that cooperative behavior is the direct result of evolutionary processes. Gintis (2009), for instance, claims that just such a process has occurred and resulted in innate cooperative tendencies in the human species.

Gintis (2000b) shows that given certain conditions and a group-selection model, cooperative behavior can evolve. Suppose that a population is divided into small groups, where cooperative behavior gives an evolutionary advantage. Suppose further that there is a mechanism for *altruistic punishment* which group members can apply to noncooperators, and that the mechanism has a strong negative impact on the individuals punished, but only a relatively small cost for the punisher. Then cooperative behavior will arise in groups with the punishment mechanism, and, given the evolutionary advantage, will spread across the population. Gintis (2009) builds on this model, suggesting on the basis of the existence of multiple equilibria in many games that social norms are also required to ensure that cooperative behavior arises and uncooperative behavior is punished.

I will follow Gintis and his coauthors in assuming that cooperativity has an innate element; this is sufficient to explain why the normative assumption of communicative cooperativity arises in the first place. But this innateness does not mean that cooperative behavior invariably arises in every interaction. Everyone has met individuals who violate Gricean principles when it suits their purposes, and many have also stopped trusting those individuals as a result. Thus a means of understanding the mechanism used for punishment is needed, as well as a way to understand the linguistic devices which can play a role in helping to avoid such punishment.

The key is to consider repeated interactions, something that we have not yet done in our game-theoretic models in this chapter. Intuitively, if one interacts with a noncooperator, one is less likely to cooperate with that individual thereafter. This consideration is irrelevant in one-shot interactions, but as games are played repeatedly, the possibility of "tit-for-tat" mutual backscratching/punishment behavior across game iterations is introduced (e.g. Nowak 2006). Clearly, if one interacts multiple times, expectations about how one's reputation may impact the future behavior of the other players can come to influence what one will choose to do. The application to Grice is obvious: if one wishes to be trusted, one must behave (in general) as a Gricean cooperator, even though in the short term one might gain a selectional (utility) advantage by behaving otherwise. This is one way of understanding the results of Gintis (2000b); we require a notion of altruistic punishment, which, in order to be applicable, in turn requires that the theory make available a notion of repeated interactions.

The basic intuition at work in this discussion can be stated as follows: if I play a game with you once and never again, I have every reason to do things that are bad for you and good for me, given that I am not concerned with what happens to you. For this reason, unscrupulous sellers have incentives to cheat and amoral speakers have reason to lie if doing so will bring them benefit; these cases will be presented in some more detail shortly. But if the game will be played again, clearly this kind of behavior does not benefit the noncooperator. This corresponds to the case of "the boy who cried wolf." The individual who was tricked the first time—by buying a shoddy product or believing a lie—will not make the same mistake again.[8] This observation opens up a larger range of possible actions more in keeping with what we find in general

---

[8] This assumes that the tricked individual remembers what happened the first time, is able to identify the other game player, and recognizes that the situation is the same, a point we will return to below.

situations of buying and selling and of communication. Games which are played more than once are known as *repeated games*; as we will see in this section, looking at repeated games gives a much clearer picture of why something like cooperation should arise even in noncooperative settings.

For a concrete example, consider the case of an unscrupulous agent in a sales transaction. Suppose that we have a two-player game, where one player provides a good and the other player is a consumer who must decide to buy the good or not. The dynamics of this scenario are complicated in various respects, but one choice that must be made by the producer is the quality of the goods that are to be sold. Plainly it is cheaper to produce poor-quality goods than high-quality ones; plainly, also, the purchaser prefers to buy high-quality goods, given that the price is the same. What are optimal actions in this scenario? Suppose first that the interaction takes place only once and that the two participants will never have any further contact. In this one-shot interaction, it is obviously best for the seller if he is able to unload shoddy goods on the purchaser, as this will yield a higher profit. The purchaser (by assumption) knows this. It is therefore to her advantage never to buy anything from the seller, as doing so will give her a loss: she will end up paying for poor-quality goods. This result is exactly what we expect in necessarily one-off buying scenarios such as people selling possibly fake luxury goods out of the backs of cars in the city. The seller has no incentive to sell something of good quality and the buyer, given the usual world knowledge, is not going to be tricked.

This situation can be modeled in game form as in Figure 2.1. This graph represents a game of buying and selling in extensive form. Each node represents a decision point of some game participant, here the seller S and the buyer B. It is a dynamic representation, in that the choices of players determine a path through the nodes of the tree. The seller has two possible actions, to produce (sell) high- (*H*) or low- (*L*)

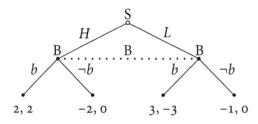

FIGURE 2.1   Buying watches off the street

quality goods. The buyer also has two choices: to buy (b) or not buy ($\neg b$). In this game, the assumption is made that the buyer cannot determine what choice the seller has made in his turn, so the quality of the goods is not verifiable before purchase. This uncertainty is represented by the dotted line between the two "daughter" nodes of the S-marked node; nodes connected in this way are referred to as *information sets*.

The pairs of numerals at the "leaves" of the tree represent the utilities or payoffs to the game players. The first numeral is the payoff to player 1, the seller, and the second numeral is the payoff to player 2, the buyer, just as with the normal-form matrices seen in the previous section. In this game, the payoffs work as follows: the seller and buyer both receive a payoff of 2 units if a purchase of high-quality goods is made, but if a buyer buys goods of poor quality, the seller gets a higher payoff (3 units) and the buyer loses 3 units. If the buyer chooses not to purchase anything, she has no gain or loss, but the seller loses the cost of acquiring the goods: 2 units in the case of high-quality goods, and 1 unit in case of poor-quality goods.

The optimal actions of the players are, as usual, found by examining any Nash equilibrium of the game, the state(s) in which no player can improve her situation by changing only her own move (so her move is a best response to the moves of the other players, who are of course also playing their best responses). The Nash equilibrium of this game, given a single round of play, is that in which the seller produces low-quality goods and the buyer does not make any purchase. The informal reasoning is as follows. Suppose that the buyer chooses to buy. Then the seller can increase his payoff by producing poor-quality goods, so he will choose to do so given that he knows the buyer will buy. From the other side, since the buyer can also perform this reasoning, she can guess that the seller will provide shoddy goods and she will choose not to buy them. In other words, the combination of poor quality and no purchase is the option which maximizes the payoffs for each player, given that each player is working to maximize his own payoffs.

When this game is transposed out of the one-off setting and (indefinitely) repeated, the result changes. In the buying–selling game, a natural strategy for a purchaser is to not buy goods known to be of low quality. Let us suppose that when a buyer encounters low-quality goods, she chooses never to buy anything from that seller again. Then, given the payoffs in the buying–selling game in Figure 2.1, it will take only four iterations of the game for the seller to lose all the gains he received from selling a poor-quality product in the first round ($3 + {-1} + {-1} + {-1}$). It is easy to see that if the producer anticipates more than two interactions with the buyer, it is worth cooperating from the start in this instance, for if the buyer behaves in a punitive manner, the second interaction will already erase the difference in payoffs from the initial cooperative and noncooperative moves. This holds with the caveat that the seller values future gains identically to present ones. The temporal aspect of value is usually modeled via a *discount rate* δ ($0 \leq \delta \leq 1$) which progressively lessens the value of a payoff as game iterations progress. The claim in the main text assumes that the discount rate $\delta = 0$; if $\delta > 0$, recovering losses will take a bit longer. Thus, the greater the discount, the greater the incentive to behave noncooperatively.[9] In general, in repeated games, cooperative behavior becomes the norm if a sufficient number of interactions are expected to take place, the players expect each other to play strategies that penalize noncooperative behavior, and the discount rate is sufficiently low.

Consider again the game in Figure 2.1. As we saw earlier, the seller has every incentive to produce a shoddy product, given that the game is to be played only a single time. But suppose the game is to be played again. There are sixteen possible results across the two games, depending on the choices of each agent in each instance of the game. But strategies for repeated games are not computed across the entire game sequence; as might be clear, understanding them in this way would eliminate the generality of the idea, for it would require that the number of game repetitions be prespecified in order to state a strategy. Instead, strategies for repeated games are stated as functions of the sequence of prior game instances (known as *stage games*, though I will also use the terms *iteration* and *repetition*): $f(h)$, for h a history of game iterations. (I will specify these in some more detail as we proceed.) Strategies can thus be of arbitrary complexity with respect to the content of histories.[10]

In general there are two types of strategies for repeated games. One type ignores the behavior of the other players and uses the same move(s) regardless of what they do; such strategies are rarely optimal for obvious reasons, and will be ignored in what follows. The other type changes behavior depending on what is observed in particular instances of game play. A well-known strategy of this kind is to behave in an iteration in the

---

[9] See Myerson (1991) or Mailath and Samuelson (2006) for details.
[10] Binmore (1992, chapter 8) provides a clear introduction to games of this kind. (Thanks to a reviewer for calling this treatment to my attention.)

way the other player did in the previous iteration (the *tit-for-tat* strategy, though this term is slightly misleading in the present context, where the players have different moves available to them).[11] Another option is *generous tit-for-tat*: copy the opponent's previous move, but shift to cooperation with some positive probability.[12]

Returning to the example, let us suppose that in the first instance the seller chooses to produce a low-quality product and the buyer makes the purchase. In the next round, the seller again has incentive to produce a poor product, just as before. But now, given the result of the last round, the buyer knows that the seller is playing L. This means that the buyer has no incentive to play b but instead has reason to play $\neg b$. In this case, the payoffs for each player across the two iterations of the game are, summing over the utilities of agent $a \in \{B, S\}$ with strategy s in round i (and ignoring discount rates),

$$\sum_{i=1}^{2} U_a(s, i) = (2, -2).$$

Obviously, for each round this game is extended, the seller will lose 1 unit of payoff, while the buyer's payoff will remain constant at -2. The intuitive interpretation of this situation is that, in iteration 1, the buyer tests the product and learns it is of low quality, and therefore chooses not to buy any more. This is an instance of a so-called *grim strategy*, on which a player plays a particular way until some preset trigger; for example, one might stop cooperating on learning that another player is not playing a cooperative strategy. In the present setting, this amounts to having the observation that the product is of low quality serve as a *grim trigger* for the buyer to stop making purchases (cf. Mailath and Samuelson 2006).

Plainly, if the buyer is playing any sort of sufficiently punitive strategy, it is advantageous in the long run for the producer to make a high-quality product. Such a strategy need not be grim. For instance, one might play a strategy on which one does not cooperate for some fixed number of moves after observing an instance of noncooperative play; once the sequence of uncooperative moves eliminates the benefit gained

---

[11] There are also variations on the tit-for-tat strategy, e.g. making noncooperative moves for n iterations after any instance of a noncooperative move, and then returning to cooperative behavior.

[12] In general, generous tit-for-tat is the best option for prisoner's dilemma games, as shown by evolutionary simulations done by Martin Nowak and colleagues: see Nowak (2006) for discussion and references.

by the seller from the first instance of uncooperative play, it is no longer rational not to cooperate. This is an example of the sort of punishment discussed by Gintis.

Exactly what the best option is will depend on what is required for cooperation to become the best move of the other agent. This in turn depends on two factors: first, the payoffs involved in the game, and second, the weight attached to present versus future profit on the part of the agents. If a player values a payoff in an early round sufficiently higher than a payoff in a late round, it will be better for that player to pursue a noncooperative strategy. The upshot is that, for any agent, cooperation will be the best option iff the other agent plays a strategy such that the sum of the payoffs modified for discount rate is higher over the expected number of iterations when a cooperative strategy is played than not. In games of complete information it is possible to compute a strategy so that cooperation becomes the equilibrium state. Thus, given the combination of reputation and punishment, cooperation is rational.

One key observation about repeated games, already implicitly assumed (via the notion of "indefinite repetition"), is that it is necessary to assume that games are played over an infinite horizon for cooperativity to arise. If players know when the final interaction will be, the best strategy for any player will always be to defect in the final turn n; given that other players have complete information about all players' utilities (and consequently their optimal strategies), their best option is to defect in turn $n - 1$. The final result is that no cooperation arises at all (Selten and Stoecker 1986).[13] It therefore must be assumed that the games in question are infinitely repeated, or at least infinitely repeatable in principle. From an intuitive perspective, this is sensible: in general, people engaged in interactions do not know exactly when their final interaction will be, particularly in conversational settings: it's not the case that I can (politely) unilaterally end the conversation—there is always the possibility that my interlocutor will continue talking. Thus

---

[13] This fact relates closely to the so-called Centipede Game, in which players pass a sum of money back and forth, which increases with each turn. Given backward induction, if any player knows the exact number of turns, she will defect just prior to the last turn in order to maximize her payoff; if all players know the number of turns, each will try to defect earlier than the other, resulting in the sum of money never being passed along at all and each player settling for the lowest possible payoff. See Kreps (1990) for details.

there's no point at which an uncooperative move is safe.[14] I will assume infinite horizons in what follows.[15]

2.3 Signaling games and reliability

The above shows how a combination of repeated interaction and (possibly) genetic or cultural predisposition can lead to cooperative behavior in various organisms. But we have not yet said anything about communication. In order to see how cooperative behavior might arise in communicative settings, it is first necessary to see how communication is modeled in game theory. Standard practice across the social sciences and theoretical biology is to use signaling games, which I will introduce next. Building on this discussion, the next chapter will discuss how cooperative communicative strategies can be defined in such games, and, finally, show how they can arise and be maintained in a repeated-game setting.

How should communication be modeled in a game-theoretic setting? In the simplest case, a communicative act involves two participants: an agent who sends a signal, and an agent who receives and acts on that signal. For the cases we are most directly concerned with, the signal will be an utterance of some linguistic material; but any model capable of handling this case will also be able to represent other sorts of communicative acts. The general game type used to analyze such acts is *signaling games*. Such games have been used in various fields, including theoretical biology, political science, and economics; they are widely accepted as the optimal model of communicative action within the game-theoretic framework.[16]

---

[14] The theory of politeness of Asher and McCready (2014, i.a.), which also crucially involves repeated games, makes the same assumption.

[15] Thus the payoff received by the players a and b are specifiable as follows for 2-player games, for game repetition n for $i \in \{1, 2\}$:

$$U_i(a, b) = \lim_{N \to \infty} \frac{1}{N} \sum_{n=1}^{N} \pi_i(a_n^1, a_n^2),$$

so the expected value of a repetition of a repeated game is the expected payoff per game iteration as the game sequence extends toward infinity, given the moves of each player in those iterations. This definition comes from Binmore (1992) and was already (implicitly) used above.

[16] In this book I will not give anything like an exhaustive discussion of signaling games; I will only provide what I take to be the essential points relating to my discussion of cooperativity and trust (to be used in the analysis of hedging). For more detailed discussion

Communication ordinarily requires the speaker to have knowledge that the hearer lacks. The speaker knows (or believes) something about the world, and tries to alter the information that the hearer has by passing this knowledge along. While there are outlying cases, for example when the point of a speaker's utterance is a side effect of her speech such as introduction of a discourse referent or signaling something about her attitudes (e.g. Barker 2002; Shan 2005), in general there is an informational asymmetry between speaker and hearer which is reflected directly at the level of communicated content.[17] Signaling games represent this fundamental difference in a direct way. They involve two agents, the signaler and the receiver. The signaler observes the state of the world and, on the basis of that state, sends a signal chosen from an existing set of options; the receiver observes the signal and, on the basis of the signal, selects an action from an existing set of possibilities, as usual.

Strategies in signaling games are different from what we have seen so far. In the simple games we have examined up to this point, strategies are just choices of action, though they may involve sequences of actions. It is possible, though non-optimal, to model communicative acts in this setting; the comparison between this case and signaling games may be instructive, so I will provide such a model. As we will see, the prediction made here is that in many cases communication is not useful.

Recall that in the game in Figure 2.1, the seller's optimal action was to first choose L. Suppose that we allow the seller to communicate something about the quality of the good before the buyer can choose whether or not to purchase it. The seller, as before, has the option to produce poor-quality goods or not. But he now can also signal to the hearer that his goods are of high quality, or choose not to do so.[18] We can assume that this signal comes with an associated cost, which can be represented by decreasing the payoff to the seller when the choice is made to advertise quality. The buyer now has the option to believe the seller, or not, as before. This whole situation can be modeled by letting the seller have two actions at the beginning instead of one (Figure 2.2).[19]

see, for example, Franke (2009, 2011) and Sobel (2012), as well as discussion in game theory textbooks (Binmore 1992 is a straightforward and technically undemanding example).

[17] Here I would like to sidestep complex issues about "what is said" and what counts as included in communicated content; by communicative content I mean essentially semantic content derived directly from the conventional lexical meanings of words. See e.g. Borg (2007) for some discussion of this point.

[18] Glazer and Rubenstein (2004) provide discussion related to persuasion in games.

[19] Nothing much changes if, instead of a sequence of two moves for the seller, we use only a single move with four possible choices instead: $A + H, A + L, \neg A + H, \neg A + L$.

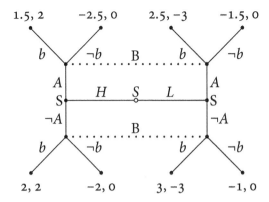

FIGURE 2.2   Advertising on the streets

In this game, the seller first decides whether to produce/sell high- or low-quality goods. He then has the option to advertise high quality or not. The buyer, of course, cannot distinguish between states in which the advertisement is truthful and those in which it is not. She can only see if the advertisement has been made. This is represented via the two information sets: each corresponds to two states of the world, an "advertising" state and a "non-advertising" state. The buyer then chooses whether to buy or not. Note that the payoffs in the case where no advertisement is made are as before; I assume that the cost of advertising is half a unit for the seller, while the buyer incurs no penalty, but there is no special benefit either.

What are the optimal strategies in this game? Note that, just as before, the seller has no reason to produce high-quality goods. The buyer, as a result, has no reason to believe the advertisement. This means that the best action is just as before: no purchase. This, in turn, means that the seller has no reason to advertise; all the communicative act can achieve is the loss of half a unit of utility for the seller. The seller's optimal strategy is therefore $L; \neg A$. Here we have a sequence of actions as equilibrium strategy. (In equilibrium, communication is useless; we will see the reason shortly.)

Strategies in signaling games are not sequences of this kind. They involve a different kind of complexity. The reason is that they specify the communicative behavior of signaler (speaker) and receiver (hearer) in a variety of situations, and so must take into account multiple possibilities, some of which may not be realized in a particular interaction. Suppose for instance that the sender has two signals available, u_1 and u_2, and that there are two possible states of the world, s_1 and s_2. (Here u_2 could be interpreted as the negation of u_1, for example.) A sender strategy must take into account both possible states. Similarly, the receiver must have a response available to both u_1 and u_2, so both possible signals must be taken into account by the receiver's strategy. Consequently, strategies in signaling games are functions: for the signaler, functions from states to signals, and for the receiver, functions from signals to states. Thus in the simple game indicated here, there will be four sender strategies and four receiver strategies. Here, for the sender, each strategy σ_i indicates what signal is sent in state s_1 and s_2; conversely, each receiver strategy ρ_i indicates what state is chosen in response to signals u_1 and u_2.

$$
\text{Sender strategies}:
\begin{bmatrix}
 & s_1 & s_2 \\
\hline
\sigma_1 & u_1 & u_2 \\
\sigma_2 & u_2 & u_1 \\
\sigma_3 & u_1 & u_1 \\
\sigma_4 & u_2 & u_2
\end{bmatrix}
\quad
\text{Receiver strategies}:
\begin{bmatrix}
 & u_1 & u_2 \\
\hline
\rho_1 & s_1 & s_2 \\
\rho_2 & s_2 & s_1 \\
\rho_3 & s_1 & s_1 \\
\rho_4 & s_2 & s_2
\end{bmatrix}
$$

Clearly some of these strategies are more conducive to communication than others. Strategies σ_3 and σ_4 have the sender always use the same signal, regardless of the state of the world; since the signal is not conditioned by any external factors, it cannot be understood as carrying information about the state. From the side of the receiver, ρ_3 and ρ_4 ignore the input signal and always yield the same choice of state; intuitively, this means that the receiver extracts no information from the received signal. Such strategies cannot be said to play a role in communication.[20]

Communicatively optimal strategies are those which covary with the input, whether it be state or signal. But since this is an interactive setting, the optimal strategy depends on the behavior of the other player. In this game, the optimal strategy pairs are $\langle \sigma_1, \rho_1 \rangle$ and $\langle \sigma_2, \rho_2 \rangle$; these pairs (and only these) allow recovery of the actual state by the receiver, for, in all cases, the output of the receiver strategy will be identical to the input to the sender strategy.

The above discussion is intuitively right, but holds only under certain conditions. Not all payoff structures support these equilibria. Payoffs are determined on the basis of the state of the world and the action selected by the receiver. As with other game types, the payoffs clarify the degree

---

[20] They are known as *pooling equilibria* because, with the right (or wrong) choice of solution concept (and probabilities), they can be involved in Nash equilibria, though degenerate ones from the perspective of modeling communicative practice.

of cooperativity that can be expected from players in both one-off and repeated game settings; as usual, players will cooperate with each other to the degree to which payoffs are correlated. However, in this context cooperation has a rather different meaning. Since receivers are expected to act on the basis of the signals they receive, their cooperativity is not much at issue. Instead, the notion of cooperativity here usually involves the credibility of the signaler: to what degree is the signal sent by a particular speaker trustworthy? This issue has been one main focus of work on signaling games, with a clear result (Crawford and Sobel 1982; Rabin 1990; Farrell 1993; Farrell and Rabin 1996): signals are credible to precisely the degree to which interests are aligned.

Take the case of fully aligned interests. Here, the sender wishes the receiver to get correct information about the state. Situations like this will arise often: for instance, suppose that I have left my umbrella at your house, you are coming to work now, and I want you to bring my umbrella iff it is raining (if it's not raining, I have to carry it, and it's a hassle). Then I want you to recover the correct state from the signal I send you about the state of the weather. This can be modeled by assuming that each player gets a maximal payoff just in case the actual state $s = \rho(\sigma(s))$, and otherwise each gets a smaller payoff.[21] In this situation, the sender has an incentive to send a signal from which the receiver can recover information about the actual state; given some knowledge about the strategy likely played by the receiver, this will entail use of either σ_1 or σ_2. In models of language, the choice between the two is usually determined by the assumption that the signals have conventional meanings, which influence the choice of strategy: supposing that $[\![u_1]\!] = s_1$, if the sender is taken to be credible by the receiver and sends u_1, then the receiver should employ a strategy which maps u_1 to s_1. Here, it is assumed that the sender does not send signals with false conventional meanings; otherwise put, he is constrained in the signals which can be sent (e.g. van Rooij 2008). Of course, this assumption is defeasible, and cannot be made in the present context, where we would like to *derive* truthful behavior. But it arises naturally if it is assumed that the receiver—at least as a default—acts as if the conventional meaning of the signal were true, which is indeed a reasonable strategy if interests align.

If interests are not aligned, the situation changes. Again, take the extreme case where interests diverge completely. Suppose that,

---

[21] As usual, the exact numbers of the payoffs don't matter much, only the relation between them.

unlike the previous scenario, the sender gets a positive payoff only if the receiver chooses state s_1, but the receiver's payoff is negative in that scenario and positive only in s_2. What are optimal actions in this case? The receiver only has incentive to pick state s_2, for otherwise payoffs are negative. As a result, she will always choose s_2, meaning she will employ strategy ρ_4. Given this, it doesn't matter much what the sender does: regardless of the input signal, the receiver will choose s_2, so the sender strategy can vary arbitrarily. Communication fails completely in this case.

We can identify an intermediate case in which the receiver would like to select the "true" state, but the sender has an incentive to induce her to pick one or the other state. Suppose that the sender prefers the receiver pick s_1. Now there are two distinct cases. In the first, the actual state is s_1, in which case the receiver also prefers that state and interests are aligned. In the second, the actual state is s_2, and interests diverge. The sender thus has an incentive to send a false signal, u_1 (supposing that u_1 conventionally indicates that the actual state is s_1). Since the receiver does not know the actual state and only observes u_1 in both cases, no positive information can be extracted from the signal, and so again the receiver must resort to a probabilistic strategy with respect to her choice of state.

The upshot is that cooperative behavior, in a Gricean sense, can be expected if interests are aligned, but cannot be if they are not.[22]

---

[22] Is cooperation necessary for communication? Asher and Lascarides (2013) provide a signaling game-based model in which implicatures can be generated even in the absence of cooperation. They distinguish three distinct levels of cooperativity: meaning-level cooperativity, rhetorical cooperativity, and (genuine) Gricean cooperativity. A speaker who is meaning-level cooperative follows norms of communication with respect to linguistic content (cf. Lewis 1969). A speaker who is rhetorically cooperative follows norms of communication with respect to expected patterns of discourse: answering questions if they are asked, and so on. Gricean cooperators are genuinely cooperative in our sense (at least, and perhaps more). The discussion of this book (so far) is concerned only with cooperativity at the Gricean level.

Asher and Lascarides take Gricean cooperativity to be too strong a condition for implicature generation, observing that implicatures still arise when interlocutors are not taken to be cooperative. Their aim is to characterize those implicatures that can be taken to be "safe": reasonably inferable even in cases where the speaker is judged not to be a Gricean cooperator, where such judgements take place on the basis of prior probabilities and reasoning about utilities. Something like their model will be necessary in addition to the current theory as well: my aim here has been to explain (following the work of e.g. Skyrms) how Gricean cooperativity might arise. In the next chapter, I will show, based on the idea of reputation, when it is appropriate to take someone to be cooperative in the Gricean sense. Of course, if they are *not* judged cooperative, other measures involving safety in interpretation must be taken. We thus see that the Asher and Lascarides model and my own have different objectives and augment each other. (Thanks to an anonymous reviewer for suggesting a comparison of the two systems.)

Given the discussion of the previous section, this should not come as a surprise to the reader. In other types of games, as well, agents will act to maximize their utilities; if the other player must lose out in order for me to maximize my payoffs, so much the worse for the other player. The same holds, of course, for signaling games. Viewing this signaling game as a more adequate model of the communicative portion of the game in Figure 2.2, sincerity is not expected of the sender here either; this is the reason the game in Figure 2.2 is in equilibrium when no communication takes place. But, as we've seen, this obstacle to cooperative behavior can be overcome if the game is repeated, in particular when the number of repetitions to be played is not known. Just as before, even if a speaker has an incentive to have the hearer believe something false about the world, doing so has a high probability of triggering a situation where his utterances will no longer be believed, given what we've seen about human behavior in repeated game settings (see Gintis 2009; Bowles and Gintis 2011). Thus, given that it is useful to the sender to have his signal acted on, he will ultimately not gain by sending verifiably false signals if the game is to be repeated enough times. Such will be the case, even in the simple games discussed above where interests only partially align, if there is a sufficiently high probability that the receiver strategy will lead to a best outcome for the speaker in the indefinitely long term. This observation can be used to explain the Gricean Maxim of Quality: lying will not ultimately result in gains for the speaker under certain assumptions about game structure.[23]

2.4 Summary

In this chapter it has been shown that the possibility of repeating games allows for an analysis of cooperation in even antagonistic settings. For the communicative case, we saw that signals could be trustworthy in two situations: where interests are aligned, and when communication is repeated (given the existence of a punishment mechanism, even one as seemingly mild as the loss of future trust). The analysis has been fairly informal. I have not touched on one key issue, the formal analysis of reputations themselves, as the histories known by the players about each other's moves, and thus what is tarnished by a noncooperative action by player 1 in each of the games above. But from the above

---

[23] Compare van Rooij (2003b) on the value of truthfulness in signaling games.

discussion it already seems that we might expect linguistic correlates of reputational phenomena. Specifically, if reputations are so important in judging cooperativity, and being judged cooperative is important to individuals engaged in communication, we would expect to find grammatical phenomena designed to manipulate reputations. A mechanism allowing speakers to avoid being judged uncooperative would be highly useful, and, given the evolutionary basis I've assumed for cooperative behavior, would thus be expected to evolve if such things are possible. The next chapter will argue that there are indeed just such phenomena, namely hedges, and fill the gap in the discussion of the present chapter by providing a formal model of reputations.

3

Trust and reputations

In the last chapter, I introduced some aspects of game theory relevant for deriving cooperation in strategic interaction. As we saw, cooperation in such contexts is dependent on the interests of participants in the interactions that are taking place: if they have the same interests, they will naturally cooperate, and if not cooperating can harm them in the long term, they also will cooperate if they are sufficiently reflective. We also saw that considerations of reputation within a game-theoretic setting can influence whether or not a particular agent should choose to cooperate. None of these things are perhaps extremely surprising to the reader. Further, this discussion has been fairly abstract. For a theory of cooperation that can be useful in linguistic pragmatics, one would like a way to apply it directly to communication, and more specifically to the case of Gricean cooperativity in communication. Further, it would be worrying if such a theory lacked applications at the level of analyzing particular linguistic constructions or behavior. The aim of this chapter is to propose a detailed theory and apply it to one such construction: hedges, and shield hedges in particular. As we will see, the result leads directly to a formulation of Gricean cooperativity, which will be built on for further applications in the next chapter.

3.1 Hedging and disclaimers

The basic phenomenon of hedging is a familiar one. Here, a speaker explicitly disavows responsibility for some aspect of a statement. The following definition comes from dictionary.com: "to protect with qualifications that allow for unstated contingencies or for withdrawal from commitment."[1] The rhetorical strategy is well known. I will proceed in a moment to elaborate on the phenomenon and examine its various realizations—for instance, the use of modal operators and modifiers.

---

[1] At http://dictionary.reference.com/browse/hedging?s=t.

I will spend the most time examining those that will be my focus in this work: the *shield hedge* exemplified in (3.1), and related phenomena in advertising. Before doing so, though, let us consider the phenomenon from a conceptual viewpoint.

(3.1)   I could be wrong, but Mary (should be) coming tonight.

Hedging raises puzzles from the perspective of information transfer. Suppose that I indicate to you that the signal I am sending might be false, as in (3.1). This indicates that I am attempting to give you information about which I am uncertain. The first obvious question is whether you should believe the hedged content. After all, I explicitly indicate that it might be false. What incentive do you have to believe it? Further, how could such a discourse move be felicitous? It looks very much like a violation of Gricean Quality of the same kind as Moore's Paradox.

(3.2)   (Asserted) *p* but I do not believe that *p*.   (Moore 1952)

We may also ask: is a discourse move of this sort a cooperative action? Intuitively, it is, or might be; the answer presumably depends on existing knowledge about my utility function and how it correlates with your own. If our utilities are correlated, you are likely to judge me as cooperative, in that I have an incentive to give you correct information, even though it is questionable; if they are not, you are likely to guess that I am trying to avoid possible repercussions of my actions.

What then (if anything) can be said about what a hearer ought to do with content like this in the general case? And what precisely is the pragmatic function of hedges from a formal perspective? The rest of this chapter is devoted to these questions. I will suggest that these situations amount to a request to the hearer that the signaler should be exempted from negative consequences to his reputation resulting from truth or falsity of the utterance. This is the benefit to the speaker—given the hedge, damage to her reputation can be avoided, which is of obvious use given the discussion in the last chapter. This idea is cashed out formally in a model of reputations based on repeated games. The question of what credence the hearer should put in information flagged in this way will be delayed to later in the book (chapter 9); as it turns out, this problem instantiates a much larger class of pragmatic problems about transmitted information which is uncertain or otherwise marked as coming from a particular source, itself with a particular degree of reliability.

Why should hedges exist? Suppose that a speaker has a reason to communicate content about which he is uncertain. Doing so is a potentially dangerous action. After all, if he turns out to be wrong, he will be taken to have violated Gricean Quality by saying something either (a) false or (b) on the basis of insufficient evidence. This might well result in reputational damage. Of course, all involved realize that speakers are fallible, and that there is no guarantee that anyone is always right in what they say; but cooperativity, as a normative strategy, means that a speaker should take care to avoid such violations, and, by not doing so, leaves himself subject to penalties. But there still might be a compelling enough reason to take the risk. For instance, if the usefulness of the informational content (its Relevance) is large enough, not making the assertion also might be penalty-worthy—not disclosing life-or-death information could be a very bad idea, even if the information is not fully certain. Thus, paradoxically, a cooperative speaker may find herself having to risk violating some subaspect of the norms of cooperativity. Fortunately, speakers have a way to signal that they do not wish to take responsibility for the signals they use. This strategy is, of course, that of *hedging*.

The phenomenon of hedging is widely studied in linguistics, mostly in pragmatics and applied linguistics (Lakoff 1973 is an early reference; for more recent work, see e.g. the papers in Kalenbock et al. 2010). Some typical examples of hedging expressions are shown in (3.3).

(3.3)   a. John is *sort of* stupid.
         b. *I suspect that* it is cold outside.
         c. *I might be wrong, but* Palin is not going to be elected.
         d. *This might not be true, but* she doesn't really care about you.

The function of all the italicized expressions in (3.3) is to "soften" the content of the speech act made (here all assertions), or to guard the speaker from being accused of saying falsehoods.[2] In this book we will be concerned only with hedges of the second type, called *shields* by Prince et al. (1982) and exemplified by (3.3c) and (3.3d). It is obvious that the use of these expressions is similar to that of disclaimers in advertising. The speaker's goal in hedging is to avoid being held responsible for the content of his utterance if it proves to be false, just as the goal of a disclaimer in an advertisement is to avoid being held responsible if the actual product is less satisfactory than the advertisement makes it out to be.

---

[2] This is the case for the hedges considered in this chapter; in the following chapter(s), we will see hedges that address different aspects of the speech act performed.

Why limit attention to shield hedges? The reason is that hedges of the other kind, such as *might*, *suspect*, and *sort of*, have a much more direct effect on the content of the sentence they appear in. A speaker who uses (3.3b) does not assert that it is cold outside; but a speaker who uses (3.4) does in normal contexts.

(3.4)   I might be wrong, but it's cold outside.

As a result, the kind of hedging that is being performed in (3.3) and (3.4) is very different. Shield hedges, as their name indicates, act to shield the speaker from possible negative consequences of her assertion, which is nonetheless carried out. Other hedges work to weaken the content of the assertion to something that a speaker is willing to assert. That compositional phenomenon is rather well understood (in the extensive work in linguistics and philosophy on epistemic modality; see Portner 2009 for an overview of work in semantics, and Weatherson and Egan 2011a for a collection of representative recent work in philosophy); but the way in which shield hedges function is not, which is reason enough to focus on them.

When the speaker's intent is to avoid repercussions stemming from possible inaccuracy of what she reports, shield hedges appear to always take the form of a parenthetical clause indicating uncertainty, followed by the content to be asserted. Schematically, they have the structure "$\Diamond_a \neg \phi$ but ϕ", where ϕ is the asserted content, and $\Diamond_a \neg \phi$ represents the possibility (according to the speaker a) that ϕ may in fact be false. Such a logical form is both consistent and, on the face of things, has nothing to do with hedging; it is, in principle, possible to simply assert the possibility of falsity of ϕ together with ϕ, though it is pragmatically incoherent. As mentioned above, such a statement looks Moore-paradoxical; I will argue in chapter 5 that this paradoxical character triggers a reasoning process on the part of the hearer which yields a hedging interpretation in the presence of a contrastive marker like *but* and a parenthetical indicating possible falsity from a first-person perspective. For now, I will simply assume that particular utterances are unambiguously marked as hedged or not hedged and postpone the derivation of such interpretations to chapter 5.

Some people find sentences like (3.3c,d) to be infelicitous. The impression is that the speaker is being inconsistent: asserting p but at the same time indicating a lack of commitment to p. For these people, the power of hedges is insufficient to avoid a Moorean violation of norms of assertion, in more or less the way in which Grice would lead us to expect might arise. Even for such speakers, the variants in (3.5) seem to be fine.

(3.5)   a. I might be wrong, but I think Palin is not going to be elected.

b. This might not be true, but it seems like she might not really care about you.

Here we have a kind of "dual hedge," where a statement about epistemic possibility is hedged. This kind of hedging has puzzling aspects from the perspective of much work in philosophy (and, to a slightly lesser degree, in linguistics). In this body of work, it is usually assumed that epistemic modals are asserted from a particular perspective, by default that of the speaker. But it seems strange for someone to hedge a statement about their own epistemic state; it seems to imply an implausible uncertainty about one's own beliefs, at least on standard views of the interpretation of epistemic modals. I will give a detailed analysis of this case in the following chapter. There, I will also discuss cases of hedging that lie outside the realm of assertion.

The discussion above might seem to lead to the conclusion that hedging is concerned solely with the truth of the hedged utterance, which predicts that nonassertive utterances cannot be hedged. This appearance is deceptive. When one considers hedges from a pretheoretical perspective, truth-oriented hedging is highly prominent; this impression is heightened by other hedging strategies than the use of shield hedges, for example the use of epistemic modals or embedding under attitudes, which are (for these cases at least) plainly truth-oriented. But the domain of hedges is in fact much more extensive. As chapter 4 will show in detail, hedging does not directly aim at the literal truth or falsity of a particular sentence, but instead relates to the *implicature* of truth that arises from the assertion of that sentence; as such, other implicatures can also be hedged if the content of the hedge itself induces this interpretation. These observations indicate that the domain of hedging could well be wider than only assertions, which turns out to be correct, as the following examples show.

(3.6)   a. (?) You might not know, but what's the GDP of Namibia?

b. If you happen to know, what's the GDP of Namibia?

(3.7)   a. ? I'm not sure whether you can do this, but stop and pick me up on your way home.

b. If you have time, can you stop and pick me up on your way home?

In this book, my focus will be on assertions, but I don't see why my model should not admit extension to other speech acts, given the obvious changes in denotations, sincerity conditions, and so on.

Are there analogues to hedging outside the realm of linguistic speech acts? Clearly, yes. The most obvious lies in advertising and in strategies that are often used to avoid possible consequences of inaccurate advertisements.

There are many kinds of advertisements: audio, two-dimensional, video-based. One common kind of advertising involves pictoral images. One provides an image purportedly of one's product and thereby represents the product as having the characteristics of the pictured object. This is a reasonable way to advertise objects for sale. However, it is often the case that the actual object lacks some, or even most, characteristics of the object in the image. Most people have probably had the experience of ordering a hamburger, bowl of noodles, or salad on the basis of beautiful pictures on a menu and being disappointed when the food appeared. Juicy-looking hamburger images may correspond to small, sad actual hamburgers. Crispy-looking lettuce images may correspond to brownish, wilted actual lettuce. Part of the reason for this discrepancy presumably involves the varying quality of ingredients available on a given occasion for replicating the image. But there is a puzzle here: why is it that, even though it is common knowledge that these images may not correspond to reality, they still sway us in our purchases? And why, knowing that we know that the image may not correspond to reality, do the sellers continue to provide such images? Notice that these questions are similar to those that arose in chapter 2 in the context of the credibility of signals in cases where it is not clear whether or not the interests of signaler and receiver align.

That chapter concluded that considerations of reputation can, in many cases at least, partially guarantee credibility. The case of advertising is not at first glance necessarily similar. An advertiser may not care about its reputation in precisely the same way: it may, for example, not expect any further interaction with a particular (potential) customer, so its reputation may not be that important as a motivator. However, this does not mean that corporations are exempt from considerations of lost credibility. Reputations may well be important in many cases, especially given the bad publicity stemming from false advertising, as from any other instance of bad corporate practice. Further, the existence of regulatory agencies and other watchdogs with the power to levy fines or other punishments is a clear incentive for advertisers to avoid demonstrably false communications. Thus, although the reason might be different, advertisers have incentive to avoid the consequences of (potentially) false claims, just as human communicative agents do.

I have suggested that hedging is a means of avoiding such consequences. What might be an analogue of hedging for the advertising case? The answer seems to be *disclaimers*, slogans which can be found on advertisements that indicate that the advertisement may not completely correspond to reality. Most if not all disclaimers attach to pictorial advertisements. In Japan, many (if not most) product images on labels, menus, etc. are accompanied by the following phrase:

(3.8)   Shasshin-wa   imeeji desu
        photograph-Top image is
        'The photograph is an image.' (lit.)

This expression has a rather complex meaning, though at first glance it appears to be a simple tautology, since all photographs are by definition images. The sense of *imeeji* 'image' at issue here is different. It refers to a kind of idealized version of the product for sale.[3] Semantically, the sentence can be paraphrased as something like (3.9).

(3.9)   The photograph represents an idealized version of the object it depicts.

In general, such images will be idealized in a positive manner (given the purposes of advertising), though it is not in principle necessary that they are: semantically speaking, it is perfectly possible for an *imeeji* to look less attractive than the product it represents, though such situations will rarely arise in practice for obvious reasons.[4]

The use of (3.8) is rather close to the following English phrases, which are found in much the same contexts: together with photographic advertisements.

(3.10)   a. Actual product may differ (from picture).
         b. (Actual) contents may vary.

Disclaimers act precisely like hedges in terms of their pragmatic function, by insulating communicators from potential negative consequences of error. In the case of advertisements that are judged to be

---

[3] From the *Kojien* dictionary definition of *imeeji*: *atama no naka ni ukaberu, mono no sugata no arisama* 'a picture of the form of an object arising in one's mind' (Shinmura 2008).
[4] Thanks to Makoto Kanazawa for discussion on this point.

inaccurate, such consequences might include the imposition of penalties by some regulatory agency on the business producing the advertised project or service, or simply a future lack of trust by consumers, resulting in a loss of profit. I take it that whatever mechanism is used to analyze the case of hedges ought to be able to analyze disclaimers as well.

I should note before proceeding that the analogy between hedges and disclaimers is not perfect. In the domain of hedging, we find both shield hedges and "softeners" such as epistemic modals which reduce the strength of the assertion. In pictorial advertising, there does not appear to be any analogue of "softening" hedges like *might*. The reason is that *might* has the function of indicating a reduced confidence in the sentential content, from within the sentence itself; this sort of modification of images simply does not exist.[5] It therefore might be that the phenomenon of shield hedges instantiates a more general communicative mechanism in a way that "soft" hedges do not.

In the remainder of this chapter I will provide a uniform account of disclaimers and shield hedging in terms of *reputations*, understood as representations by game participants of the past behavior of (themselves and) other participants, which in turn lead to expectations about players' future behavior. The basic idea is that a hedge or disclaimer requests an exemption from negative consequences to reputation stemming from the hedged utterance.

3.2 Reputations

To understand what hedges do, we need to model two things: the reputations of agents in repeated games, and the action of disclaimers and hedges, conceived of as operators on reputations of a particular sort. Much research has been done on reputations in game theory, as can be seen from a glance at the relevant portions of Mailath and Samuelson 2006. In this book I will not require most of this apparatus. Instead, I will make use of a very simple model of reputations based on records of the past actions of players.

We will begin by viewing reputations as derived from simple *histories*: sequences of objects of the form *act* selected from A, the set of possible actions for a given agent in a given (repeated) game.[6] These objects

---

[5] I will return to the case of epistemic modals in the next chapter.

[6] Allowing any action from A is the most general version of the model. Shortly, I will restrict it to communicative acts in particular, which will change the way in which histories are represented, as we will see.

are records of an agent's actions in past repetitions of the game. Each iteration of the game will introduce a new object in the sequence via a concatenation operation, namely the action of the agent in that game iteration. This sequential structure is not strictly speaking necessary. One could also model reputations as sets of past actions (or, more carefully, multisets, so that the required proportions of action can be calculated, as will be discussed below), as in one formulation discussed by Mailath and Samuelson (2006). But I think it is desirable to have the extra structure provided by sequences, as it gives a way to model changes over time in the behavior of agents.

When games are complex, histories will be n-tuples of sequences instead of single sequences, each object in the tuple representing the history of the agent's actions at one choice point of the game. More formally, things look as follows.

(3.11)   a. **History of play for a single move.**
$H_a^{g,n} = \langle act_a^1, \ldots, act_a^n \rangle$, for the move at a given choice point in game g by agent a, for game repetitions $1 \ldots n$.

b. **History for a game.**
$H_a^{m,g,n} = \langle H_a^{1,g,n}, \ldots H_a^{m,g,n} \rangle$, where game g has m choice points for agent a.

Observe that $card(H_a^{i,g,n}) = n$ for all $0 < i \leq m$ in game histories of the form $H_a^{m,g,n}$ (here, $card$ is a cardinality predicate). Histories of the form above are assumed to be common knowledge of all game participants (and free from error). Relaxing these assumptions yields various refinements (cf. Camerer 2003) which I will put aside for present purposes.[7]

Histories are created by a simple process of concatenation:

(3.12)   **Making histories.**
a. **Histories of moves.**
Suppose we have a move history $H_a^{g,n}$ and a plays ACT at iteration $n + 1$. Then $H_a^{g,n+1} = \langle act_a^1, \ldots, act_a^n, ACT \rangle$.

b. **Histories of games.**
Suppose we have a game history $H_a^{m,g,n} = \langle H_a^{1,g,n}, \ldots H_a^{m,g,n} \rangle$. Then $H_a^{m,g,n+1} = \langle H_a^{1,g,n+1}, \ldots H_a^{m,g,n+1} \rangle$.

---

[7] For instance, one could limit the number of prior repetitions to which a given agent has access, in order to see what happens when agents are assumed to have limited memory, or allow agents to make errors about histories to some degree. I will not consider these complexities further here, but they are an interesting avenue for future research.

A player's reputation in a game is derived from his history in that game. The basic idea is simple. We merely view a player's reputation with respect to some choice as his propensity, based on past performance, to make a particular move at that point in the game. Such propensities are computed from frequencies of this or that move in the history. In particular, the propensity of a player a to play a move m in a game g at choice point i is just the proportion of the total number of game repetitions in which the player chose the action m at choice point i, so

$$F_{H_a^{m,g,n}}(move, i) = \frac{card(\{act \in H_a^{m,g,n}[i] | act = move\})}{card(H_a^{m,g,n}[i])},$$

where $H_a^g[i]$ denotes the restriction of the history to that tuple associated with i. The above number can be viewed as a probability: in effect, the information that the game participants have about a's likelihood of choosing move m. In this model, the reputation of the player is identical with the propensities obtained in this manner about his past actions, and thus the probabilities associated with his future moves.

For example, suppose we have a simple game with two players, A and B, who each can make a single move, a or b. Suppose that the game is repeated three times and that A always plays a and B plays a twice and finally b. The histories of the players then look as follows.

(3.13)   a. $H_A^{1,g,3} = \langle\langle a, a, a \rangle\rangle$
        b. $H_B^{1,g,3} = \langle\langle a, a, b \rangle\rangle$

The propensity of A to play a is $\frac{3}{3} = 1$, so B can reasonably expect A to play a again, on the assumption that A is following the same strategy as he did in previous rounds. Conversely, B's propensity to play a is $\frac{2}{3} = 0.66$, so the situation is less certain for A in the next round.

We can also define a player's reputation with respect to the strategies played in individual game repetitions, when games are complex. A single-game strategy σ (of the set of possible strategies for player a, S_a) can be considered as just a sequence of moves at choice points, so a tuple $\langle (act_1, i_1), \ldots, (act_n, i_n) \rangle$. An agent's reputation with respect to a strategy then is just the propensity that agent has for playing the entire sequence of moves associated with the strategy. We then have, for $\sigma = \langle (act_1, i_1) \ldots (act_n, i_n) \rangle$,

$$F_{H_a^{g,n}}\sigma = F_{H_a^{g,n}}\langle (act_1, i_1), \ldots, (act_n, i_n) \rangle.$$

In the following, our attention will mostly be focused on single-move strategies, due to the use of signaling games.

This sort of computation about propensities is of course the simplest available variety of induction about future behavior on the basis of past performance. It assumes that future behavior will work identically to past behavior. As a result, if one views the propensities I have been discussing in a probabilistic manner the theory essentially uses a frequentist interpretation of probabilities to judge the probability of a future action.[8] It is worth making this assumption explicit for future reference.

(3.14)   **Inertia Assumption.**
            The future actions of game players will be similar to the actions they have taken in the past. In particular, for a strategy σ of player a, $F_{H_a^g,n}\sigma = P(H^{g,n+1} = \sigma)$, for the probability function(s) P used by players in calculating future actions.[9]

More complex sorts of induction are also available, but in this book I will not consider them, as adjudicating between the various possibilities (together with the relevant background) would be a book-length project in itself (though see Kulkarni and Harman 2011 for extensive discussion). I do not think that moving to a more complex form of inductive reasoning would impact my analysis of the general function of hedges, though it might alter general conclusions about the propensities and reliability of a given agent. In any case, I will provide one way to add complexity later in the chapter by means of differentiating the situations in which a particular action is taken.

Note that the notion of an agent's propensity for a property above yields a real number in the interval $[0,1]$. This number can be viewed as a point on a "propensity scale"; an agent has a propensity for using strategy σ iff his propensity to play σ exceeds a contextually set degree s, the contextual standard for having that propensity. This sort of analysis is widely used in linguistics for the analysis of adjectives (cf. Kennedy 1999 and references therein); Kennedy (2007) puts the view to work in the analysis of natural language vagueness. I make use of a contextual standard because it already seems vague how often one must play a strategy to count as having a propensity to play it, meaning that a degree-based analysis which is able to incorporate a picture of vague predication is directly applicable. I will thus say that

---

[8] See e.g. Binmore (2009) for more on interpretations of probabilities.
[9] For the moment, we can remain agnostic about whether players use the same probability functions, though it seems highly unlikely that they really do; later in the book these functions will be indexed to agents for just this reason.

$$Prop(a, \sigma) \text{ iff } F_{H_a^{g,n}}\sigma \succ s,$$

where s is the contextual standard for propensity-having. This just says that a has a propensity to play strategy σ if, in the past, he has played σ with a probability above the standard s (itself in $[0, 1]$), as computed by frequency.

Relevant for our purposes are the properties of cooperativity and truthfulness. Strategies can be characterized as *cooperative* or *uncooperative*. Here I will call a strategy cooperative, $Coop(\sigma)$, if it yields a best outcome for both players over an infinite horizon of game repetitions.[10] A strategy for signal-sending will be called *truthful*, $Truthful(\sigma)$, if the conventional meaning of the signal matches the sender's knowledge of the state of the world (in the way discussed for signaling games in the previous chapter). We will use these notions extensively in what follows. For example, an agent can be said to have a propensity to play a particular strategy; if he has that tendency and the strategy is cooperative, the agent can be said to be cooperative too. Again, it seems vague what counts as cooperative in terms of frequency, calling for an analysis in terms of standards.

This idea can be generalized. Consider cases where the agent plays a variety of different strategies, all of which are cooperative, but plays none of them with sufficient frequency to count as having a propensity to play that strategy. Here we still want to say that the agent is cooperative. To allow for this situation, we can define cooperativity and truthfulness for agents as follows.

(3.15) $Coop(a)$ iff $\displaystyle\sum_{\sigma \in Coop} F_{H_a^{g,n}}\sigma \succ s$

(3.16) $Truthful(a)$ iff $\displaystyle\sum_{\sigma \in Truthful} F_{H_a^{g,n}}\sigma \succ s$

According to these definitions, a player is cooperative (truthful) just in case the sum of the player's propensity for playing each cooperative (truthful) strategy exceeds the threshold for being considered to have a propensity. This is just to say that an agent is cooperative (truthful) if her propensity to play a group of cooperative (truthful) strategies is sufficiently high. The situation where an agent always plays a single

---

[10] I assume that agents have access to this information, and so tacitly that they are able to make this calculation. As always, the situation in the abstract model may or may not reflect the capabilities of actual individuals.

strategy with the relevant property falls out as a special case. Hereafter I will call a player who uses a truthful strategy *reliable* and refer to the player's propensity for truthfulness as *Rel(a)*, the reliability of the agent.

For an example, consider a speaker who consistently tells the truth, but occasionally either gets things wrong or lies. Let's suppose for concreteness that $H_a^g = (TTTF)^{23}$ (understood as 23 repetitions of $TTTF$), where as discussed above T indicates that the current state $t \in [\![S]\!]$, the conventional denotation of the signal S. Thus a is consistently truthful in 0.75 of the game iterations. Then, if $s < 0.75$, the speaker a will be judged truthful and hence cooperative; the receiver is then justified, under most strategies, in believing the next utterance of a, and indeed further utterances unless a sends signals of type F a sufficient number of times to drive $\sum_{\sigma \in Truthful} F_{H_a^g, n}\sigma$ below s.

Of course, the procedure described here depends on being able to know when an instance of testimony counts as untruthful. The computation cannot be carried out if it is not clear whether the utterance content properly tracks truth. Since this is not always possible, there is going to be some uncertainty left in any given history. This is a problem for the analysis to the extent that we believe that all instances of testimony ought to play a role in making decisions about truthfulness and, by extension, cooperativity. It seems that in general such judgements are made on the basis of partial information: we examine only those instances of testimony which can be determined to be accurate or inaccurate. Those we cannot check are just left out of the computation until they can be gauged for reliability. This means that the computations of cooperativity and truthfulness above (like other kinds of judgements made over histories) should really be restricted to only game iterations which have a determinate second element from the perspective of truth judgements (T or F). This amounts to excluding elements i with the property that $\pi_2(i) = ?$ from computations of reliability.[11]

Let us now consider a second example of how agents might make use of histories, and thus reputations. Recall that in the buyer–seller game without advertising, the seller had the choice of two moves: producing an object of low quality or one of high quality. The first move, as we saw, is not a cooperative move, as it reduces the payoffs to the buyer.

---

[11] Note that this observation also explains the relative gullibility of children: in many or most cases, children don't have a way to check for truth outside of testimony, and so only have a very limited set of data on which to make judgements about truth. Often, this will lead to continuations of initial cooperativity that last much longer than what we find for adults. See chapter 9 for further discussion.

The buyer, conversely, had two moves, buying the produced object or not; here, buying is a cooperative move, as buying increases payoff to the seller, and not buying reduces payoff and so is not cooperative—a slightly peculiar result of the way in which I have defined cooperativity, which is largely tailored for communicative contexts. What should each player do in this situation?

The obvious answer is: if both players have propensities to play cooperatively, then they should both play cooperatively, and if either player does not, then the other player should not. Roughly, playing cooperatively is a good strategy if $Coop(S)$ & $Coop(B)$, and otherwise it is not. (This of course assumes that the contextual standard is set sufficiently high.) We may characterize the situation by saying that, if the seller is known to be cooperative at iteration i, then the buyer should play a cooperative strategy at $i + 1$, and the same, *mutatis mutandis*, in the other direction. In other words, a rational player will have a strategy of the form $Coop(i) \rightarrow play_j(\sigma)$ such that $\sigma \in Coop$, if such a σ exists, for $i, j \in \{S, B\}$. This strategy has the form of a function from histories to moves, as described in the last chapter; note also the close resemblance to the optimal strategies in the image-scoring games of Nowak and Sigmund (1998a,b), as might be expected given the close relationship between the two models. As discussed in the last chapter, in the image-scoring model, each player is assigned an "image score": a cooperative move causes the player's score to rise, and an uncooperative one causes it to fall. Player strategies then dictate cooperation, or not, on the basis of the image score: strategies mentioned by Nowak and Sigmund include cooperating with players when their image score exceeds a certain threshold, or when it exceeds the score of the agent deciding whether or not to cooperate. Plainly, their notion of thresholds is very close to the propensities which have been implemented in this chapter.

Other strategies are of course possible. A more conservative version of the above buyer strategy sets the standard at a fixed point, say 0.8, and plays b only if the seller's "cooperation rating" exceeds that point: that is, the buyer only buys if she is very confident that the seller is being cooperative. The opposite direction is also possible: a gullible or unthrifty buyer might set the standard at 0.2, so that the buyer is willing to take a chance if she thinks there is even a fairly small possibility that the seller is cooperating. For a strategy ignoring standards altogether, the grim strategy discussed in the previous chapter has B playing $\neg b$ if $F_{H_S^g}(L, i_1) \neq 0$—which will be the case (only) if the seller has ever produced low-quality goods. One could also define purely quantitative strategies that make use of the sequential structure of histories, so that, for instance, *B* could play *b* iff *S* played *H* for the past five moves, while anything prior to that is ignored. Many other possibilities can be defined. But, once again, they all depend on the past history of the other game participants. This further reinforces the observation that one's history, and thus one's reputation, is very important to one's future payoffs. As we will see, it is this importance that leads to the existence of disclaimers and hedges.

3.3 How to maintain your reputation

In the last section I provided a simple model of reputations for repeated games. Now we will use this to analyze the work that disclaimers and hedges do. The main idea is simple: adding a hedge or disclaimer keeps the information in that game repetition from being entered into one's reputation.

In a game where the payoffs of one player depend on the actions of the other (or another, in games of more than two players), it is always best to play a strategy that depends on the other player's actions. In repeated games, this is also true, of course. This means that the best strategies available for the second player in the repeated versions of all the games above depend on the second player's knowledge of the first player's probable actions; these can be guessed at based on that player's history via the Inertia Assumption. Recall that in some of the games we have seen it is in fact the case that the best outcome for each player over a sequence of repetitions comes about if they cooperate, although the individual games are not games of coordination in the sense that the players have identical optimal outcomes. What this means is that, for repeated games, the first player has an incentive to maintain his reputation for cooperation at a high level. If he does not, he can expect that, at some point, the second player will stop cooperating and, again over time, the probability of a net loss will increase.[12]

---

[12] This part of the argument assumes that the players do not know each other's strategies. If they do, the details of the situation will change. For example, if the first player knows that the second player will stop cooperating if his reputation for cooperation drops below 0.6, he will work to maintain his reputation just above that level. Still, since the optimal strategies depend on the other player's actions and thus reputations, there will be a point at which reputation maintenance becomes essential, so the outcome is essentially similar.

What does this mean for the best actions of the players? It means that, if there is a way to keep one's reputation for cooperating at a high level, there is incentive to use it. The obvious way to do so is to actually cooperate—and it does seem that this is the only way to keep a good reputation for cooperating in the buying–selling game. But the case of communication, and thus of other games where signals are sent such as advertising, is different. Here, one can send a signal that the world is a certain way, but also communicate that the signal may not be accurate. This amounts to sending a second signal with a metalinguistic character. By sending signals of this metalinguistic kind, one can exempt oneself from damage to one's reputation, given that some other conditions are met. This signal is not available for application to actions—actions change the world directly and cannot be insincere or false. It is instructive to compare inferences drawn from information that cannot be provided insincerely within for example biology, such as that gained from observation of the size of a competitor (e.g. large size indicates strength) or coloration (e.g. brightly colored tail indicates maleness); these are called *indices* by Maynard Smith and Harper (2003) and contrasted with *signals*, which can be insincerely used. In sum, actions speak louder than words; but the reputation created by language is somewhat malleable.

My view is that disclaimers and "shield"-type hedges are metalinguistic signals of this type. They indicate something like this: "the signal I am about to send may be false." Of course, this assumes that the content of the signal is something that can be true or false at all. This is the case for pictorial advertisements that purport to accurately represent a given product; it is also the case for verbal advertisements that indicate (truth-conditional) features of the product. Other types of content will be considered in chapter 4, with respect to both linguistic content and advertising. In this chapter I will only consider hedges which work on content of the former and simpler type.

There are several ways to model the idea that disclaimers and hedges serve to protect reputations in the current framework, of which I will consider two. The first is to complicate the game structure by adding an additional choice node for the first player, which indicates whether or not a disclaimer is produced.[13] This simply takes the game to be of

---

[13] What I will say here also applies to the equivalent game formulation where the first player has three possible initial moves, i.e. $\neg A, A + D$, and A, instead of separating advertising and disclaimer into separate moves.

a different kind than before. The idea then would be that, instead of computing the frequency of the strategy of advertisement and good products, with the resulting definition of cooperativity, we compute the frequency of accurate advertising with respect to the disclaimer; false advertising with disclaimers is then taken to be a cooperative strategy as well. I prefer not to take this route for two reasons. First, this picture gives the disclaimer a character that is the same as an ordinary move. While this may not be exactly wrong, I think its effect is more subtle and that this should be reflected in the model. Second and perhaps similarly, this route makes it necessary to decide whether false advertising with disclaimer counts as a cooperative strategy or not.[14] It is not obvious to me that there is a clear answer to this question. In general, I feel that the disclaimer asks that the current signal be exempted from the question of cooperativity completely, though doing so has an impact on the effectiveness of the communication, as will be discussed in detail in chapter 9. Consequently I will propose a different analysis that directly formalizes this intuition.

I propose that disclaimers and hedges request that the current game not be included in the player's history. If I am not confident in my assertion that p, I may hedge, for I do not want to be put on the record as a liar. If I take the best possible photograph of my product but doubt that the actual product will always live up to the hype, I may put a disclaimer on the photograph, for I do not want to have consumers lose confidence in my truthfulness, or (even worse) be sued for false advertising. The disclaimer essentially says: do not hold me accountable for what I am signaling here.

This idea can be formalized in a number of different ways. The simplest is just not to add the current game result to the history sequence at all: to ignore it completely. It will therefore not count as either positive or negative in the computation of cooperativity. Formalizing this idea is as simple as altering the definition of history construction, something easily accommodated in the current formalism. I will now indicate how this can be done. Recall that the original mechanism was as in (3.12), repeated below as (3.17).

(3.17)   **Making histories.**

  a. **Histories of moves.**

  Suppose we have a move history $H_a^{g,n}$ and a plays ACT at iteration $n + 1$. Then $H_a^{g,n+1} = \langle act_a^1, \ldots, act_a^n, ACT \rangle$.

---

[14] The fact that this question arises directly is, however, a nice feature of the analysis.

b. **Histories of games.**
   Suppose we have a game history $H_a^{m,g,n} = \langle H_a^{1,g,n}, \dots$
   $H_a^{m,g,n} \rangle$. Then $H_a^{m,g,n+1} = \langle H_a^{1,g,n+1}, \dots H_a^{m,g,n+1} \rangle$.

Let us assume that the presence of a disclaimer flags the entire game as "disclaimed." I denote the resulting *disclaimed games* with a predicate of games D, applying to game iterations g_i. Then we can define the following.

(3.18)   **Disclaimed histories.**
   a. **Disclaimed moves.**
      Suppose we have a move history $H_a^{g,n}$. Then $H_a^{g,n} = H_a^{g,n+1}$ iff $D(g_{n+1})$.

   b. **Disclaimed games.**
      Suppose we have a game history $H_a^{m,g,n} = \langle H_a^{1,g,n}, \dots H_a^{m,g,n} \rangle$. Then $H_a^{m,g,n} = H_a^{m,g,n+1}$ iff $D(g_{n+1})$.

This instantiates the first strategy; disclaimed games are simply not entered into the history at all. Is this the right way to go? It seems intuitively clear that signals bundled with disclaimers are used later when evaluating the trustworthiness of other signals with disclaimers, and likely for evaluation of whether the speaker counts as generally cooperative as well. Chapter 9 will concretize this intuition by privileging (in general) nondisclaimed content over disclaimed content in terms of information update. But this move is not compatible with the first strategy. Another, more reasonable-looking, possibility is to add the result of the game to the histories of the players, but (for the signaler) to flag it so that it does not enter the general computation of cooperativity. This is easily enough done. On a second version of this general strategy, one might place the "disclaimed" signals in a separate history of their own. These two strategies appear to be notational variants, given the right mechanism for making cooperativity judgements, though I will spell them both out for completeness. Either looks to be a reasonable way of handling the problem of constructing histories with disclaimed information.

The second strategy can be formalized by introducing a second history for games that have been disclaimed. Each player's history is then a pair $H_a^{m,g,n} = \langle Hn_a^{m,g,n}, Hd_a^{m,g,n} \rangle$ of ordinary histories and the histories of disclaimed games.

(3.19) **Histories of the disclaimed.**

(i) Suppose we have a history $H_a^{m,g,n} = \langle Hn_a^{m,g,n}, Hd_a^{m,g,n}\rangle$. Then $H_a^{m,g,n+1} = \langle Hn_a^{m,g,n+1}, Hd_a^{m,g,n}\rangle$ if $D(g_{n+1})$ does not hold.

(ii) Suppose we have a history $H_a^{m,g,n} = \langle Hn_a^{m,g,n}, Hd_a^{m,g,n}\rangle$. Then $H_a^{m,g,n+1} = \langle Hn_a^{m,g,n}, Hd_a^{m,g,n+1}\rangle$ if $D(g_{n+1})$.

Here we have simply added the results of disclaimed games to the history provided for disclaimed games, while history-making for ordinary games is as before. In this second strategy, the way to calculate cooperativity and truthfulness is as before, but when interested in truthfulness in disclaimed games in particular we can check the second element of the history tuple for propensities with respect to truthfulness rather than the first. In this strategy, it is also necessary to modify the definitions of frequency, propensity, etc. to act only on the first members of history tuples by replacing all instances of H_a^g in the definitions with $\pi_1(H_a^{m,g,n})$, except when checking disclaimed histories, in which case we use $\pi_2(H_a^{m,g,n})$. These changes are trivial and I will omit them here.

For the third option, the mechanism of history creation can be as in (3.19), but we should modify the way that truthfulness is calculated. The current mechanism calculates the proportion of the total number of repetitions where the signal sent matched the state of the world. Here, we would like to calculate the total number of truthful signals, but ignore signals from disclaimed games only if they are inaccurate. This means that we must take both elements of the history tuple into account in our calculations. From this perspective truthfulness can be defined in two steps, first by adding the number of instances of truthful strategies in normal games to the number of truthful instances in disclaimed games, and then taking this proportion as the frequency of truthful strategies in the total history while excluding those signals that are both nontruthful and disclaimed from the comparison class. The result can then be evaluated with respect to (3.16). This means that we must redefine the notion of frequency for cases like these.

The required notion of frequency is this one.[15]

$$F^3_{H_a^{m,g,n}}(move, i) = \frac{\begin{array}{l} card(\{a | a \in \pi_1(H_a^{m,g,n}[i]) \ \& \ a = move\}) + \\ card(\{a | a \in \pi_2(H_a^{m,g,n}[i]) \ \& \ a = move\}) \end{array}}{\begin{array}{l} card(\pi_1(H_a^{m,g,n}[i])) + \\ card(\{a | a \in \pi_2(H_a^{m,g,n}[i]) \ \& \ a = move\}) \end{array}}.$$

[15] "F^3" is mnemonic for "frequency for strategy 3."

Using this definition for the computation of truthfulness gives the desired results. As I said above, I will not try to adjudicate beween these ideas here; I suspect that there is not a right answer about which is the correct one, and that each has its uses in particular contexts.

Let us examine a case study. Consider the agent with a history of the form $(TTTF)^{23}$ from the previous section; this agent, as we saw there, has a propensity for truthfulness of 0.75. Now suppose that this agent sends a message of type F The resulting history will have the form $(TTTF)^{23}F$; calculating a's propensity for truthfulness now yields 0.741. This is not a very significant difference, but as such moves stack up the danger of being judged uncooperative rises. Thus a might choose to disclaim her signal in the last case. If disclaimed, we have $D(F)$ for iteration 93 of the game; on any of the above interpretations of disclaiming, this iteration is then left out of the reputation computation, and the speaker's "index of truthfulness" remains 0.75 after all.

Before proceeding, a few points ought to be clarified. First, I want to emphasize that the kind of reputation analyzed here—records of a given individual's past behavior—does not exhaust all the factors that can contribute to an individual's reputation. Clearly there are many other considerations that play a role. Consider the case of an honest politician who has never taken a bribe or performed any other questionable act (as far as anyone knows). We are still likely to consider the person as corruptible or perhaps even corrupt, despite our lack of any evidence other than her politicianhood. Conversely, no amount of evidence can make us think they are honest given that we already believe them dishonest.[16] The reason for this individual's reputational difficulties is precisely and only the fact that she is a politician, and that we, with our knowledge of political systems, are disposed to believe that politicians are by nature dishonest. The example shows that, under the right circumstances, other information can override induction-based reputational considerations; but such information does not play a role in the operation of hedges or disclaimers, and so I will not incorporate it into my model just yet.

For a preview, though, I will incorporate this sort of default judgement about trustworthiness into the theory in the second part of the book, where more general considerations about the reliability of information enter the picture. There the main focus is on evidential sources, and on how judgements about the reliability of such sources impact the use and interpretation of evidential constructions. Clearly different

---

[16] Thanks to Hsing Chien Tsia for the example.

evidence sources are associated with different levels of reliability in general, but sufficient good (bad) performance can upgrade (downgrade) a particular source in context. We will see there that the testimony of different individuals can be associated with different levels of reliability, as can the reliability of the information transmitted by the disclaimed moves of that individual. As I will show, it is possible to go to an even more fine-grained level, and consider the particular reliability of moves disclaimed in certain ways as opposed to others: the content of p in a bare statement of "This is probably wrong, but p" might be pegged as less reliable than "I think this is right, but it might not be; anyway, p." The result of this second part of the theory is that the act of hedging does not solely correspond to the disclamation operation D, but turns out to have a more continuous character when its effects are considered together with rankings on information sources and the changes in those rankings that induction over histories can induce. The particular case of testimony is discussed in detail in chapter 9.

3.4 Discriminating among situations

The model as presented so far is extremely abstract. Interactions are viewed as instances of game repetitions, and no more; reputations retain only information about the actions taken by players, and no more. Even if we suppose that the games themselves, and so the choice set available to each player, are common knowledge of all players (meaning that moves can in some sense be judged for cooperativity or other properties), information about the actions taken by players over the life of the repeated game is clearly not the only information taken into account in making judgements about the future actions of others. One might consider, for instance, the context of use: perhaps a given agent is reliable in certain kinds of situations but not others; for linguistic actions, the content of the utterance should also play a role, as an agent might be knowledgeable about some domains and not others, or have a tendency to lie about matters relating to his family but nothing else. A model with the resources to discriminate between situations of use or contents of utterances would be far more useful than the skeletal one I have given so far. In this section, I want to add some parameters to the model in order to reflect this fact.

I will proceed as follows. I will first enrich the model of histories with the extra parameters mentioned in the preceding paragraph, after which

I will show how they can be used to yield a somewhat more sophisticated picture of how judgements about cooperativity and reliability can be made.

In order to enable the sorts of induction we might require, it is sufficient to enrich the content of histories. As presented so far, histories of interactions are tuples of action sequences: for a game g with n choice points, $H_a^{m,g,n} = \langle H_n^{1,g}, \ldots, H_n^{m,g} \rangle$, where each $H_n^{i,g}$ is in turn a record of the actions taken at point i by the relevant agent, and so a simple sequence of actions $\langle act_1, \ldots, act_n \rangle$ for n repetitions of the game. These representations of histories are rather impoverished. It is not possible to recover any information from them about the situation in which a particular game instance occurred, or the actions a given agent took in situations of a certain kind, or any kind of contextual information at all. More complexity is needed in the model to make such reasoning available.

Fortunately, it can be added straightforwardly by complicating the individual "entries" of the histories. I will also take this opportunity to tailor the history entries a bit more closely to their intended application in information acquisition. Thus, rather than using sequences of simplex actions, we can instead let each game repetition introduce a 3-tuple to the history sequence, consisting of a proposition, a truth value, and a set of properties. This set can be taken to contain information about the communicative acts themselves, and also properties of the situations in which the act was performed, so, strictly speaking, we really have a set of properties of the particular game iteration. This gives a new representation for the entries of individual game iterations g_i, of the form

$$\langle \varphi, v, \mathcal{P} \rangle,$$

where φ is the propositional content of the communicative act, $\pi_2(g_i)$ is its truth value, which may be indeterminate and so can be identified with one of the elements of the set $\{T, F, ?\}$, and $\mathcal{P}$ is a subset of the set of properties of game iteration or of the action taken there, $\{P | P(g_i)\}$; for purposes of generality, I take it that this set can be quite heterogeneous and contain any predicate which concerns itself with g_i. Thus, move histories will now be sequences of tuples of this form instead of sequences of simple actions, and game histories sequences of move histories (1-tuples in cases of games with only one choice point). In what follows, I will generally write $\mathcal{V}$ for $\{T, F, ?\}$ to avoid typographical clutter.

It is not trivial to say what properties are going to be in $\pi_3(g_i)$. This is in part an empirical question; considerations about salient features of utterance situations and about psychological factors relating to what properties human beings find significant enough to store in long-term memory must be taken into account. Exactly what properties should be included in $\mathcal{P}$ appears to be an instance of Fodor's version of the Frame Problem (Fodor 2000), the question of what is relevant for a particular inference in the general case. This problem arises in many other places in pragmatics: the computation of sets of alternatives, of implicatures, of relevant alternatives (see McCready forthcoming, b for some discussion). Answering this question is not easy, and perhaps not even possible with the instruments made available by the linguistics toolbox. In any case, it is certainly beyond the scope of this book. For the purposes of the present project, I will have to leave the question of what to include in $\mathcal{P}$ underdetermined; I will assume a black-magical mechanism that takes care of the problem.[17] It is also going to be necessary to close $\mathcal{P}$ under inference, for otherwise we won't have access to some kinds of composite properties which will be needed in the second part of the book.

However, it is at least possible to specify something about the content which *must* be there. If we limit attention to features that appear relevant to present analytical purposes, it is clear that these sets must at least contain those properties of the move and of the game situation which are both useful for making later judgements about the agent and recoverable from observation. For instance, in the case of signaling, we will require information about the propositional content of the signal (assuming as usual that signals have conventional meanings), which should be included in $\mathcal{P}$. We should also have at least information about the general purpose of the conversational interaction and of the degree of interest that the conversational participants have in fulfilling it, or what is at stake in the conversation in the sense of Stanley (2005). We might also have derived information, such as the degree to which the utterance contributed to resolving the conversational purpose: its relevance, in the sense of van Rooij (2003b). Here, we see interaction between properties of the context and properties of the content proper.

---

[17] The problem seems intimately connected with the issue of determining what the question under discussion is for a given discourse, or trying to understand what other conversational participants are aiming to achieve, in itself a book-length issue at the very minimum.

Therefore, I will allow $\mathcal{P}$ to remain unspecified except for requiring that it contain information about the action types (for comparison with other similar types), for example what kind of propositional content is being communicated, and also information about the situation in which the action was used, for instance information about the topic of discourse, context of utterance, or known speaker goals. These sorts of information seem like reasonable candidates for things that one could expect conversational participants to recall, and, with them, it's possible to separate out instances of histories that are relevant for the current computation, as desired.

There are many applications for enriched histories, as many as there are reasons to restrict attention to certain situations when making predictions about future events. Here I will focus on cases which are obviously relevant to considerations of cooperativity and reliability. I begin with a case where the particular context of utterance is relevant to evaluation of reliability, choosing as exemplar the evaluation of utterances by a teacher who is known to be an unreliable colleague, but who is a cooperative individual in the context of nonprofessional interactions. It is easy to find similar cases with respect to content. Again, we can consider an expert in a scientific field with a terrible moral character, but who is extremely reliable when attention is restricted to his area of expertise.

Let's begin with the case of a professor, called Amelia, who is invariably truthful about all issues when speaking with friends and family, but who has a commitment to avoiding work-related responsibilities which results in her being highly unreliable in her communications when they might result in added work. Amelia is now asked to chair a committee and says that she is busy. Is this statement likely to be true? This is something that we would like to be able to derive from the records we have of her previous interactions. Let us suppose, as before, that those interactions are modeled as instances of signaling games. Then we have a history $H_a^{m,g,n}$ supposing n iterations of the signaling interaction. We can assume for simplicity that games here consist only of single utterances, so each repetition contains only one choice point for the sender (Amelia); thus $m = 1$ and the sole element of $H_a^{m,g,n}$ is a sequence of elements $h_a^{g,i} = \langle\langle\varphi_1, v_1, \mathcal{P}_1\rangle_1, \ldots, \langle\varphi_n, v_n, \mathcal{P}_n\rangle_n\rangle$, where $v_i \in V$. Suppose as before that we can classify the signaling moves s_i into two categories based on the state of affairs that held at the time of utterance, yielding a set of cooperative moves, i.e. truthful signals, and a set of uncooperative moves, i.e. signals whose conventional meaning fails to properly represent the state of the world (and, as proposed before, ignoring those elements g_i such that $\pi_2(g_i) = ?$). Then Amelia's reputation for truthfulness is based on whether for any given iteration g_i the signal s she sends in i conventionally represents the actual situation t, so whether $t \in [\![s]\!]$. All this is familiar.

To analyze the Amelia case, we proceed in two steps. First, it is necessary to determine at what level predictions should be made about the reliability of Amelia's utterance. At least two relevant possibilities are available. First, one could consider the general reliability of what she says, which means considering her entire reputation, the whole history of her (discourse) moves. But given the scenario, this method will not be very efficient: since her behavior is dramatically different in work and non-work situations, an agent who is aware of this fact should consider only the relevant type of situation in judging the reliability of her current utterance. The second possibility, then, is to consult the properties of each move $\mathcal{P}$ to see which type of situation the move falls into, and then restrict Amelia's reputation to only the relevant situation type; since here the relevant distinction is between cases where $W = \lambda x[x$ was produced in a work-related situation$]$ holds of s and those where it does not. Since we are considering Amelia's reputation in a situation related to her professional responsibilities, the restricted reputation will consist of the triples $\langle \varphi, v_i, \mathcal{P} \rangle$ such that $W \in \mathcal{P}$.

Now, given what we know about Amelia, we can expect that her propensity for truthfulness in the history restricted to W-utterances will prove to be quite low, meaning that it will likely fall below s; thus the claim she has made of being unable to chair the committee will be disbelieved, with whatever consequences that may have. This will be so even if her overall propensity for truthfulness is quite high. Concretely, suppose that she has a history h of length 1000, of which 100 elements have the property that $W \in \pi_3(g_i)$. Let Amelia's propensity for truthfulness computed with respect to h be 0.9, as every element such that $W \notin \pi_3(g_i)$ is such that $t \in [\![s]\!]$ $(=\pi_1(g_1))$ for the state t relevant at utterance time. This means that she has been untruthful in every g_i for which $W \in \pi_3(g_i)$; therefore, computing her propensity for truthfulness with respect to the restricted history of moves made in contexts satisfying W yields an index of 0, which will be below even the most liberal standard for ascribing a propensity for being truthful.

Next, a case where information about the content of the utterance is relevant. Take a standard kind of case from the epistemological literature on testimony (e.g. Audi 2002) where a particular individual is very reliable about issues in a given area and not very reliable elsewhere. The canonical example might be a sort of absent-minded scientist type. Let us instantiate this example as a researcher, Bob, who is up on the semantics–pragmatics literature, has excellent intuitions, and so on, but otherwise more or less fails to function in daily life. An extreme case, he cannot manage even to remember the weather outside after entering a building. Consequently most of what he says is not truth-conducive, unless the discussion involves semantics or pragmatics, in which case he is always spot on.

This case can be analyzed in a way exactly analogous to the Amelia case; the differences will only involve the sort of restriction that needs to be induced on Bob's history with respect to signaling games. Thus, consider the predicate $SP = \lambda x[$the content φ of x concerns semantics or pragmatics$]$;[18] we are then interested in distinguishing those elements g_i of Bob's history such that $SP \in \pi_3(g_i)$, just as with W for Amelia above. Then, supposing that Bob performs no better than chance on any given iteration g_j where $SP \notin \pi_3(g_j)$ but is truth-conducive to a degree of 0.95 otherwise, and further supposing a sufficiently high proportion of non-semantics/pragmatics discourse, Bob will be judged as unreliable in general, but highly reliable when the discourse concerns semantics and pragmatics. Thus, adding the relevant restrictions enables a fine-grained means of making judgements about speaker cooperativity and reliability on the basis of past interactions. We will see more applications of the information contained in the 3-tuples that make up game histories in the second half of the book.

There are further problems concerning restrictions that have to do with interest relativity (see Stanley 2005): the stakes at issue will often determine how specific the kinds of contexts are that we are going to want to take into account. The higher the stakes, the more stringent our computation is likely to be. In general, we might expect to find restriction of attention to game iterations where the stakes are qualitatively similar to those of the current context, in addition to judgements about general reliability; perhaps standard shifting will also play a role.[19] The analysis of such restrictions thus must involve both

---

[18] This of course presupposes that x is a signal, for otherwise it will have no content in the relevant sense.

[19] The relationship between shifting standards with respect to phenomena like gradable predicates and restriction of histories of evidence acquisition seems to be a potentially promising area for investigation, but one I will not be able to enter into here.

utterance contexts and the question under discussion, as well as game-theoretic considerations about utilities. This is complex, and I will have to leave it for future work.[20] In the next section I will examine some remaining foundational issues that arise in the context of the picture of disclaiming I have developed, after which we will turn, in the next chapter, to consider some other kinds of hedges and consequences of hedging.

3.5 Residual issues

Several questions are left unresolved by the above. Here is one. Suppose that two agents are playing the communication game for the first time of a series with an indefinite number of iterations, and suppose further that it is not clear from contextual cues whether the speaker is cooperative or not.[21] What should the receiver do on observation of the sender's signal—trust the signal or not? The analysis I have given has nothing to say about this case: there is no history to rely on, and so there is no information about the cooperativity of participants in the interaction. The Gricean view (presumably; see chapter 1) is that, as a normative matter, the hearer should trust the signal. In the following I will give two possible explanations of the reason why.

The first is just that an initial move of "trust" opens the door to maximizing future benefits. The hearer does not know the speaker's strategy; he could be sending a false signal for personal gain, or honestly trying to communicate. If he is indeed trying to communicate, but she chooses not to act on his signal, he is likely not to cooperate in (at least) the following round—indeed, if the sender is using any sort of tit-for-tat style strategy he will be pushed into noncooperativity by a noncooperative move of the hearer at this stage. The reason is that after the initial stage of the game, the sample size of the game history is of cardinality 1, and so whatever move the hearer makes will induce a propensity calculation yielding either 1 or 0, depending on the move. As a result, if the hearer hopes for cooperation in (immediately) subsequent rounds, she should cooperate on the first round. The same goes for the speaker. The result of strategies that try to maximize utility over the long

---

[20] Thanks to Sara Moradlou for helpful comments relating to this point.
[21] As previously mentioned, the influence of contextual cues, and their necessity or lack thereof for questions of trust in testimony, has been a major focus of research on this topic since the work of Hume and Reid. These topics will be taken up in full detail in chapter 9.

term is then cooperative behavior in the initial stage. A similar result is derived for prisoner's dilemma games in the image-scoring model of Nowak and Sigmund (1998b). In general, here again, we find that an initial noncooperative move will induce a low image score which in turn will cause the probability of cooperation by the other player to drop on optimal strategies.

The second explanation assigns a larger role to habit or convention. Speakers are ordinarily assumed to behave cooperatively in the sense of Gricean cooperativity; this is how the familiar calculations associated with Gricean reasoning and conversational implicature go through. One of the Gricean virtues is to follow the Maxim of Quality, which states in part that one should not say things that one believes to be false. If one makes the assumption that conversational participants respect Quality, then we would expect truthfulness in signaling; further, this expectation will lead us to expect truthfulness on the first round of a repeated game. Otherwise stated, our expectations about the conventions of communication lead us to gamble that whatever new agents we encounter obey these conventions. This gamble also leads to cooperative behavior in initial game stages.

These two analyses can be teased apart by considering games that do not involve signaling. The Gricean story only has to do with communicative conventions; it has nothing to do with economic maneuvering or standard prisoner's dilemma games (at least in any direct way). The first analysis predicts that cooperative behavior will be the norm in *all* repeated games, given the right payoff structures, known number of repetitions, mutual knowledge, and so on; the Gricean analysis predicts cooperative behavior in communicative settings, but has nothing to say about what might happen elsewhere. Therefore, if cooperative behavior arises in the initial stages of economic settings as well, the Gricean story, while not necessarily wrong, must be augmented by a separate analysis of economic (and other) cases. As it turns out, it is known that cooperative behavior is best (payoff maximizing) in economic settings as well for repeated games (Mailath and Samuelson 2006). This shows that the Gricean assumption is actually best considered a special case of a more general interagent dynamics—at least for the Quality case discussed here, but likely also for the other "submaxims," if they are considered as instances of general cooperative behavior.[22]

---

[22] It is less easy to use an image scoring/reputational analysis for gauging cooperativity of the kind involved in computations of e.g. Quantity or Manner, for the simple reason that,

It is worth noting here that this may well be the initial motivation for advertising as well. By advertising, the signaler indicates some degree of confidence (possibly feigned) in his product. If the claim of the advertisement turns out to be false, some reputational damage to the advertiser would take place; the bare fact of advertising then indicates some substantial degree of confidence in the claim. By this move, the advertiser should intend to make the receiver believe that there is a reason to move directly into a cooperative equilibrium. This, again, makes some sense if one makes reference to an initial convention of cooperation, which yields an initial move on which the advertisement is believed.

Within the model(s) developed, then, we have good reason to expect initial cooperative moves. This observation shows the usefulness of the game-theoretic approach to pragmatics. As we have seen already, there is a good deal of research using game-theoretical tools in such areas as the rise of conventional meaning (Lewis 1969) and Gricean notions in pragmatics (van Rooij 2003b, 2004), as well as other areas such as nonliteral communication and mutual belief (e.g. the papers in Benz et al. 2006a). Here we can see that assumptions about mutual cooperativity are also derivable using game-theoretic techniques. This is not a new observation; it is made both implicitly and explicitly in the work of van Rooij, for example. The present work, though, shows that the results carry over to new settings like the present one.

Nonetheless, this situation does not necessarily arise for all possible cases. So far we have considered only cases of games without signaling and games with signaling but without the possibility of disclaimers. What happens when we also have the option of signaling via a hedge that our other signal(s) may be false? Here the situation is different. The result about the preference for initial cooperative moves in repeated games depended on the expectation that the signaler, because of a desire to maximize his expected payoffs in later rounds, would play a cooperative move in the first round. But this expectation only arises because of the possibility of later penalties for noncooperative initial moves. If that iteration of the game is disclaimed, then (according to my analysis) any noncooperative moves are not entered into the history

---

here, the question of whether a speaker is cooperating or not will not be in any sense a binary phenomenon. While there has been investigation of prisoner's dilemmas with continuous payoffs (also known as "trader's dilemmas," e.g. Le and Boyd 2007 for recent work on the evolutionary dynamics), I am not aware of research on the effects of reputation in such games (see also Fullam et al. 2004), though it would clearly be of interest for Gricean pragmatics.

of the player who made them. This is so for any of the three analysis strategies I outlined.[23] But if the move is not put in the history, then the signaler need not fear retaliation, and so the player receiving the signal has no reason to expect a cooperative initial move anymore. Why then would any player, signaler or receiver, choose to cooperate in this sort of situation? We might call this the puzzle of initial cooperation, which is slightly less tractable than the puzzle of cooperation in games without disclaimers. It seems that the standard tools of the theory of repeated games do not account for this case, unlike the case of signaling without disclaimers discussed above.

In this case, I think the natural analysis does involve Gricean cooperation as such. We can think of Gricean cooperation in a number of different ways. It can be considered a normative rule: one *should* be cooperative in conversation. It can also be thought of as a simple propensity for conversational participants. I prefer the latter formulation—though even that can have a normative foundation. It brings to the fore an interpretation of cooperation on which it arises due to external factors. It is a choice for speakers, but not one that is necessarily based on any rational considerations. This in turn suggests an evolutionary interpretation: people cooperate because, over long time periods, those individuals who cooperated had higher average payoffs than those individuals who did not; of course, this is formulated most obviously using evolutionary games (Skyrms 1996; Gintis 2000a). Such evolutionary interpretations are of course compatible with the general picture of cooperativity as payoff maximization proposed here. On this understanding, Gricean cooperation is built into the communicating individuals as a (strong) default mechanism. It can be stated as follows.

(3.20) **Cooperation by default.**
        If there is no evidence to the contrary, assume the other conversational participants are (Gricean) cooperators.

Evidence to the contrary might consist of having properties associated with noncooperative, or untrustworthy, individuals: being a politician (as in our earlier example), having physical features associated by societal convention with untrustworthiness, or other things. This sort of issue has been examined by scholars working in the philosophy of testimony.[24] Here, there are two basic positions: the so-called Humean

---

[23] The obvious analogue should also be so for other analyses of reputation like that of Nowak and Sigmund (1998b).

[24] Chapter 9 has full details on this topic.

view, on which trust is the natural default position, and the so-called Reidian stance, on which trust is predicated on the observation of properties indicating trustworthiness. One observation to come out of the debate between the two is that, in general, we do not choose to trust or not in a vacuum: we almost always have some kind of information that can lead to guesses about the trustworthiness of our interlocutors (e.g. van Cleve 2006 and other papers in that volume, and McCready forthcoming, a for an initial application to hearsay evidentials). This observation is usually used to support a Reidian view, but I think it can just as well serve to explain why we sometimes choose not to trust, despite taking trust as the default position.

If we think of cooperation as a default, we can see why it occurs in initial moves of games with disclaimers. Since the receiver of the signal has no evidence that the signaler ever gives false information, by default she will assume that the signaler is a cooperative agent, and so that the signal is truthful. She will then take the signal at its face value and perform a cooperative move. Again, this can be thought of as a special case of a larger phenomenon: perhaps cooperation is the default in general, and not just in games of communication. Nonetheless, something like the above principle seems to be necessary to derive initial cooperation in games with disclaimers. This principle can be thought of as introducing the assumption that the initial probability of a propensity to cooperate is high, in the absence of defeating factors (in the sense of nonmonotonic logic; see Pollock and Cruz 1999); such initial probabilities and how they interact with histories will be considered in detail in chapters 8 and (for the particular case of testimony) 9.

We thus arrive at initial cooperativity via a process of evolution, itself predicated on rationality to the extent that evolution can be viewed as a process of utility maximization. Default cooperativity is then maintained by rational agents by their behavior and by using mechanisms such as hedges. However, disclaimers and hedges are extremely powerful. As we saw in the last section, they can change the whole abstract picture of a game; more concretely, they can in principle be used to avoid penalties for the wildest and most unbelievable utterances. This means that there is a potential for abuse, and for speakers to use hedges in intuitively uncooperative ways. However, when one examines the actual use of disclaimers and hedges, this situation does not really arise. Speakers hedge utterances they are not fully certain about, but they do not make statements that have no credibility whatsoever, hedged for safety. Similarly, advertisers may "upgrade" their product image via a disclaimed signal, but it would be too much for them to represent their product with a completely inaccurate image known to be false by all concerned as long as it is disclaimed. One thus would like to know what constraints there are on the use of hedges and disclaimers.

McCready (2008d) discusses a case that has some commonalities with advertising: trademarking the names of new products. In that work I analyzed trademarking as a naming process with the effect of creating new kind terms called *unnatural kinds*. Two restrictions on trademarking can be easily identified. The first is that one cannot trademark an existing kind term. I could not trademark the name "Potato Chips©" because *potato chips* is already the name of a natural kind. The second is that the name cannot be misleading. McCready (2008d) mentions the unnatural kind "100% All Natural Australian Beef©," which named a product containing 95% or more all natural Australian beef; this term, it seems, is currently out of circulation, because it constitutes what can only be construed as a deliberate attempt at deceiving people who encounter it. Indeed, both restrictions involve deception. If there is excessive potential for confusion about what qualifies as an instance of the new kind—or whether the newly created kind is a new kind at all—the creation will be disallowed.

Disallowed in what sense? The restriction is not semantic, because one can easily produce tricky product names, as in the case above. Instead, it is a restriction on legitimate uses of the kind creation operator: otherwise put, it is pragmatic. I would like to claim that a similar sort of pragmatic restriction is present for disclaimers and hedges. The essential point is that hearers do not tolerate abuse of the mechanism.

Suppose that a signaler uses a disclaimer or hedge along with a signal which not only is false, but is egregiously false. An egregiously false signal is one which does not come close to describing the world. I will forego a real formal definition, but a first pass is that such a signal is one that, given the available evidence of the signaler, has a possibility of less than chance of being true, so it is a signal that the signaler has reason to believe is probably false.[25] For instance, if it is sunny outside, and I come and tell you "I'm not positive about this, but it might be raining," I have produced an egregiously false signal by this criterion,

---

[25] A more adequate definition in the context of representations might involve a quantitative measure on the accuracy of a representation. If the representation proves to be sufficiently "distant" from the represented object, it can be construed as inaccurate; if the inaccuracy is extreme, we would have an instance of egregious falsehood. Thanks to Yasutada Sudo for discussion of this point.

together with a hedge. In this case, you are not likely to let me slide on the consequences of telling you a falsehood. The reason is that, if you are aware of my evidence (or when you become aware of it), it becomes clear that the inaccuracy of my signal was not an honest mistake.

Generalizing from this case, we arrive at the following principle of disclaimer/hedge use.

(3.21) **Propriety Principle.**
        Games can be disclaimed only when the signaler is engaged in honest communication.

The Propriety Principle is based on intentions and depends on the signal receiver recognizing whether the intentions of the signaler are honest or not. In general, it will take an egregiously false signal for the hearer to conclusively determine that it is not being followed, though borderline cases may often arise.

Why would something like the Propriety Principle arise? It seems to be another instance of the general tendency to punish uncooperative individuals. Such a tendency is well documented within behavioral game theory (e.g. Camerer 2003). There, it has been shown many times[26] that people tend to punish others whom they perceive as being unfair or excessively self-interested. It has further been shown that this tendency on the part of the human animal can contribute to the rise of altruistic behavior, together with its maintenance (cf. Nowak 2006; Gintis 2009); indeed, Bowles and Gintis (2011) have claimed that the possibility of punishment is one crucial factor in the evolution of cooperative behavior. Thus the existence of something like the Propriety Principle is to be expected. Indeed, for the particular case of communication, it seems to be an aspect of the epistemic vigilance discussed by Sperber et al. (2010).

We should now consider a related problem: when should a speaker *not* hedge? Obviously, when hedging would violate the Propriety Principle. But what about cases where the violation is not so extreme? There seems to be an incentive to hedge quite generally. After all, hedging makes communication safe: one cannot be blamed for one's actions any longer if they are hedged (within reason at least). The decision of whether or not to hedge is wholly the speaker's. But this question can be answered in a straightforward way. Suppose that there is a cost to hedging, as there was for advertising in the model of sales presented in Figure 2.2. The existence of such a cost is obviously sensible: it

---

[26] See Camerer (2003) for detailed references.

takes some effort to produce an utterance, and presumably the cost of production will increase proportionately to the complexity of the utterance (or of the content). Models incorporating cost of utterance have already been used in game-theoretic pragmatics to model politeness, among other phenomena (van Rooij 2003a). Given a cost for hedging, production of a hedged utterance will be more costly than production of a nonhedged utterance. Supposing a model roughly analogous to that in Figure 2.2, even in the case that communication is successful a speaker who hedges will get a lower payoff than one who does not. Thus, in the absence of uncertainty about whether a hedge is needed, it pays not to hedge. Thinking again in terms of standard game-theoretic models of evolution, the proportion of speakers who hedge when it is not required will tend to diminish within the population with respect to speakers who do not incessantly hedge. Incorporating costs thus can account for one deviant speaker type, which hedges when it is not required. Another reason not to hedge will appear in chapter 9: in general, hedged communications are assigned a lower degree of reliability than nonhedged communications, for hedging indicates a relatively low speaker confidence. Thus, not hedging is more likely to successfully result in a change in hearer beliefs. For the speaker whose aim is information transmission (as reflected in the payoff structure), not hedging is likely an optimal strategy.

We can see from this discussion that the Propriety Principle only addresses one face of a general problem: when hedging is appropriate. There are two sides to the issue. One might hedge incorrectly when the hedged information is excessively certain: this case is accounted for by assigning costs to hedges. One might also hedge inappropriately when the information is too *uncertain*: this case falls under the rubric of the Propriety Principle. It seems correct that the two types of wrong hedging are analyzed via distinct mechanisms, as the wrongness involved is, intuitively, due to these discourse moves having quite different kinds of negative effects. When then is it appropriate to hedge? The answer seems to be: when the speaker is not fully certain that the information to be transmitted is true, but is sufficiently uncertain that it is false. Presumably the exact boundaries of the hedgeable zone will vary from situation to situation in the usual, vague way, with the goals of the conversation and the inclinations of the conversational participants. The crucial point is that the relevant uncertainty not be too great, and yet not too small.

The question of what penalties apply to a signaler who fails to follow the Propriety Principle is an interesting one. We can easily imagine three possibilities. The first is that the game in which the violation occurs fails to be disclaimed, and so the noncooperative move is noted on the record. This seems a rather mild penalty; in fact, if this is the only penalty, the speaker has little incentive to avoid violations, as using a disclaimer will never give a worse outcome than a disclaimer-free noncooperative move. I do not think this is realistic. The second option is stricter: detection of a violation of Propriety means that any future attempts by the signaler to disclaim game iterations will fail, and every move will go on the record. In other words, receivers will no longer trust that the signaler is using the disclaiming mechanism in an honest and cooperative manner and will not allow its use anymore. This situation seems very common. The final possibility is that a detected violation causes all future attempts at disclaiming games to fail, and further all games which were successfully disclaimed in the past to be placed back on the record.[27] In other words, the rejection of disclaimers is retroactive. I think that situations like this may arise as well, if a particular instance of an egregious violation is sufficiently outrageous (for example, if the probability of the claim, given the speaker's evidence, is 0.01).

3.6 Conclusion

This chapter has provided a model of reputation and used it to explain the function of certain kinds of hedges. I claimed that hedges work to keep speaker errors in truth-tracking from negatively impacting their reputations, and thus possibly their future interactions. But the reader might recall that I mentioned cases of hedging outside the domain of truthfulness or the lack thereof. Indeed, such cases are to be expected from the perspective of reputation damage. Saul (2012) indicates that lying and misleading can be viewed as equally morally reprehensible. That means that we should expect that we have hedges for "what is said," as analyzed in this chapter, but we should also expect to have hedges for other kinds of content, for errors there, deliberate or not, should also potentially lead to reputation damage. Hedges of this more general sort are the topic of the next chapter.

---

[27] This option requires use of the second or third strategy in disclaiming games, for otherwise there is no record of the content that has been disclaimed previously. If one thinks this situation arises, this is another reason to prefer one of these strategies.

Before moving on to this project, I should also note that I don't want to claim that *only* factors like those I have addressed can be relevant in the computation of reliability. Consider Lackey's (2008) first class of evidence for reliability (p. 182): particular contexts may have features which keep considerations of reliability quite stable, even though one might have different speakers addressing a single topic or domain of discourse. Examples of this kind require use of information from multiple histories, because each history is associated with a single speaker. The system I've proposed obviously has the resources to do this: one can examine multiple histories for content of certain kinds, and compute accordingly. But I won't work out the full details of how this can be done in the present work.

4

Hedging beyond truth

This chapter considers extensions of the analysis of hedging in the last chapter to a range of other phenomena that behave like hedges and disclaimers, in a general sense. The function of hedges is, I have argued, to limit the responsibility that the speaker must take for her linguistic actions. One kind of responsibility that one assumes in performing assertions is that of guaranteeing the truth of the asserted content; but linguistic communication takes place in conditions of epistemic uncertainty, and so it is perhaps unsurprising that natural language should have a mechanism for eliminating (or trying to eliminate) negative effects that might arise from errors in truth which develop out of that uncertainty. That is the gist of the last chapter.

But guarantees of truth are not the only effects of assertion. As we have already seen in chapter 2, the assertion of a sentence indicates several things in addition to the speaker's belief that it is true; this belief arises from a mutual assumption that the speaker is cooperative, but in the Gricean sense of cooperativity other things also follow from that assumption. The first part of this chapter focuses on the other implicatures arising from the Cooperative Principle, namely Quantity, Manner, and Relevance implicatures. For instance, in the case of Relevance, it follows from cooperativity that the asserted content is meant to be relevant to the hearer's goals in some way. If my analysis of hedging is on the right track, it ought to be that natural language makes some means available of hedging relevance implicatures as well, and also implicatures that stem from the other submaxims of the Cooperative Principle. I will argue that there are such constructions: so-called biscuit conditionals or "relevance conditionals"; indeed, ordinary hedges can perform this function as well. As we will see, they are highly similar in function to the more obvious hedges discussed in the preceding chapter. The result is that hedges in general act not on the content of sentences directly, but on speech acts and what follows from them; it further follows that the requirement for truth in assertion is mediated by the assumption of cooperativity via its Gricean realization. I give an analysis of their function along these lines, and compare it with existing accounts in the literature.

The second part of the chapter turns to a range of other phenomena that are not directly concerned with cooperativity, but instead with hedging specifically. We have already seen that it is possible to hedge the truth of an assertion. But what about content that is not truth-directed, or cannot on the face of things be sensibly denied? I consider two such cases. The first is that of expressive content, which by definition is not aimed directly at truth but rather at the expression of some attitude. I show that such content cannot be (Quality) hedged, and relate this fact to the nature of expressivity via the notion of *alief* (Szabo Gendler 2008a,b). This notion points up an analogue of expressive content in the domain of pictorial advertising. I then turn to the case of Quality hedging of sentences containing epistemic modals, already discussed briefly in the last chapter. The problem of such sentences is that, given a standard semantics for epistemic modality, *might*-sentences of the form (e.g.) $\lozenge\phi$ indicate that ϕ is compatible with the knowledge/beliefs of the speaker;[1] but how can it be pragmatically sensible to hedge the statement that something is compatible with one's beliefs? I argue that in such cases the speaker is actually hedging a further pragmatic effect of modal utterances, that of introducing the prejacent ϕ into the discourse as a candidate piece of information to be updated within the sense of dynamic semantics. This view supports a pragmatically mediated view of the update process, which is discussed further in chapters 5 and 8. The chapter concludes with a brief discussion of hedging of predicates of personal taste.

4.1 Biscuit conditionals

Austin (1970) discussed a construction superficially like an indicative conditional, but with what appear to be significantly different truth conditions. These are cases where the consequent is known to be true, but the antecedent describes a condition without which learning the consequent may not be of much interest to the hearer.

(4.1)   There are biscuits on the sideboard if you want some.

(Austin 1970)

(4.2)   If you care, *Independence Day* is on TV tonight.

---

[1] Or possibly some other salient individual or group of individuals; see below for detailed discussion.

Such conditionals have come to be known as "biscuit conditionals" after Austin's example. To my knowledge, no precise definition of biscuit conditionals has been given in the literature. Intuitively, one necessary condition for such conditionals is that the antecedent and consequent stand in no causal relation: the consequent is true regardless of the truth or falsity of the antecedent. This condition can be, and has been, formalized in various ways: one obvious way is via conditional probabilities, so that $A \Rightarrow B$ is a biscuit conditional just in case $P(B|A) = P(B)$. This condition seems enough for our purposes here, though it may not pick out biscuit conditionals exclusively, as pointed out by Francez (2010). However, there are also some linguistic tests available: for instance, ordinary conditionals can appear with *then* in the consequent, but biscuit conditionals cannot (Iatridou 1991; Swanson 2013):

(4.3)   a. If it is raining, then Mary probably has her umbrella.

      b. If you are hungry, (*then) there are some biscuits on the sideboard.

Another putative test, that biscuit conditionals cannot appear with sub-junctive mood, has been conclusively shown to be incorrect by Swanson (2013).

What is the proper way to think of biscuit conditionals? A widely known (though perhaps rarely supported) analysis is due to DeRose and Grandy (1999), who analyze biscuit conditionals as conditional assertions. The idea is that sentences like (4.1) only assert their consequents if the antecedent is true, and otherwise assert nothing. This is just to say that such conditionals involve a special kind of speech act. DeRose and Grandy analyze this as a means of avoiding falsehood: asserting a proposition implicates by Gricean principles that the content of the assertion is relevant to the hearer. If it is not, then a falsehood has been implicated. They note that this is a somewhat unorthodox notion of falsehood in that it arises from metaconversational princi-ples. It certainly seems like a strange objection to your statement that *Independence Day* is on TV for me to say that you have indicated something false to me, insofar as you know that I don't care about *Independence Day*. This is doubly so given the cancellability of Gricean implicatures, which is one of their defining features. But let's put these rather problematic aspects of the proposal aside for the purposes of discussion. With respect to the utility of this speech act, they say the following:

Such a conversational maneuver would allow you to make a warranted assertion should it be called for, while at the same time shielding you from the danger of committing the conversational misdeed of making an irrelevant assertion.

(DeRose and Grandy 1999: 411)

Note the similarity to our standard cases of hedging and disclaimers. Indeed, this passage suggests that the same general mechanism is at work, even down to the use of the term *shield*, which should be reminiscent of shield hedges. It looks natural, in light of this correspondence, to view biscuit conditionals as not being "real" conditionals in any semantic sense; rather they are simply hedged assertions, and the conditional clause functions as a shield hedge of a somewhat special type. Analyzing biscuit conditionals in this way allows us to avoid the need to postulate a special speech act, conditional assertion, specially for cases like these. Indeed, we avoid the problems noted by Belnap (1970) with respect to this kind of move, i.e. that sentences like (4.1) are simply judged false if there are no biscuits on the sideboard at all.[2]

This analysis, then, assimilates biscuit conditionals to hedged assertions rather than to other conditional constructions. This looks reasonable; in fact more obvious shield hedges like (4.4) look like perfectly adequate paraphrases of biscuit conditionals.

(4.4)   a. I don't know if you want any, but there are biscuits on the sideboard.

   b. I'm not sure you actually care about this, but *Independence Day* is on tonight.

Of course, this cannot be the end of the story. We have to say something about exactly what is being hedged here, and why the content that is hedged in this case seems to differ from what is hedged in the more "object-level" cases of hedging discussed above.[3] Another question that the literature often attempts to answer is why the hedges in these cases take the form of a conditional clause. The usual goal is to unify biscuit "conditionals" with other, more standard, conditionals. But as (4.4) shows, other constructions than conditionals can certainly do the same job. I will put this question aside for the present, but return to it in chapter 5 in the context of more general considerations about pragmatic interpretation.

---

[2] Unlike DeRose and Grandy, I share Belnap's intuition about this case.
[3] It is also necessary to indicate how the nonstandard interpretation of the conditional clause arises; I will take up this task in chapter 5.

In the cases above, what is being hedged is rather clear: as DeRose and Grandy note, it is the implicature of relevance that arises as a side effect of the assertion of the "consequent." In fact, though, it need not always be relevance that is hedged, an observation that often plays a surprisingly small role in the literature on the topic. As far as I can see, any Gricean implicature arising from assertion can be targeted for hedging, not just implicatures of relevance. Here I represent the content implicated by the consequent (or, as I claim, the hedged assertion) together with the relevant Gricean maxim, below the example.

(4.5) a. If I'm not wrong, it's raining.   (Quality)
      ↝ It's true that it is raining

    b. If you care, *Independence Day* is on tonight.   (Relevance)
      ↝ You care that *ID* is on tonight

    c. (*Where are you from?*) If you're interested in my nationality, I'm from the US.   (Quantity)
      ↝ You are not asking about my home town or planet of origin

    d. If I've got the order right, John got into bed and took off his shoes.   (Manner)
      ↝ John got into bed before he took off his shoes

In the above, implicatures arising from each of the Gricean maxims are hedged: in addition to Relevance implicatures, it is also possible to hedge Quality, Quantity, and even Manner implicatures as well. This suggests that one would not want to restrict attention to the Relevance case, as DeRose and Grandy (1999) and also (mostly) Siegel (2006) do. Of course, one might try to assimilate the other three cases to ordinary indicative conditionals, but this seems to go counter to intuitions about the meaning of "conditionals" like these, where the "consequents" certainly appear to be asserted in the usual biscuity way. We can take it, then, that the hedged content in the above is just one or another of the implicatures that arise from the assertion.

It should be noted that in the case of Quality this could also be viewed as a presupposition: given that one follows e.g. Searle (1969) and takes the truth of φ to be a precondition for asserting φ (in the guise of belief),[4] and further understand such preconditions as introducing presuppositions, it does seem that a presupposition is being hedged.

---

[4] One might also take it to be part of the normative conditions for assertion, as in e.g. Williamson (2000). I will not enter here into the question of whether we should view compliance with such normative conditions as presuppositional or as generating an implicature, though the latter seems more immediately plausible.

In fact we can find other cases that might be analyzable as instances of presupposition hedging, as in the following.

(4.6) a. If John really does have a daughter, then his daughter sure never does come around.

   b. If (as you claim) Burkina Faso is a monarchy, then the king doesn't have very much power.

These, of course, are the standard cases of presupposition binding à la van der Sandt (1992) and Beaver (2001). It might be possible to view these as hedges as well. The idea would be that conditionals of this form are also hedges, and that hedges are metalinguistic operators able to apply to all sorts of non-truth-conditional content. There seems to be nothing obviously wrong with this sort of analysis; it brings out the commonality of all the cases we have seen, in that in each the "consequent" is asserted, but some side effect of that assertion is cancelled. If correct, this picture would have substantial implications for how we should analyze presupposition and especially for dynamic semantic analyses of this issue.[5] I will not argue for the idea further in the present context, instead returning to our original questions.

Thus, in biscuit conditionals and related hedging constructions, the hedged content is the nonliteral content of the asserted sentence. By nonliteral content I mean that content which is not at issue: at minimum, implicated content, as in the standard biscuit conditional cases, but perhaps presuppositional content and even conventionally implicated content as well.[6] These, then, are cases where a metalinguistic device—hedging—is used to disclaim "metalevel" content. So these cases, while they have a different character than the initial cases we looked at, are not fundamentally different in nature: just as before, some aspect of an utterance is disclaimed. The difference is that here the fact of the sentences being uttered is completely inescapable, because the disclaimed content results directly from the actual fact of utterance.

The second question was how to determine what is being disclaimed. How can we tell if in a given utterance the disclaimer is of the content of the utterance or of some side effect of its performance? The answer to this seems, in most cases, rather obvious: it will depend completely

---

[5] Heim (1983) is an early exemplar; Beaver (2001) provides a nice summary in addition to an analysis; another source of interesting discussion is Schlenker (2009).

[6] Though we will see in section 4.2 that expressive content lies outside the reach of the disclaiming operator.

on what the content of the hedge is. If I hedge with "If you care" I am hedging the Relevance implicature; if I hedge with "If you're interested in my nationality" I am hedging the Quantity implicature, and so forth. The content of the hedge itself thus determines what is being hedged. Of course, the question of how one can tell whether to read a conditional as biscuity or not also depends on content: as stated above, a biscuity interpretation results if there is no sense in which the consequent can be understood as depending on the antecedent. Siegel (2006) writes that what is needed is "a discourse-coerced construal rule that will effectively apply only when needed to accommodate what would otherwise be anomalous interpretations" (Siegel 2006: 192). I think this is essentially right; again, I will consider the details of how this should be spelled out in chapter 5.

A slightly more complex case is that of hedges like "If it's true," "I might be wrong," or "I don't know if it's true," in that, here, it is not clear whether the content is being hedged or the implication that the content is true (via Quality, or possibly norms of assertion) is being hedged. However, the two dovetail quite neatly. If I hedge a piece of content I also call into question its truth, and thus the Quality implicature, and vice versa. The simplest view of how hedging works is then that it is always the implicature that is blocked; on such a view, we need not define separate mechanisms for the case of Quality hedges and all other types of hedging, so hedging can be viewed as a single phenomenon. What we are dealing with is an instance of the use of some linguistic content to block commitment to implicatures arising from inference about cooperative language use: basically a preemptive cancellation of implicated content. The essential idea of the treatment in chapter 5 is that use of the disclaimer functions to block the application of particular default inferences, via additional inferences that arise from the use of the disclaimer itself.

Comparing my proposal with other available accounts of biscuit conditionals is instructive. We have already discussed the view of DeRose and Grandy (1999), but it is obviously not the only one on the market. Here I will discuss two others: that of Siegel (2006), and that of Predelli (2009). Doing so will give additional insight into the nature of biscuit conditionals, and on how a hedging view can help us understand their behavior and the environments in which they appear.

Siegel (2006) provides the following paraphrase for the biscuit conditional in (4.1).

(4.7) If you are hungry, then there is an assertion a and a proposition p such that a is an assertion of p and p = "there are biscuits on the sideboard."

This differs from the conditional assertion account in the following way: the assertion is claimed to exist given the truth of the antecedent, but is not actually made; it is a "potential literal act." Predelli (2009) has noted that this analysis makes the peculiar prediction that according to the speaker, given that the addressee of (4.1) is hungry, there exist assertions and propositions, which is an unexpected ontological commitment. Presumably naive speakers do not intend to make such claims with the use of biscuit conditionals. But let us put this problem aside, though it is not a fully trivial one; as Predelli indicates, the truth or falsity of (4.1) only depends on the existence (or not) of the biscuits, and has nothing to do with more esoteric domains.

    As I see things, there are two main questions for the Siegel analysis. The first involves the interpretation suggested in (4.7). How should we understand the notion of a "potential literal act"? What is it to be an assertion that is not made? The second worry is empirical and involves the evidence for the theory. If it turns out that the consequents of biscuit conditionals are not asserted, clearly one should prefer an account stated in terms of a potential literal act to an assertion account, whether it involve conditional assertion or not. Siegel has several arguments that the consequents of biscuit conditionals are not in fact asserted. Since my analysis is predicated on the assumption that the consequents of biscuit conditionals are not only asserted but asserted unconditionally (though hedged), if Siegel's arguments are correct here, this would be telling against my view. I will show that the evidence is not at all conclusive. After considering these issues, we will turn to an examination of some of the complex data Siegel provides, which will lead to a deeper understanding of biscuit conditionals on the view I am proposing.

    The first worry is about the proposed paraphrase in terms of potential literal acts. What do we mean by a potential literal act? We must assume the existence of an infinite set of potential acts (given the cardinality of the set of meanings expressible by grammatical sentences of natural language), which are not necessarily made, yet are accessible. Even if we do not worry about ontological issues, one wonders what other phenomena might necessitate this kind of treatment. Siegel reminds us of Krifka's (2001) analysis of "conjoined speech acts," where multiple question acts are performed: but these acts do not need to be viewed as nonliteral, and indeed this domain does not exhibit the Boolean structure we might expect of a domain of fully independent objects.[7] It is also difficult to see how the account can avoid pragmatic stipulation: since the acts are potential, they fail to carry implicatures, since such arise from speech acts;[8] it is then necessary to stipulate that the literal act, if performed, would be "relevant."

The literal act analysis also carries with it some odd commitments (as already pointed out by Predelli 2009, and above). Given her use of a pure conditional analysis, Siegel (like DeRose and Grandy) must use a somewhat peculiar conception of truth, on which the content of implicatures is tied directly to truth-value. In regard to the case where A and B are both false (in $A \rightarrow_{BC} B$), she writes (p. 178): "If it is not true that the listener is hungry, then just about any assertion about pizza will not be relevant." However, it does not seem that difficult to imagine cases in which it could be relevant that there is pizza regardless of the hearer's hunger or lack thereof, for instance if speaker and hearer need a piece of pizza for a science project. In such cases, the analysis predicts that the conditional should be true if material implication is used; in fact, however, the utterance seems odd, as the antecedent does not seem to have the proper relationship to the consequent. In general, it's not clear that the judgements speakers have about biscuit conditionals track truth together with relevance in the way predicted.

Siegel is aware of this issue, and writes (p. 179): "Since the failed felicity presupposition is about the truth of the assertion, some speakers will speak of such sentences as false, since, of course, there is no natural language predicate 'serious presupposition failure.'" This is an interesting picture, in that implicatures arising from speech acts are being implemented as standard presuppositions (Heim 1992; Beaver 2001; Schlenker 2009). This move is somewhat natural if we want to select a way to understand felicity conditions in terms of the standard categories of object-level meaning (truth conditions, presupposition, etc.). Note that we do get projection of ordinary presuppositions from biscuit conditionals:

(4.8) If you care, I just saw some boy walk off with Jerry's backpack.
$$C(h) \Rightarrow \partial \exists x[Bpk(x) \wedge R(j, x)] \wedge \exists y[Boy(y) \wedge steal(y, x)]$$
$$\dashrightarrow \exists x[Bpk(x) \wedge R(j, x)] \wedge [C(h) \Rightarrow \exists y[Boy(y) \wedge steal(y, x)]]$$
(after projection)

---

[7] As Krifka notes, disjunctions, for example, are impossible.
[8] Or so I assume, after Grice (1975) and his followers; see Chierchia (2004), among others, for a different view.

A similar issue is raised by the discourse effect of biscuit conditionals. Worryingly, if one wants to uphold the intuition that the consequents of biscuit conditionals are asserted, we need an extra assumption: that the bare fact of the existence of a (potentially relevant) literal act leads, effectively, to its performance.

(4.9)   If a potential literal act is assertable, then it is asserted.

This inference does not seem at all justified, and it is hard to see how it might be justifiable; the relevance of a question does not mean that the question is asked, for example. In general, the analysis depends on a kind of automatic deployment of speech acts: asserting existence of a (relevant) speech act implies performance/performability of the speech act, and consequent truth of its content (together with relevant implicatures). But why then does this sort of interpretation not always arise?

The last problem mentioned does not arise for Siegel if the consequents of biscuit conditionals are not asserted at all, as she suggests. Siegel takes this position on the basis of three empirical arguments. The first involves Japanese facts related to the adverbial *yokumo*. The analysis here is flawed for reasons independent of assertion or lack thereof. The second is predicated on entailments: she argues that biscuit conditionals do not entail their consequents. I will provide some arguments against this via alternate analyses of the data on which her claim is based. The conclusion will be that whether such entailments go through or not depends on exactly what is being hedged. The final argument involves truth-value judgements of biscuit conditionals. However, the intuitions she cites seem to be controversial, as we will see.

The argument from Japanese involves the adverbial *yoku(mo)*, which has a highly complex meaning: it takes a proposition, and expresses that the speaker is surprised by its truth, and has some emotive attitude toward it; further, it requires that the content it applies to already be in the common ground (see McCready 2004). The argument itself has two parts. The first involves the claim that *yokumo* cannot appear in assertions. This claim is made by Siegel on the basis of some distributional constraints on *yoku(mo)* that I observed (McCready 2004), although actually I explicitly do *not* take assertion to be the relevant factor, but instead a constraint on actuality (see that paper for details). Given that these are the right constraints, it's not clear that the argument goes through. Putting this aside and supposing that there is indeed a requirement for assertive environments, if the consequents of biscuit conditionals are asserted, *yokumo* should be able to appear there; but it cannot. Thus, the consequents of biscuit conditionals cannot be asserted. It does indeed appear that the data supports the argument, as shown by (4.11).

(4.10)   Kinguzu-wa yoku   uruhuzu-ni katta-mono-da
          Kings-Top   surprise Wolves-Dat won-Nom-Cop
          'The Kings, amazingly to me, defeated the Wolves.'

                                                    (Siegel 2006: 175)

(4.11)   *Nani-ga   okotta   ka kikare-tara   kinguzu-wa yoku
          what-Nom   happened Q asked-Cond Kings-Top   surprise
          uruhuzu-ni katta-mono-da
          Wolves-Dat won-Nom-Cop
          'If they ask you what happened, the Kings, amazingly to me, beat
          the Wolves.'

However, there are problems with the argument. The first is clear: the inference just does not go through. The fact that *yoku(mo)* cannot appear in the consequents of biscuit conditionals is compatible with multiple analyses. Any number of confounding factors could be in play. Thus, the incompatibility does not lead directly to the conclusion of a lack of assertive force. A more promising possibility than assertion (given the analysis of McCready 2004) can be seen by considering the meaning of the adverbial. *Yoku(mo)* requires a speaker to find, or have found, the content in its scope surprising, and to have an emotive reaction toward it: much like exclamatives in a semantic sense (Zanuttini and Portner 2003; Rett 2008). This does not appear compatible with biscuit conditionals at all. To see this, consider the invented class of "biscuit exclamatives," where (in my terms) an exclamation is hedged.

(4.12)   a. *If you're interested, WHAT A CRAZY PARTY!

          b. ?? If you're hungry, THERE'S SOME PIZZA IN THE
             FRIDGE!!

The sentence in (4.12a) shows that WH-exclamatives cannot appear as biscuit-conditional consequents, and (4.12b) shows the same for propositional exclamatives. This restriction might follow from a number of factors: plausible reasons might be the requirement for low (prior) probability, or the unnatural quality of trying to hedge while excited. (It also might follow from the common-ground requirement of *yoku(mo)*, which might also hold for exclamatives.) Whatever the reason, it seems clear that Siegel's argument is not as clean as one might like, and the conclusion cannot be taken to be definitive, meaning that consequents might be asserted after all.

Siegel's second argument against assertion accounts is that biscuit conditionals do not exhibit the entailments that one would expect if such analyses were correct. Specifically, she worries that, if biscuit conditionals are indeed assertive, then $A \rightarrow_{BC} B$ should entail B; but this is not necessarily the case. Indeed, it is true that biscuit conditionals need not entail their consequents (assuming with Siegel that (4.13) is a biscuit conditional, which does not seem perfectly clear):

(4.13)   If we can believe Gordy, a lot of women want to date racecar drivers.

   ↛ A lot of women want to date racecar drivers.

However, I think that this evidence does not speak against assertion accounts, as long as such accounts are of the right form. Clearly, the antecedent (4.13) is meant to call into question the quality of Gordy's testimony. As such, it is a Quality hedge; such hedges are meant, on my analysis, to disclaim Quality implicatures, so that (4.13) should be read conditionally on the reliability of what Gordy claims. This analysis makes Quality hedges over testimony interestingly close in function to hearsay evidentials (cf. Aikhenvald 2004; McCready forthcoming, a). Perhaps it is reasonable to think of biscuit conditionals as an evidential strategy for languages like English which lack overt evidentials. Though I will not pursue this point further here, I will return to it in chapter 9 after discussing evidentials further in chapters 6, 7, and 8. In the present example, the (presumed) unlikelihood of the consequent, together with the way in which the antecedent is phrased, make it seem very unlikely that the speaker actually believes the consequent, which in turn leads to an obvious violation of the Propriety Principle. A hedging analysis can therefore treat (4.13) as introducing an additional implicature via Gricean flouting, namely that the consequent is in fact false. The hedging view, then, makes available a simple and natural view of when biscuit conditionals assert their consequents, and when they do not.

A similar analysis can be given of Siegel's example (4.14). Predelli (2009) argues that this one should be evaluated as (literally) false, though Siegel's informants apparently give the opposite judgement. I agree with this judgement. The point is that we are allowed to evaluate this example without making the assumption that the speaker means to tell the truth. It is a familiar fact that informants can confuse judgements of truth and falsity with judgements of pragmatic infelicity, and so it may not come as a surprise that someone might judge (4.14) true because it lacks the expected inappropriateness, due to the flouting quality of the hedge.

(4.14)   If you want to hear a big fat lie, George W. and Condi Rice are secretly married.

There appears to be a solid argument in favor of treating the consequents of biscuit conditionals as asserted, which to my knowledge has not been made in the literature. This argument comes from anaphora. It is well known that nonspecific indefinites introduced in conditional consequents cannot serve as antecedents for anaphora.

(4.15)   If a farmer owns a big piece of property, he usually keeps a donkey. # It lives a free and easy life.

But such anaphoric dependencies are perfectly felicitous in the case of biscuit conditionals.

(4.16)   a. If you're hungry, there are some$_1$ cookies on the table. They$_1$ are ginger snaps.

   b. If you're free, I'm going to a$_1$ party tonight. It$_1$ starts at midnight.

In the context of dynamic semantics, this means that either the conditional consequent is not embedded under any semantic operator that blocks dependencies, or that some element in the second sentence is enabling some sort of subordination. The second possibility looks unlikely: there is no obvious operator (a modal or a generic, cf. Roberts 1989; Carlson and Spejewski 1997) which could play such a role. The first possibility thus looks to be right. But this isn't consistent with the consequent not being asserted, for if it's not, it has no way to introduce the required discourse referent to enable anaphoric dependencies. I conclude (once again) that the consequents of biscuit conditionals are indeed asserted.

The analysis I have proposed can easily account for many of the other examples in the literature. Below are some instances from Siegel's paper. (4.17b,d) are obvious instances of relevance conditionals, where a relevance implicature is being hedged. (4.17a,c) are problematic for any approach which takes biscuit conditionals to invariably hedge relevance.

(4.17a) involves a hedge over appropriateness of a speech act: in the case that the speaker's observation is unwelcome, some consequences of this infelicity are avoided (or at least that is the intent; Brown and Levinson 1987). (4.17d) is slightly more complex, though the basic idea is the same. Here, the speaker indicates an explicit awareness that her speech act is not welcome, and proceeds to disregard any possible consequences and perform the speech act anyway. It may not be quite right to characterize this case as a hedge per se, but clearly the first clause is making reference to possible effects of asserting the second clause on the reputation the speaker has for cooperativity (or lack thereof).

(4.17)   a. If I may say so, you're looking lovely tonight.
         b. Although you probably don't care, your skirt is too short.
         c. Since you're interested, John is a Catholic.
         d. You don't care what I think, but your skirt is too short.

It is also worth noting that one can hedge speech acts other than assertions. For instance, consider the following cases. The examples in (4.18) are commands or requests with a precondition hedged: that the hearer is able to perform the requested action. The examples in (4.19) are questions with, again, a precondition hedged: that the hearer knows the answer.[9] Such cases are obviously closely related to the conditional questions discussed by Isaacs and Rawlins (2008), though my analysis is rather different from theirs. But it is difficult for Siegel to get these cases if she limits the domain of "potential literal acts" to assertions. If this domain is to include all sorts of potential acts, then she can give an analysis analogous to that of biscuit conditionals, though issues might arise about how to distinguish the different kinds of act-objects, and even of individuation conditions for such acts: for instance, does there exist more than one object corresponding to distinct uses of the same content, as in the case of indirect speech acts? Fortunately, one need not make decisions about these issues on my analysis.

---

[9] Although such cases raise new puzzles of their own. Why for instance are sentences like (i) and (ii) infelicitous?

(i) # I might not really want you to do this, but take out the trash.
(ii) # I really don't want an answer, but who came to the party?

The reason appears to be analogous to Moore-paradoxical sentences of the form "ϕ but I don't believe that ϕ"; as in such cases, the speech act performed is inconsistent with the denial of the precondition for the speech act. For the hedging cases, it appears that it's not consistent to deny speaker-controlled conditions on speech acts. The analysis looks straightforward given a notion of speaker control in speech act conditions; see Kaufmann and McCready (2008) for this notion for a limited domain of speech acts.

(4.18) a. If you have time/don't mind, please get me a coffee (too).

b. If you're able to/it's not too heavy for you, move the table to the center of the room.

(4.19) a. If you happen to know, what time is it now?

b. If you're willing to tell me, where did you and Jane go last night?

Let us now turn to the analysis of Predelli (2009). According to Predelli, a sentence can be evaluated against two types of background context. Both are notions of "admissible context" for the use of a sentence: the first is essentially that of Kaplan (1989), according to whom contexts of use (CU) for a sentence must satisfy certain conditions, such as having a speaker.[10] Predelli accordingly gives the following definition. Here C is the set of all contexts and A is some appropriate condition on the use of s (e.g. truth).

(4.20) $c \in CU(s)$ iff $c \in C$ and the agent of c utters s under appropriate conditions A at the time and possible world of c.

This notion of context is relevant for any pragmatic use. The second notion is a notion of context for "relevant" uses of a sentence ($CGRU$). This is obtained by augmenting the notion of context of use CU above with an additional (set of) condition(s) R, defined as whatever "derives from one's favorite account of conversational relevance" (Predelli 2009: 300).

(4.21) $c \in CGRU(s)$ iff $c \in C$ and the agent of c utters s under appropriate conditions A and R at the time and possible world of c.

With these notions, Predelli can give his analysis, which is interesting in that it makes a distinction between truth and contextual effect. According to him, a biscuit conditional $R \Rightarrow B$ (R some condition) is true if its consequent is true. But its antecedent has an effect on the relevance of the use of that sentence: it requires that the context of relevance checking ($CGRU(s)$) makes the antecedent content true as well. The antecedent of the biscuit conditional has no effect on truth conditions (formally it is taken to be an identity function), but it changes $CGRU(B)$ to $\{c|c \in CGRU(s)$ and $True_c(R)\}$ in the conditional's local context (so that the

---

[10] See Predelli (2003) for extended discussion of issues relating to such conditions.

effect does not last beyond the conditional scope). This can be viewed as an attempt to implement the discussion of expressive correctness found in Kaplan (1999).

An obvious problem with this formulation is that it makes reference only to relevance, while, as we have seen in some detail above, there are many biscuit conditionals that (in my terms) hedge other kinds of pragmatic content. But this problem is merely the result of Predelli's limiting attention to the standard cases in the literature, which could be fixed by adding conditions to the definition of admissible context. One must wonder, though, in what sense the Predelli view counts as a full theory, given that he has not given us anything like a definition of what an admissible context might be; he says only that it satisfies whatever one would like to say about relevance. I find this rather unsatisfying, but his desire seems to be to provide a framework and a framework alone, so I will not press this point. In any case, I believe that there are more substantial issues.

The first issue involves the nature of the pragmatic content involved in biscuit conditionals. Predelli takes the common Ramsey test view of conditionals and applies it to expressive correctness. This amounts to a kind of unification of biscuit conditionals with other pragmatic conditions on meaning, exactly parallel to the way in which dynamic theories of presupposition work (Beaver 2001). For Predelli, then, biscuit conditionals institute a change in context comparable to the role of conditionalizing over ordinary content. This is, of course, one of his goals: he wishes to treat biscuit conditionals together with ordinary conditionals. Whether we are happy with this consequence depends essentially on whether we think biscuit conditionals are true conditionals or not. I have argued that they are not, and that their analysis should go in a different direction; to the extent that I have been convincing, we should be skeptical about taking biscuit antecedents to be analogous to "ordinary" presupposition satisfiers, just as we should be about the part of Siegel's analysis that implements this view.

The second worry involves Predelli's goal of treating biscuit conditionals as expressive, and thereby unifying them with speaker adverbials like *frankly*, pejoratives, vocatives, and the other things that are more unambiguously expressive (see, among many others, Kaplan 1999; Potts 2005; McCready 2010c for more on expressive content, as well as the following section 4.2). These expressions have certain traits in common, some of which were discussed above: for example, they do not interact much with semantic operators (compared to "vanilla" content), they act on contexts in a highly direct and unmediated way, they have an "essentially" expressive character, much as "I" has an essentially indexical character (Perry 1979), and so on. Biscuit conditionals do not seem to pass any of these tests, and the mechanism Predelli proposes to analyze them also lacks features that would seem to be necessary for the analysis of expressives. In this sense, his analysis looks to fail on its own terms.

This worry is somewhat substantiated by considering Predelli (2013), where he gives a more general analysis of expressives along the same lines. The discussion there proves to be illuminating about the relation between expressive content and biscuit conditionals. Although he explicitly disavows the details of all the specific analyses he proposes and thus does not commit to a semantics for any particular expressive, he gives a slightly more concrete proposal for the interjection "alas" in his chapter 7. His goal here appears to be showing how his general view on expressive content is supposed to work, and how it can guarantee certain inferences that follow from his expressivist semantics; but, as it turns out, his proposal, though tentative, is already enough to show that the analysis he proposes in Predelli (2009) for biscuit conditionals does not really treat them as genuine occurrences of expressive content. Section 2 of his chapter 7 is a formal sketch of a theory of "alas"; in the key area of use-conditions, he provides a clause aimed at deriving the expressive content of connectives. Since expressive content found in conditionals is independent of at-issue content (on which more detail in the next chapter), he takes the use-conditions introduced by sentences of the form $s_1 \, k \, s_2$ (for k a connective) to be the conjunction of the use-conditions introduced in s_1 and s_2. But this is, of course, inconsistent with the treatment of biscuit conditionals I have outlined here; the whole point of such conditionals is that their use-conditions are *not* those of the sentences that comprise them. Taking biscuit conditionals to conditionalize over use-conditions thus is not obviously compatible with Predelli's (2013) general theory of expressive meanings, unless one wishes to claim that biscuit conditionals are a separate construction entirely, which obviates the point of trying to treat them using a conventional semantics for conditionals in the first place. I conclude that there is no strong evidence for a genuinely expressive treatment.

Still, Predelli does seem to be onto something: there might be a sense in which biscuit conditionals are expressive after all, on a different sense of "expressive." Here is a candidate. Biscuit antecedents are expressive in that they *act* on a context, altering it, rather than behaving like ordinary content. But the kind of expressivity they evince is not like that of pejoratives, greetings, or exclamations. Rather, it is more like the expressivity of speech acts, with their performative character. Biscuit conditional antecedents are in a sense *antiperformative*: as I have argued, they exempt a speaker from certain consequences of the speech act which she performs. This kind of metalinguistic character is similar in some respects to that of adverbials like *frankly*, but such adverbials are supplementary in Potts's (2005) sense: they comment on some main content, rather than affecting it directly.[11] Biscuit antecedents, conversely, do not comment on the content that follows them so much as they modify the effect of its use. They are not supplementary; they are metaconversational.

Summing up, this section has proposed an analysis of biscuit conditionals on which they consist of a shield hedge and an assertion (or other speech act). I argued that this view retains some positive features of other, existing, analyses, while in the end providing a simpler and more natural treatment.

4.2 Undisclaimable content and expressive meaning

So far the discussion has gone as follows. We first looked at general considerations of cooperativity, communicative and otherwise, and how such considerations admit a characterization via reputations in repeated games. This characterization was then used to account for one kind of hedging involving situations in which the speaker was unsure of the truth of the content of her utterance. Generalizing, we then examined one kind of situation in which other sorts of content is hedged: namely, so-called biscuit conditionals, where various kinds of implicatures (involving relevance in the standard examples) are hedged. From this perspective, it became clear that what is hedged in standard cases of shield hedges is not in fact the truth of the utterance content itself, but the Quality implicature that is induced by a speaker's *use* of that content in the utterance.

I now want to extend this discussion to consider other kinds of content. Up to here, we have talked exclusively about hedging with respect to the content of entire utterances, and the implicatures which those utterances directly generate: namely, for instance, that ϕ is true

---

[11] This is the source of the controversial "independence" constraints discussed by Wang et al. (2005) and Amaral et al. (2008), among others.

after an utterance with content ϕ. Interestingly, there are many cases where what is hedged is not a simple implicature of this kind, but one relating to a *side effect* of the utterance. This can be brought out clearly by considering utterances which might not reasonably be expected to be "hedgeable": for instance, statements about the mental state of the speaker, her preferences, or metalinguistic effects of what is said and what has been taken to hold for the purposes of the discourse. Consideration of these cases gives us a deeper understanding of how such processes work, and of hedging itself.

Up to this point we have been talking exclusively about advertisements that represent objects in the world, and about communicative acts that aim (in principle) to provide accurate information. Obviously, such content does not exhaust the full repertory of either advertising or communication. Some advertisements are meant to have a more subtle communicative effect, though one which is often realized as rather crass advertising, and some communicative actions do not involve the transmission of propositional content. In this section, I will first discuss advertising that does not have truthful communication as its primary intent. I will then show that, just as before, an exactly analogous case can be found in natural language. As a result, a general theory of the two types can be provided in terms of a distinction between "at-issue" and "expressive" meanings.

It is easy to find advertisements that do not directly aim to represent the advertised object. Indeed, it seems that such advertisements are probably more common than advertisements which make factual claims. So far we have considered only pictorial advertisements that appear on for example packaging or menus, where the object being sold is explicitly represented. But pictorial advertisements in for example magazines or on television do not usually aim to show exactly what the product is like. Instead, they try to leave the viewer with a positive association to the product. One example is advertisements with celebrity endorsements, where the intent is for the viewer to extend any positive feelings she may have for the celebrity to the endorsed product; here, it is often the case that the celebrity has certain properties that may be relevant to the product, for instance as when athletes endorse a particular brand or model of sneaker, or a supermodel appears in an advertisement for skin cream. Another kind of case arises when an image one might view as positive or attractive is provided, such as someone climbing an attractive mountain in an ad for hiking gear, or a woman draped across the hood of a vehicle for an automobile advertisement.[12] Let us call advertisements of this type *associative*.

In this sort of context, it doesn't make much sense to talk about truthfulness or accuracy of representation. No one would take seriously a consumer's claim that the advertiser was uncooperative because the car one bought lacked a woman on the hood. Similarly, the relation between the famous athlete and the shoe is not meant to be one that is either reproducible or that has any concrete implications about the effect of the shoes. What is the sense of advertisements like these? For an answer, we can consider cases in purely linguistic communication in which conveying content about the facts—truth-conditional content— is not the primary motivation.

For an example, take the utterances in (4.22), which exhibit behavior similar in some respects to the above.

(4.22) a. Ouch!   (Kaplan 1999)
       b. Damn, man!
       c. Whoah!

Use of these expressions is not intended to describe the world directly. No propositional information is communicated, except as a side effect of the speech act. My goal in making any of the utterances in (4.22) is not to assert anything about the world; full discussion of this point can be found in Kaplan (1999) and Potts (2007), but the fact is already brought out clearly by the observation that these utterances do not have truth conditions. They indicate the speaker's mental state but not in a way that invites objective consideration. The sort of content carried by these expressions is known as *expressive content*, and has been a focus of much recent work in linguistics and philosophy (e.g. Kaplan 1999; McCready 2004, 2005; Potts 2005; Richard 2008; Potts et al. 2009, among many others; some details of these analyses will be discussed in chapter 5).

We can also find cases where expressive content mixes with "ordinary" truth-conditional content. Most obvious is the case of expressive modifiers like *damn* or *fucking*, as in (4.23a,b), a sort of case studied extensively by Potts (2005, 2007). Less obvious perhaps are cases where, arguably, a single term carries both expressive and truth-conditional content, as in pejoratives and certain honorifics (4.23c,d). Cases like this are discussed by Bach (2006); Gutzmann (2008); Williamson (2009); McCready (2010c), among others.

---

[12] Thanks to Sarah Zobel and Anna Pilikova for discussion of some examples here.

(4.23) a. I lost my *damn* keys.
      b. Give me the *fucking* money.
      c. Some *bum* tried to talk to me on the street today.
      d. Yamada-sensei-ga irasshai-masita.
         Y-teacher-Nom   came.Hon-Pst.Hon
         'Prof Yamada came.' (and Prof. Yamada is to be respected)

I think these cases are rather close to the associative advertisements above. In these cases, some of the sentential content is intended to represent some fact about the world (or, in the case of the imperative, to alter it in some way). For example, (4.23a) represents the world as one where the speaker has lost her keys, and (4.23d) represents the world as one where Professor Yamada has come. Simultaneously, though, the speaker indicates her attitude toward something: toward the state of the world or the fact that the keys have been lost in (4.23a), or toward Professor Yamada in (4.23d). Crucially, only the first part can be challenged as false. The second part, the expressive content, is just not the right sort of thing to be challenged—it merely indicates something about the speaker's attitudes, but not in an objective, questionable way.

This fact is reflected in the behavior of operators when applied to sentences containing both expressive and so-called "at-issue" content. As noted by Potts, operators only have effects on the at-issue content, leaving the expressive content untouched.[13] Let us write the at-issue and expressive contents as a pair, following Potts (2005) and others; this is meant to express the intuition that two dimensions of meaning are involved here, which can be modeled in a multidimensional semantics à la Potts, or by other means.

(4.24) a. A: I lost my damn keys.
        B: That's not true.
       $= \langle \neg lost(a, keys), \{damn(keyLosing)\}\rangle$
      b. I didn't lose my damn keys.
       $= \langle \neg lost(a, keys), \{damn(keyLosing)\}\rangle$

So negation applies only to the at-issue content in any pair like the above.

The same holds for trying to hedge utterances that contain expressive content. The expressive content projects from the hedges: the only thing that is hedged is the at-issue content.

---

[13] This actually is not always true; there are contexts, such as in the scope of certain attitudes, where operators do have effects on expressive content as well (Wang et al. 2005, 2006; Bach 2006; Amaral et al. 2008). I will put this fact aside here; we cannot embed advertisements under attitudes anyway, nor disclaimers.

(4.25) a. I might be wrong about this, but I'm pretty sure it's going to fucking rain tomorrow.
$\implies$ speaker is in emotional state characterized by $[\![fucking]\!]$[14]
$\implies D(sure(s, rain(tmrw)))$[15]

   b. I might be wrong about who that was out there, but it looks like that asshole is waiting for you again.
$\implies$ speaker doesn't like referent of DP
$\implies D(waiting(that\_guy))$

Again, we may represent this as a pair of meanings, where the disclaiming operator D applies only to the at-issue member. Here the representations of the expressive meanings are very rough; see Potts (2007) or McCready (2012a) for more detailed proposals.

(4.26) a. $[\![(4.25a)]\!] = \langle D(rain(tmrw)), \{irritated(rain(tmrw))\}\rangle$
   b. $[\![(4.25b)]\!] = \langle D(waiting(that\_guy)), \{dislike(that\_guy)\}\rangle$

It has also been shown by Potts that expressive content has impact even when it is quoted: it is the mere use of the word that causes the expressive effects. These effects cannot be cancelled; they persist even if they are explicitly disavowed by the speaker. In this sense they are like, for example, screams or shouts: when I scream "I'm not angry!" at you, you are unlikely to believe me. The reason might be that the effects produced supersede the linguistic despite their symbolic nature: expressive meaning goes straight to the gut. Potts, in a nice phrase, talks about expressive content being "inflicted on" the hearer; this suggests direct connections to advertising, which we are now in a position to explore.

   What happens when we see an attractive advertisement, for example the aforementioned woman on car? The reader who finds little appeal in this scenario is welcome to substitute whatever strikes his or her fancy here: change the woman to a man, remove the human and substitute a beautiful beach in the background, or whatever. One may separate out what can be taken to be the literal representation from that which cannot be understood literally. For example, in the scenario, we know that (some token of) the car(-type) is for sale, and the woman/man/beach obviously is not. This means that it is impossible

---

[14] This could be positive or negative, or otherwise; see McCready (2012a) for relevant discussion and analysis.
[15] See the next section for more on disclaiming sentences with epistemic modals and epistemic attitudes.

to construe the advertisement as a completely literal representation. We find it easy to distinguish embellishments of this kind from images meant to convey the character of the product. But what is the purpose of the embellishments? They are meant to give a positive association to the product.[16] This positive association is supposed to increase the probability that a consumer will select the product over its competitors.

What is the nature of the positive association? We have established already that the blonde herself (or what have you) is not part of what is represented as being for sale, so the association is not a literal one: "if you buy this car, you will get a blonde/beach." Rather, the intent is to provoke a reaction in the viewer, in the sense of stimulus and response. For susceptible people, the image of something attractive will produce sensations of attraction. The hope of the advertiser, however crass it may be, is that this attraction will extend to the product. But note that (again for susceptible people) this reaction will arise in a way independent of rational faculties; it is a reaction by the body to stimuli produced for the body. As such, it is in a way independent of symbolic content. It is also difficult to resist, as it bypasses rational processes: this is the source of its (presumed) effectiveness. Again, this is much like expressive content.

From this discussion, it seems reasonable to conclude that the aim of associative advertising is to induce *alief* in the viewer.[17] Alief is a kind of mental state discussed by Szabo Gendler (2008a,b), which is distinct from such "conscious" states as belief, desire, or knowledge. It arises in situations where people have what amounts to a preconscious response to certain stimuli which results in certain kinds of action or reaction. Szabo Gendler provides many examples: for instance, the reaction of fear or panic people have when standing on a transparent platform above a large drop (despite knowing it to be safe), or the disinclination of experimental subjects to eat chocolate shaped like dog feces, despite having seen the chocolate before it was shaped into that form. These responses are not rational, but nonetheless arise. The similarity to what happens upon the observation of pictorial advertisements is clear.

Szabo Gendler takes alief to be a four-place relation between an agent, a (mental) representation, an affective state, and behavioral response. For instance, upon observing and consequently forming a representation of a feces-shaped piece of chocolate, one may find oneself in a

---

[16] Thanks to Anna Pilikova and Henk Zeevat for discussion here.
[17] I am grateful to an anonymous reviewer for bringing this connection to my attention.

state of feeling disgust, and with certain physical responses of avoidance coming online. Alief can also be viewed in a two-place manner:

(4.27)   S alieves R when S's R-related associations are activated and thereby rendered cognitively, affectively, and behaviorally salient.   (Szabo Gendler 2008a)

It is interesting to consider the connection with expressive content here. Many or even most expressives have content which clearly relates to states of alief rather than states of belief: such is obviously the case for such items as expressive adjectives and pejoratives, which specifically function to indicate emotive states of the speaker with respect to some phenomenon, but possibly for other expressions as well. I cannot pursue this issue here in full detail.

Suppose that the alief-inducing representation comes with a disclaimer: (3.8) repeated below as (4.28), or the like.

(4.28)   Shasshin-wa   imeeji desu
         photograph-Top image is
         'The photograph is an image.' (lit.)

What gets disclaimed in this case? Recall that a disclaimer in the formal model proposed in the previous section is asking that the current game iteration not be taken into account when we calculate things like trustworthiness and cooperativity. But we can already deduce that the presence of the attractive individual or background in the advertisement is not meant literally. This means that the disclaimer should actually have little effect at least on this part of the content. We would not take the disclaimer to indicate that the blonde we purchase may not resemble the one in the advertisement, for we already know that the blonde is there only for advertising purposes. All this is just to say that, while we would take under advisement that the car for sale might not resemble the pictured one in every particular, the gut reaction of attraction or excitement produced by the image in the susceptible would remain.

These observations lead to the following picture. An image in associative advertising carries a dual message, one part of which is representational, one part of which merely packs a sensual punch. When associative advertisements are disclaimed, the disclaimer applies in some sense only to the representation: the "sensual" content is somehow untouched. It may be clear that the above relates closely to the distinction between expressive and at-issue content. Expressive meanings are, as Potts puts it, "inflicted" on the hearer independent of the hearer's choice of whether or not to accept an assertion; the sensual content of an associative advertisement is inflicted in precisely the same way. At-issue content can be hedged, while expressive content cannot; the same holds for the corresponding parts of associative advertisements. I therefore propose that we view advertisements—and visual representations in general—as having components that correspond to expressive and at-issue parts of linguistic meaning. We get something like the following for the "blonde on car" advertisement (where v is the viewer):

(4.29) $\langle represents(image, product), \{alieve(v, attractive(product))\}\rangle$

When disclaimed, the second part of the meaning remains untouched.

(4.30) $\langle D(represents(image, product)), \{alieve(v, attractive(product))\}\rangle$

If correct, this analysis has some interesting consequences. First, it indicates that expressiveness is not a property only of linguistic communication, but of symbolic or representational communication in general. This might not be a surprise. We have already seen that one can generate implicatures from the use or lack of use of disclaimers together with pictorial representations: using a disclaimer, when use of one is not otherwise mandated, implicates that the representation is probably relatively unlike the actual object. The opposite implicature can also arise. If use of disclaimers is common, lack of a disclaimer may implicate accuracy of an image; indeed, one can even strengthen this by making this explicit: "this photograph is not an *imeeji!*"[18] But it is also the case that not using an image at all can generate implicatures, for example that the product is so unpalatable that any positive representation would be far over the line into obvious insincerity (cf. section 3.5); that the producers expect the product already to be well known; that no representation can adequately capture the flavor of the product, etc. As usual with particularized implicatures, the precise content will depend on context (Levinson 2000). If images can generate implicatures, it might be no surprise that they can be associated with different kinds of content as well.

This picture raises some other interesting questions. One is what the pictoral analogue of a presupposition would be, or if such a thing could even exist. Could the presupposition of a picture *of something* be that it *represents that something*? Or is this part of, as it were, the assertion of the picture? Alternatively, is the presupposition simply that

---

[18] Thanks to Yasutada Sudo for discussion on this point.

the represented object *is representable*? These appear to be properties of the medium, rather than of any given representation, however. It is also interesting to speculate in this context about the nature of expressive content. The discussion above suggests that expressive content—in the realm of images—is content which produces a prerational response in the observer. How far does this picture carry over to other instances of expressive content? It does seem to fit the cases of profanity and pejoratives rather well; but it is not so obvious that it is right for expressions like honorifics, where the content is in some sense less immediate or primitive. Perhaps we should take honorifics to class with conventional implicatures like appositives rather than with the true expressives. These topics go well beyond the scope of the present work, but they appear to be interesting issues for future exploration.

4.3 Disclaiming side effects: epistemic modals

This section considers the possibility of disclaiming the side effects of utterances, viewed as operations that take place alongside the introduction of truth-evaluable or expressively evaluable semantic content. Side effects are induced by the utterance of a variety of sentence types and linguistic objects. For example, the use of indefinite descriptions has the side effect of introducing discourse referents (Karttunen 1976), and the use of vague or contextually sensitive expressions such as gradable adjectives can have the side effect of setting a standard for the truth of the expression, as analyzed in detail by Barker (2002). I believe that these particular side effects can be hedged as well (something I will say a bit more about in the conclusion to this chapter), but my focus in this section will be on the side effects of using modal sentences and self-ascribed attitudes, as in (4.31).

(4.31)   a. It might be raining.
         b. I think it is raining.

The literal claim of these sentences on standard views of epistemic modality (detailed below) is that it is compatible with the information that the speaker has that it is raining. The interesting questions for the purposes of our discussion are: why is it often deemed more natural to hedge sentences like (4.31) than sentences free of intensional operators? And, more puzzlingly, what could possibly be the point of hedging a claim about one's own information state?

(4.32)   a. I'm not sure, but it might be raining.
         b. I'm not sure, but I think it's raining.

The mere fact of these cases is already interesting in light of what is, to my knowledge, the only direct discussion of hedging in philosophy (excluding DeRose and Grandy 1999). Sorensen (2006) claims that hedges can function as a test for possession of a truth-value. If something cannot be hedged, it must be truth-valueless. Sorensen considers only hedges like "might," and so examples like "John might be bald"; but the same likely holds for shield hedges as well. If it does, then cases like those in (4.32) are bad news for analyses that treat modal sentences as truth-valueless expressions of some speaker attitude or propensity, and similarly for some popular treatments of predicates of personal taste and moral or deontic claims (e.g. Gibbard 2003), which use a similar treatment. Another kind of apparent counterexample involves hedges of utterances with purely expressive denotations, such as the classic Kaplanian examples of *ouch* and *oops* (Kaplan 1999):

(4.33)   This might not be appropriate, but oops.

However, it is not completely clear that such examples should be treated on a par with the other examples of hedges I have discussed: (4.33) sounds rather metalinguistic compared to the hedges we have seen so far. But if cases like these are indeed analogous to other cases of hedging, then we find further issues for Sorensen's thesis.

   Putting this point aside, let me turn to the hedging of epistemic modals and attitudes. Note first that it is not at all difficult to hedge sentences containing such expressions. In fact, for some speakers, it is obligatory. For speakers of this type (whom I will call *strict*), hedged nonmodal assertions sound strange; for these people, it is necessary to modalize the asserted content for the hedge to be good, a point already mentioned in chapter 3.

(4.34)   For strict speakers:
         a. # I might be wrong, but John is coming to the party.
         b. I might be wrong, but I think John is coming to the party/John might be coming to the party.

It seems that for these speakers the asserted clause simply indicates too high a degree of commitment or confidence without the modal. But we now have a puzzle. What is being hedged, actually, when one hedges a modal sentence? On standard accounts of modal meaning, in fact, the hedge (at least in the form here) is perfectly consistent with the modal sentence. Consider two standard accounts of modality in the semantic literature, both making use of a possible-worlds-based framework: that of Kratzer (1981) and that of Veltman (1996). On the Kratzerian account, a sentence with a possibility modal is true iff there is some epistemic alternative to the actual world in which the sentence is true. Kratzer defines notions of modal base and ordering source: we can simplify matters and put aside the ordering source here for the purposes of illustration, so we are left with something like a standard modal logic analysis of possibility (cf. Chellas 1980).[19]

(4.35)   Simplified Kratzer/modal logic for epistemic possibility modals:
$\mathcal{M}, w \models \Diamond_e come\_party(john)$ iff $\exists w'[wR_{epist}w' \rightarrow come\_party(john)(w')]$

The speaker, obviously, need not be highly confident in her assessment for this sentence to be true. She need only consider John's coming tonight possible in view of her knowledge (beliefs), even if the possibility proves to be quite remote. Note that this is perfectly compatible with her being unsure whether John is coming, for there may be epistemically accessible worlds in which John does not come as well.[20] The same result is gained by considering the Veltman account, a dynamic semantics for modality. In dynamic semantics, meanings are viewed as context change potentials, the possibilities for information change induced in the agent who updates her information state with that meaning. For the case of epistemic modality, information states can be viewed as sets of worlds, states or points of evaluation: the set of states considered to be live possibilities by the updating agent. In Veltman's dynamic semantics, the possibility modal is viewed as a global test on information states, passed for a proposition φ if there is some state (world) verifying φ in the information state. More formally (where $\sigma[\varphi]$ indicates the result of updating σ with φ, and propositions are also viewed as sets of worlds, as usual):

(4.36)   Veltman semantics for epistemic possibility modals
$$\sigma[\Diamond\varphi] = \begin{cases} \sigma & \text{if } \sigma \cap \varphi \neq \varnothing \\ \varnothing & \text{else} \end{cases}$$

---

[19] For our needs here, what matters is only that the truth of an epistemic modal claim depends on the compatibility of the modalized content with the relevant set of accessible possible worlds. No ordering is required.

[20] Indeed, there should be: if there are not, then the speaker should state that John is or must be coming, for reasons of Gricean Quantity.

Thus an information state will pass a modal test if there is a possible world in which the modalized sentence is true, and otherwise it will fail. This, of course, means that a given information state can be perfectly compatible with both a proposition and its negation, given that both are modalized. Indeed the following is consistent in both the Kratzer and the Veltman semantics, as (obviously) is desired.

(4.37) $\lozenge \phi \wedge \lozenge \neg \phi$

We can now ask the question of what exactly is being hedged in the case of modals. Unfortunately, this proves to be a somewhat fraught issue, as the obvious answer cannot be correct. If an epistemic modal claim is about (in essence) the compatibility of some proposition (that in the scope of the modal) with the information known or believed by the speaker, then how can it be coherent to hedge that claim? It would be tantamount to an admission that one does not know what one knows: paraphrasing, "I might be wrong about what my information is." But this just seems the wrong interpretation, and further is one that is pragmatically incoherent. This is puzzling.

One possible response to this puzzle might be to cite the work of DeRose (1991) (among others) on epistemic modals.[21] On this view, epistemic modals do make claims about the compatibility of their prejacents with an information state, but the relevant information state is not necessarily that of the speaker, but can be relative to some other contextually salient individual, or even the joint (or private) knowledge of the members of some salient group. The view, then, is a standard contextualist one about epistemic modality. How could it be used to analyze the present case? Recall the problem: we have sentences of the form "Possibly p, but I might be wrong"; schematically, this should be analyzed as $\lozenge \phi$, but with a hedge, where the hedge means, roughly, $\lozenge \neg \lozenge \phi$. If the modal operator indicates compatibility with the speaker's information, then the sentence should be inconsistent or at least pragmatically bizarre, for it should mean that the speaker isn't certain about the content of her own information state; but this is inconsistent with standard assumptions about knowledge or belief. Here, though, the advocate of a DeRose-style contextualist theory has a way out of the problem. He can claim that the individuals (or groups) whose epistemic states are at issue in evaluating the two modal operators are distinct. One has to be a bit careful here in choosing the individuals who can

---

[21] Thanks to an anonymous reviewer for this suggestion.

serve as possible modal evaluators, for just anyone won't do: there has to be at least an element of hedging. One reasonable kind of claim might involve different aspects of oneself, so the sentence *It might be raining* might be paraphrased as "possibly *rain*, according to that part of me that has watched the news, but perhaps it's not possible that *rain* after all, according to that part of me that has examined the state of the sky".[22] This looks rather reasonable, and avoids some of the complexity which might otherwise follow.

But it turns out that this move won't help much, as it depends on an illicit kind of context shift. Many authors have called into question the validity of appealing to certain kinds of shifts in context in epistemological explanation. In general it is not that easy to shift contexts. For instance, writing about the well-known problem of shifts in quantifier domains (cf. Stanley and Szabo 2000), Swanson (2010) writes:

> Speakers regularly use "everyone" not to talk about absolutely everyone but rather about every employee, or every child, or every addressee, or what have you. But once a particular restriction on "everyone" is in place, considerable conversational pressure holds it there. The reason for this is that it takes group effort for conversational participants to coordinate on domains of quantification, and one should not ask conversational participants to engage in such an effort without good reason.

This point is well taken; it indicates that people should not shift domains without good reason. Further, it is an obvious point that shifting quantifier domains without signaling those shifts rather explicitly won't be a successful communicative strategy, in that one's interlocutors are rather likely to miss the shift, and fail to make sense of what one is trying to convey.[23] Some commentators are rather liberal in the kinds of context shifts they allow; for instance, consider the following example, which I personally find rather hard to get: B's utterance just sounds contradictory, a judgement shared by many other speakers I've consulted.

(4.38)   **Quantifier Shift** (Stanley 2005: 65)

   a. A: Every van Gogh painting is in the Dutch National Museum.

   b. B: That's a change. When I visited last year, I saw every van Gogh painting, and some were definitely missing.

---

[22] This idea has clear functional similarities to the idea of information states indexed to evidence sources presented in chapter 7, and to the "community of minds" logic of Fagin and Halpern (1988).

[23] Similar points are made in McCready (2012a) in the context of recovering the content of emotive speech; further, McCready (2012b) sketches an extension of this analysis to the case of quantifier domains, which precisely requires coordination.

But even the most liberal speakers balk at cases where one shifts horses in midstream, as it were; it is generally acknowledged that shifting contexts within a clause is not allowed. If it were, examples like this one would be possible, supposing that the antecedent is evaluated in such a way that students are quantified over, and the consequent in such a way that ancient Greek philosophers are quantified over (to make this marginally plausible, suppose that the sentence is uttered in a class on classical philosophy):

(4.39)   If everyone is here, then everyone is dead.

One can easily construct similar examples for other domains: gradable adjectives, for instance, as in (4.40), or, crucially, epistemic modals, as in (4.41) as uttered by Bond. But these sentences are all completely absurd.

(4.40)   *Context: John is an NBA center and Bill is 3 years old.*
         If John is tall, then Bill is too.

(4.41)   *Context: Bond is in Milan, and Goldfinger in Moscow; Goldfinger thinks that Bond is in London or Abu Dhabi.* (cf. Egan 2006; Weatherson and Egan 2011b)
         If I might have pizza for dinner tonight, then I might be in Abu Dhabi.

The lesson is that we cannot shift the individuals whose information is at issue in evaluating epistemic modals arbitrarily and suddenly, just as we couldn't for other kinds of contextually dependent expressions. We thus need to go in a different direction.[24]

Intuitively, it seems as if a speaker of a hedged modal claim is hedging, not the modal content, but the proposition in the scope of the modal. Semi-formally, we get the following, where $\checkmark$ indicates an available and $\star$ an unavailable reading.

$$(4.42) \quad D(\text{might}(\phi)) = \left\{ \begin{array}{ll} \checkmark & D(\phi) \\ \star & D(\Diamond\phi) \end{array} \right.$$

---

[24] Another possibility, also suggested by a reviewer, would be to make use of a different sort of semantics for modals, for example the probabilistic view ("Bayesian expressivism") espoused by Yalcin (2012). It's not obvious to me how this would solve the issue raised here, especially given that Yalcin, in that paper, ultimately advocates the use of centered worlds as input to credences, which therefore are likely (though not absolutely required) to correlate with subjective evaluations to some degree. The issues here are complex; though it is possible to combine a nonsubjective notion of probability with centered worlds (as I do in McCready 2014), the result will have a subjective component. I do not think that the nature of probabilistic views automatically allows them to evade the worries I have expressed.

The puzzle then is twofold: first, why we get a reading which doesn't seem to correspond to the actual hedged content (i.e. the modal claim), and, second, why the reading that does indeed correspond to such content does not arise.

The answer to these questions comes easily once we consider what modal assertions do to the common ground. It is folk knowledge in semantics and pragmatics that modal assertions do more than simply indicate something about a speaker's information state, though this fact is rarely explicitly stated in the literature (although see von Fintel and Gillies 2008a,b; Wang et al. 2012 for some instances). Instead, they bring their prejacents forward in some manner short of full assertion. In some contexts, indeed, they seem to count as weak claims of their prejacent content, at least in terms of the effects of their use. Consider, for example, the case of epistemic modals used to give advice, as in (4.43).

(4.43)   It might rain this afternoon. (So you should take your raincoat.)

If all that's claimed by (4.43) is that afternoon rain is compatible with the beliefs of the speaker, what relevance does that have for the hearer? Indeed, Wang et al. note that in most contexts a claim about compatibility of some proposition with the speaker's information is not very useful; more useful is the related claim that the proposition is therefore likely to be true. This idea can be cashed out in various ways, all of which are pragmatic in nature. Here, I will not take a position as to what the proper method is: von Fintel and Gillies talk about making a proposition salient via a modal utterance, Wang et al. have such propositions indicated as possibly true by means of grounding in a proper epistemological method, and I will propose yet another way in chapter 7. My intent in this chapter is only to consider the effects of modal assertions and how they interact with hedging. The basic intuition is that two actions are associated with an utterance of $\Diamond\phi$: an assertion of the modal claim $\Diamond\phi$ itself, and a "making salient" of ϕ. I will follow the literature and use the term "proffering" for making a proposition salient. Thus, we get the following. Here "$\approx$" indicates nonmonotonic entailment, which I use for reasons that will become clear shortly.[25]

$$Assert[\Diamond\phi] \mathrel{|\!\approx} Proffer[\phi].$$

---

[25] An entailment is nonmonotonic if it can be defeated by the presence of other information. An overview of nonmonotonic logics, including this notion of entailment, can be found in Nute (1994).

Something more or less identical happens in other cases where speakers express epistemic attitudes using embedding verbs:

(4.44)   a. I might be wrong, but I think Palin is not going to be elected.

  b. This might not be true, but I suspect she doesn't really care about you.

As with the "pure" modal sentences, there is an inference to the proffering of the content of the attitude.

$$Assert[\mathit{Think}(s,\phi)] \approx \mathit{Proffer}[\phi].$$

With this in place, we can ask what the hedge itself is doing. There are two possible objects which can be targeted, given the observations of the last section that pragmatic content is also available for hedging (as in the case of biscuit conditionals). The first is the modal claim, and the second is its prejacent content. Which of the two can be coherently hedged? Recall the discussion of the Propriety Principle. That principle, and the related principle involving costs of hedging, state that a speaker cannot hedge crazily, without a good reason. This principle was introduced to block speaker strategies which hedge every utterance in order to avoid possible penalties. But, as noted earlier, associating costs with hedging guarantees (in the long term) the absence of hedges on certain information. Intuitively, if a speaker has no reason to doubt a piece of content, there is no good reason to disclaim it. But why would one ever disclaim content about one's own mental state, given the existence of something like privileged access (Mitchell 1986)? Surely I have as good an idea of my own views, and information, as anyone else, so it makes no sense to disclaim except in very special situations. If this is correct, then modal claims should not be hedgeable.[26] From this, we can see how to answer the second question raised above about why the full modal content cannot be hedged: doing so would simply be incoherent, and thus is blocked by the evolutionary considerations that come along with the cost of hedging.

  The above shows why it is incoherent to hedge a (self-ascriptive) modal claim. This leaves only the reading where the prejacent content itself is hedged. The task now is to explain why this content is available

---

[26] Here I exclude those special circumstances where the claim is made with respect to someone else's perspective. For such cases hedging is perfectly coherent, for I may indeed be uncertain about someone else's information. I will disregard such cases in this paper, for I do not see that they are essentially different than hedging nonmodal claims in the sense we are interested in here.

for hedging at all. Given the discussion above, the answer to this question is also relatively clear: it is available because that content is proffered to the hearer by the nature of modal assertion. Since the asserted modal claim itself is not available to hedge, there is no choice but to hedge the proffered content.

How to analyze the action of the hedge? The first and most obvious way is to simply suppose that the hedge targets the modalized content itself. But there is something puzzling about this idea: how can it be that one can hedge content that is not actually asserted, in any sense? We might then say that the hedge applies to the entire derivative speech act itself, so that we get something like

$$D(Proffer[\phi]).$$

But this also seems unintuitive. It seems questionable that the proffering itself is hedged (however this is to be cashed out), for it certainly seems as if the modalized content is profferred, only in the somewhat hesitant way characteristic of hedged content.

In my view, the situation here is closely analogous to what we saw with hedging in biscuit conditionals. There, hedges could target side effects of the speech act performed by the "consequent"; in the modal case the relevant side effect is the proffering of the modalized content. The difference is that in the present case there is a further side effect of the proffering: the hearer is invited (as pointed out by von Fintel and Gillies 2008b) to take the modalized content as a "serious possibility," something which should be taken into account when considering future courses of action. For instance, if I am looking for my keys and you say (4.45), I might well go look in the living room.

(4.45)   They might be under the couch.

The hedge is targeting this implicature, and, in general, the nonmonotonic inference from $\Diamond\phi$ to "optimally, behave as if ϕ is a serious possibility," which in essence amounts to behaving as if ϕ were true.

We could think about the action of the hedge here as simply blocking the nonmonotonic inference itself, and so as a kind of metalinguistic hedge; this is similar in some respects to the claims made in McCready (forthcoming, a) about how update works with hearsay (or reportative) evidentials in languages like Japanese or Quechua. Evidentials of this kind indicate that the speaker heard the content in the evidential's scope from someone else, and make no stipulations regarding its truth or lack thereof. However, given something like Gricean cooperation, we might expect that the content in the evidential's scope should be believed: given that speakers are Gricean cooperators, their information should be trustworthy, and so second-hand information should also be trustworthy. But this inference doesn't seem to follow in full generality. The reason, according to McCready (forthcoming, a), is that this (Quality) implicature is blocked by another (Quantity) implicature: given that the speaker chose to assert *Hearsayφ* rather than just $φ$, some lack of confidence in $φ$ is indicated, and the two implicatures block each other's application.[27] This seems a reasonable strategy for hedges of the present sort as well. It also explains why some speakers prefer to hedge modal statements. Since the prejacent is not directly asserted but instead proffered, the path to update with the prejacent content is less direct than in a normal assertion; since update with the prejacent is fully dependent on the lack of defeaters, problems of Moore-paradoxicality are unlikely to arise. I take it that sensitive speakers are picking up on this distinction.

The above view of the implicatures of evidentials and blocking requires viewing implicatures as nonmonotonic entailments which can interfere with each other.[28] The idea would be that speakers generally follow something like the following axiom, so that when a hearer observes an assertion of "$◇φ$" she ordinarily behaves as if $φ$.[29]

(4.46) $Observe(h, Assert(s, ◇φ)) > actAsIf(h, φ)$

This axiom correctly captures the fact that modal assertions can be used to give advice, which is otherwise puzzling. The hedge should function to block the use of this axiom. How exactly? Here we need a more specific picture of how hedges function in pragmatic inference.

In chapter 3, I used a simple predicate D to indicate that a particular piece of content was disclaimed. Let me assume the existence of the following axioms, together a way of spelling out Gricean cooperativity:

---

[27] Chapter 9 reconsiders these cases from a more nuanced perspective.

[28] See Reiter and Criscuolo (1981) on the behavior of interacting defaults.

[29] Here ">" is a nonmonotonic conditional: see Asher and Morreau (1991); Halpern (2003); McCready and Ogata (2007a) for details of such conditionals.

(4.47) **Cooperativity by default.**

    a. **Quality.**

       $Assert(s,\phi) > True\phi$

    b. **Quantity.**

       $Assert(s,\phi) > Approp\_gran\phi$

    c. **Manner.**

       $Assert(s,\phi) > Clear\phi$

    d. **Relevance.**

       $Assert(s,\phi) > Rel\phi$

The intuition behind these axioms should be clear: given that a speaker asserts a sentence with content ϕ, certain things generally follow. For example, (4.47a) says that asserted content is generally true. Clearly, qualifications might be required about *actual* truth as opposed to mere belief by the speaker; I will ignore these complications here, both for the purpose of keeping things relatively simple and also because I think that some of the problematic facts about how actual and speaker-relative truth interact in communication can be solved with closer attention to the nature of the process of update and information transfer.[30] The exact details of the other axioms I have left somewhat fuzzy. (4.47b) provides a default inference to the claim that the granularity of the utterance content is appropriate to the question under discussion (Roberts 2012), so that if you ask me what I want to eat I should not answer "food"; but spelling this out fully would take us far afield. Similarly for (4.47d), which assumes a notion of relevance: I take it that such can be spelled out in terms of information content, perhaps in the manner of van Rooij (2003c), for whom relevance is measured by entropy reduction with respect to a question under discussion. All this seems straightforward, though somewhat cumbersome and complicated. The really hard case is (4.47c). It is surprisingly difficult to say exactly what is implicated by the maxim of Manner in any given instance. Here I have simply used a predicate *Clear*, which I will leave undefined, which is meant to indicate that the way a piece of content is expressed is not too difficult to follow. For present purposes I will leave things at that.

    Thinking of implicatures as default inferences is not a new idea (e.g. Levinson 2000), and is not uncontroversial (Geurts 2010). But it is

---

[30] In particular, a theory of information transfer of perspective-dependent content is needed. I think the foundations for such a theory are given by property theories of content, and the equivalent centered-worlds views (e.g. Lewis 1979; Stephenson 2007; Yalcin 2007; Stalnaker 2008). See Wechsler and McCready (2011) for some relevant discussion.

one available view, and it is one that makes it easy to see how hedges can affect the implicatures of ordinary utterances. As I have stressed throughout, the most familiar cases of hedging indicate that the speaker is not certain about the content she is putting forward; I modeled this as a request to, essentially, remove the hedged content from the conversational record for purposes of inductive reasoning about speaker reliability. But an obvious side effect of using a hedge is to alter the assumptions the hearer can reasonably make about what the speaker is doing. If I hedge the truth of my statement, it seems nonsensical to allow something like the **Quality** inference above to go through, and similarly for the other cases. Something like this seems to be the right way to think about biscuit conditionals, as I have argued. Let us therefore assume the existence of an axiom of the following form:

(4.48) $Assert(s,\phi) \wedge D(True\phi) > \Diamond \neg True\phi$

This axiom says that if a speaker hedges the truth of the content of an assertion, then one can normally conclude that the status of that content is unclear with respect to truth. With this, we can see the utility of the *specificity* property of nonmonotonic inference: given two conditionals with conflicting consequents, where the antecedent of one supersedes the other, the more specific one will win out. In the present case, that means that (4.48) will override (4.47a), and no implication of truth will arise.

It is easy to see how the corresponding cases of Quantity, Manner, and Relevance can be handled in this system. We need only introduce axioms along the lines of (4.48) but which reference the other axioms in (4.47). This is trivial. The interesting issue arises when we try to see how to be certain what is being disclaimed: whether we are seeing an instance of $D(True\phi)$ or $D(Rel\phi)$, for instance. As I suggested in chapter 3 and will elaborate on in chapter 5, in the general case this will be clear from the content of the hedge itself. For more complex or ambiguous cases, reasoning about the probable intentions of the speaker will be required, as in (4.49).

(4.49)   I might be off base in this, but it's going to rain today.

An utterance of (4.49) might represent a Quality hedge of the claim that it is going to rain, or it might indicate an uncertainty of the speaker that the possibility of rain is relevant to the hearer's goals or the goals of the conversation. Deciphering what is happening here requires some extra work on the basis of the information present in the context.

I suspect that this sort of reasoning is also best modeled by some kind of nonmonotonic inference (perhaps along the lines of McCready 2012a), but I will not try to give an exhaustive model of how it might work here.

With this in place, it is clear how to model the effect of disclaimed modal sentences. The axiom in (4.46) states that, when a modalized sentence is uttered, the interpreter will normally behave as if the prejacent content is true. But this axiom is defeasible, and can be overridden by any more specific or stronger axiom. An obvious case in which one should *not* act as if the prejacent is true is when the speaker herself indicates uncertainty about it, for example with a disclaimer. This observation corresponds to (4.50).

(4.50) $Observe(h, Assert(s, \Diamond \phi)) \land D(Assert(s, \Diamond \phi)) > \neg actAsIf(h, \phi)$

Since this axiom is more specific than (4.46), it will override it, and the proffered content will not be accepted after all, which is the desired result when epistemic modal sentences are hedged.

Summing up, in this section I have shown how hedging of modals works. In general, what is hedged in a(n epistemic) modal claim is not the modal claim itself and its corresponding claim of consistency with an information state, but rather the bringing of the modalized content into full salience. I argued that this effect is induced as a pragmatic default, which is blocked by a stronger default inference arising from the use of the hedge itself; a more sophisticated picture along these lines will be discussed in chapter 7. In the next section I want to show how the same sort of model can account for the pragmatic function of hedging more explicitly speaker-relative content.

4.4 Evaluative hedging

Before concluding the discussion of non-truth-conditional hedging, I wish to briefly mention the hedging of another kind of content exemplified by various sorts of evaluative predicates. One well-known class of such predicates involves gradability: (4.51) could be true and false in the same set of objective circumstances depending on where the standard for coldness is taken to be set. This is a familiar observation which has been made by many (e.g. Klein 1980; Kennedy 1999, among many others).

(4.51)   It's cold.

Many instances of gradable predication involve what has been called *privileged access* of the speaker to the claim made by the sentence (e.g. Mitchell 1986): the speaker is in a better position than anyone else to know whether the predicate actually holds. Consider, for instance, (4.52): clearly, the speaker knows better than her interlocutors how she feels about the taste of coconut water.

(4.52)   Coconut water is nasty.

Can gradable predicates be hedged, especially those associated with subjective judgements? It is clearly possible to do so in at least some cases.

(4.53)   I might be wrong, but it's cold.

Similar examples corresponding to modifications of (4.52), though, seem to be difficult to make coherent.

(4.54)   (?) I might be wrong, but coconut water is nasty.

The generalization appears to be that hedging is only possible for those expressions that have objective correlates in some sense. Whether some object or the weather is cold depends on some properties of the object which are then compared to some (not necessarily determinate) standard of coldness, as already discussed above (Kennedy 2007). This coldness is objectively determinate. I can measure an object's temperature. Nastiness has no such objective correlate: no measure is available for the nastiness of an object. Interestingly, though, the content seems to be slightly different from what one might expect. In (4.53), the speaker hedges her judgement that it is cold; but what is hedged is not any objective fact about the temperature or her perception of it,[31] but whether she has got the judgement right given the facts; the speaker seems to be acknowledging some uncertainty about the placement of the contextual standard for something to count as *cold* (cf. Barker 2002). This observation, if correct, shows that there remains at least one puzzle concerning what content is interpreted as hedged; my suspicion is that many more remain to be ferreted out. I will leave this task for a future occasion.

---

[31] At least, outside a set of very unusual contexts.

4.5 Conclusion

In this chapter, I have considered three cases of hedging of non-truth-directed content: biscuit conditionals, hedged expressives, and hedged epistemic modals and attitudes, as well as briefly considering hedging of more explicitly speaker-relative content. As we have seen, it is quite possible to hedge aspects of communicated content that do not directly relate to truth, or even, for the case of the proffered content of epistemic modals, are not part of the communicated content at all. All this led to a pragmatic view of hedging on which the content which is the target of the hedge depends on the content of the hedge itself via the mediation of (defeasible) reasoning about intended interpretations. Chapter 5 will take up the issue of how this reasoning proceeds, and how it can be formally realized given the observation that hedging requires certain kinds of syntactic constructions.

5

Deriving hedged interpretations

The aim of this chapter is to explain how and why certain constructions can receive interpretations as hedges in the sense of this book. As the reader will recall, there is no construction in natural language which is exclusively interpreted as a hedge, and there is no completely unambiguous way to indicate that one intends to hedge a sentence. Standard hedges have forms like those listed in (5.1), usually followed by *but* or a similar contrastive item.

(5.1) *I'm not sure about this; I might be wrong; I might be confused; …*

Schematically, we have something like the following, where the order of conjuncts is unimportant:

(5.2) $\lozenge\neg\phi$ but ϕ

The first conjunct of these constructions (that indicating the possibility of error) obviously has nonhedging uses; one could, for example, use it to respond to an interlocutor's questioning of some previous assertion. Certainly their components do not have any special relationship to hedging: *sure* or *wrong* have many uses which don't involve hedges at all. For this reason, there is a need to explain how hedging interpretations arise and whether there are any special conditioning environments that enable them. One would also like to understand why the particular expressions in (5.1) and their like are associated with hedges, and also more about the role of the contrastive expression that often appears with hedges.

I will claim that disclaiming interpretations arise from pragmatic reasoning about possible discourse moves. An examination of the kinds of expressions that are used to disclaim shows that, understood literally, they inevitably result in pragmatic incoherence of the kind observed in Moore's Paradox: a seemingly intentional violation of norms of assertion. In order to make sense of the utterance, then, some other interpretation is needed: given the right configuration, one that makes a disclaiming interpretation viable, a charitable hearer will therefore understand the utterance as disclaimed.

The chapter then proceeds to an interesting phenomenon which I have not really addressed yet in this book: the fact that, in some cases, the disclaiming effect can be limited to a particular predicate or subpart of the utterance. For example, the following sentence is naturally understood as disclaiming the coffeehood of whatever the speaker drank, but not as disclaiming the drinking itself.

(5.3)   I drank the coffee, which might not *actually* have been coffee.

This interpretation is quite similar to what we find with (5.4).

(5.4)   I drank the coffee, though it might not really have been coffee.

Here is another, similar, pair (based on an example found through use of Google). Again, we find that only part of the asserted content is hedged. (5.5) hedges the claim that the topic to be discussed is a problem; it does not hedge the speaker's claim that she plans to discuss that topic.

(5.5)   I want to address the following problem, which might not really be a { problem | one }.

(5.6)   I want to address the following problem, though it might not really be { a problem | one }.

An important observation here is that similar examples which are not parenthetical appear completely incoherent in many cases. At minimum, they are not interpreted as hedges at all in the sense I am interested in here, but rather indicate the speaker's genuine uncertainty about the nature of the substance she has drunk (for the present case). We therefore have what amounts to a non-shield hedge.

(5.7)   I drank the coffee which might not (actually) have been coffee.

This fact is not limited to subsentential hedging. Compare parenthetical shield hedges with their non-parenthetical counterparts. (Note that sometimes the parentheticality of the initial clause can be indicated by a special intonational contour rather than a comma-like pause.)

(5.8)   I might be wrong about this, but it's raining.

(5.9)   # I might be wrong about this but it's raining.

Here, the second sentence has a paradoxical flavor: it is pragmatically contradictory in precisely the same way as the usual Moore-paradox cases, despite the presence of the contrastive particle. I take this to indicate that the hedging flavor of the construction disappears in these contexts.

(5.10)   # It's raining but I don't believe it (is).   (Moore 1952)

The observation that must be explained, then, is why it is necessary for a hedge to be parenthetical.

This chapter aims at explaining this set of facts. There are two key elements to the proposal. Section 5.1 shows how incoherence of a certain kind can serve to introduce disclamation via a process of reasoning about rationally admissible speech acts; this analysis is put into a compositional framework in section 5.2, on the basis of whether a given bit of content is asserted or not. I claim that the key here is whether or not the hedge is part of the assertion. If it is, we get Moore-paradoxicality, or else an expression of uncertainty about the accuracy of some part of the content, as in (5.7). In order to avoid this incoherence, some way is needed to avoid paradoxes of assertion. As it turns out, the nonasserted quality of parentheticals gives just what is required to get a hedged interpretation, explaining why hedges are so often parenthetical. I then explore two ways of spelling out an analysis. Both are set in the system of Potts (2005). The first view, detailed in section 5.2, follows Potts in his analysis of utterance modifiers; according to this view, parentheticals are utterance modifiers which introduce nonasserted content. I show that this idea can be implemented in a way quite different from that of Potts, for whom a relation of uttering is present in the semantic representation. However, it turns out that a purely "semantic" approach has difficulties in deriving the required hedged interpretation, and also in the analysis of cases like (5.5), in which a hedge can target a particular part of an utterance rather than the entirety of that utterance. The key point for these cases is that they arise with nonrestrictive relative clauses, i.e. *wh*-appositives, but not with their restrictive counterparts. Many authors have shown that the content of such appositives is also nonasserted (e.g. del Gobbo 2003; Potts 2005; AnderBois et al. 2012), so it is to be expected on my view that they can function as hedges. But why do they only hedge a particular part of the utterance? These cases of "partial hedging" are the topic of section 5.3, which builds on the previous discussion to provide a more pragmatically balanced analysis of the derivation of hedges. A crucial ingredient of the analysis is the idea of a *minimal revision*, which is used to explain the observed partial hedges; this notion is detailed in section 5.3.

The above analyses have some interesting implications. The observation that Moore's Paradox can be avoided by allowing a nonasserted meaning for some part of the sentential content has not previously been made, to my knowledge. It raises the question of how far this strategy can be pushed. Can one overcome, for example, failed presuppositions, or other kinds of problematic speech acts? More generally, what is the relationship between charitable interpretation and the different kinds of content that are known to exist in natural language? The final section of this chapter (§5.4) discusses these questions, and some other implications of the analysis; notably the somewhat surprising consequence that, for hedging interpretations to arise, it has to be assumed (on some level) that the speaker is being cooperative: in other words, in order to get a disclamation, one must already be judged to be a cooperative speaker. This consequence is in a way paradoxical, but it puts a new light on the cooperativity assumptions laid out in the preceding chapters, and brings the strands of the hedging phenomenon together in a satisfying way.

5.1 Pragmatic derivation of disclaiming

First of all, how does the hedging interpretation arise? There are two ways to think of the phenomenon.

The first possibility is that the source of the interpretation could be semantic. Of course, there is no sense in which the lexical content of hedges is specified for a disclamative interpretation. Still, it could be the case that particular semantic contexts induce an interpretation as a hedge, or that certain constructions do. In fact, this at least initially seems reasonable, given the observation that disclamative interpretations only arise in the context of parentheticals and nonrestrictive relative clauses. This section will explore this option to see how it would work. To preview, though, I will ultimately conclude that this view by itself cannot be the correct one; the reason is that it seems to be the combination of certain kinds of content with the parenthetical setting that induces interpretation as a hedge, but either one alone doesn't do so. This makes it appear implausible that it is purely the semantics of the parenthetical construction that forces a hedging interpretation; a pragmatic component will turn out to be necessary for the story as well. Thus the analysis of this section should be taken with a grain of salt, although much of it will be put to work in the next section, where my ultimate solution will be presented.

The first and most obvious question to ask about the "purely semantic" strategy is whether there are phenomena that are comparable to what we find with the hedging constructions, i.e. constructions that receive a special interpretation despite being composed of ordinary lexical items. If so, we might think we have a reason to think that the view is right. The answer is that there clearly are; in fact, it seems to be exactly a subclass of this construction that can induce hedged interpretations in the right circumstances. Appositive clauses are the clearest case. Their content is, by most metrics, independent of that of the main clause, and as a result they have been argued to introduce conventionally implicated content by Potts (2005).[1] Consider the following two sentences.

(5.11)   a. John, a good swimmer, won the race.
          b. John, who is a good swimmer, won the race.

Both of these sentences receive roughly the same interpretation: they assert that John won the race and express in some nonassertive way that he is a good swimmer. As expected given the characterization as conventional implicature, this latter content is independent of sentential operators and cannot be denied via truth-directed denial (exemplified below using the nominal appositive case). Both of the sentences in (5.12) implicate that John is a good swimmer; and this proposition is not denied by B's utterance in (5.13b).

(5.12)   a. It's false that John, a good swimmer, won the race.
          b. If John, a good swimmer, won the race, then he was probably very happy.

(5.13)   a. A: John, a good swimmer, won the race.
          b. B: That's not true.

Compare the version without the appositive clause in (5.14), where the denial can target either the proposition that John won the race, or the proposition that John is a good swimmer.

(5.14)   a. A: John is a good swimmer and won the race.
          b. B: That's not true.

---

[1] Other approaches have been taken: for instance, multidominance in syntax (Heringa 2012) and alterations in syntactic attachment (Schlenker 2007). I will put these aside for present purposes.

These properties follow immediately in the system of Potts (2005). In this theory, composition is supposed to work quite differently for "ordinary" vanilla content and for conventionally implicating items. Notably, the former are resource sensitive in the usual way, but the latter lack the property of resource sensitivity: for conventionally implicating items, a predication of $\lambda x[P(x)] : \langle e, t \rangle$ to an object $a : e$ yields the output $P(a) : t \bullet a : e$, where "$\bullet$" is a metalogical conjunction without any specified semantics. Thus, functional application for conventional implicature returns the input to the function as well as the result of the application. Potts enforces this by means of introducing distinct sets of types for conventionally implicating meanings ("CI types") and at-issue meanings ("at-issue types"): the former are of types σ^c (σ a metavariable over types) and the latter of types σ^a, where the two sorts have distinct rules for application. For instance, ordinary application is handled by the rule (5.15) and CI application via (5.16).[2] Full details can be found in Potts (2005).

(5.15)   **At-issue Application.**
$$\frac{\alpha : \langle \sigma^a, \tau^a \rangle, \beta : \sigma^a}{\alpha(\beta) : \tau^a}$$

(5.16)   **CI Application.**
$$\frac{\alpha : \langle \sigma^a, \tau^c \rangle, \beta : \sigma^a}{\alpha(\beta) : \tau^c \bullet \beta : \sigma^a}$$

With these rules and the obvious syntax (together with some auxiliary assumptions, for instance that the appositive is given a predicative interpretation), we can get the semantic parse (5.17) for the sentence (5.11a).

(5.17)

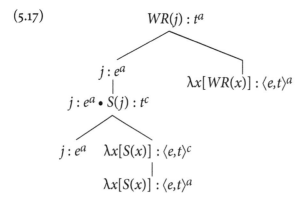

The point of immediate relevance here is the part of the tree where the appositive is integrated into the sentence. We first have the denotation of *a good swimmer*, here translated as $\lambda x[Sx] : \langle e, t \rangle^a$, which is an at-issue typed expression. In the immediately dominating node, it is altered to $\lambda x[Sx] : \langle e, t \rangle^c$, an expression of CI type. The transformation is effected by the use of a rule for what Potts calls "feature semantics": this amounts to a means of transforming the denotations of expressions for reasons that are not connected to the presence of any lexical item. In this partic-ular case, the rule is triggered by the presence of the special appositive intonation, which Potts analyzes as associated with a feature COMMA whose function is to transform at-issue into conventionally implicated content. Of course, such a rule is powerful, and can be argued to be insufficiently constrained (see e.g. Amaral et al. 2008); but our interest here is in the clear analogy with the case of parentheticals. There, as well, we have a case of what appears to be nonasserted content stemming from a special intonation.

There is, then, a parallel between the constructions we are inter-ested in and appositives, which can be brought out through a Pottsian treatment. I will show exactly how this can be spelled out shortly. But the prior question that should be addressed is whether or not such a treatment is enough to answer the questions we began with. Is an analysis treating potential hedges as conventional implicature enough to derive the fact of hedging interpretations?

It seems clear that the answer must be negative. There is no necessary connection of any kind between conventional implicature and hedging. Parentheticals are not always hedges, though the converse appears to be true. We thus must incorporate the second possible treatment, which makes use of pragmatics. On this view, the hedging interpretation arises (at least in part) as a result of some kind of Gricean reasoning or inference. The rest of this section is devoted to showing how this can be done; the combination of the result with conventional implicature will be the focus of the next section.

Suppose that a conversational agent utters $\phi \wedge \Diamond \neg \phi$. Is this a consis-tent thing to say? Above I have suggested that it is not, in that it violates a precondition on speech acts. The particular precondition I have in mind is that the speaker must believe the content that she asserts: i.e. that $Bel(s, \phi)$ is required for an assertion of ϕ.[3] Given this precondition,

---

[3] In fact, this precondition represents only one member of a family of related conditions that have been proposed as requirements for assertion: other possibilities are that ϕ be true

for the suggested assertion the precondition is that $Bel(s, \phi \wedge \Diamond \neg \phi)$, from which it follows that $Bel(s, \phi)$ simpliciter. Suppose that it is true that $Bel(s, \phi)$. On a standard semantics for belief (e.g. von Fintel et al. 2004), then ϕ is true in all the agent's doxastically accessible worlds. Presumably all these worlds are also epistemically accessible on the assumption that the agent is minimally rational and self-aware. But, as already discussed in the last chapter, for the truth of $\Diamond \phi$ it is required that ϕ is epistemically possible, i.e. true in some epistemically accessible world; if these worlds are also doxastically possible (as is the case on standard assumptions), then the possibility of $\neg \phi$ is not consistent with the truth of $Bel(s, \phi)$. This reasoning is elementary; for the case of interest, it results in a pragmatically incoherent, or even inconsistent, discourse move.

The problem here is the interaction between the precondition (of the first conjunct of the assertion) and the asserted content (of the second conjunct in particular). In order to avoid the problem, we might eliminate or alter one or both of these pieces of content. Let us consider each of these strategies in turn.

The first possibility is to eliminate the precondition that requires belief. In order to see how this could be done, we must first consider the source of the precondition. According to Searle (1969), it arises via the nature of the assertive act: something just does not count as an assertion unless it is sincere, and this sincerity requires the belief of the speaker.[4] Taking a slightly different perspective on the issue, the requirement for belief relates closely to the Gricean prescriptions on communication we have been considering in the book up to this point, in particular the maxim of Quality: one should not assert things one does not believe to be true. Now we can ask what a speaker might do in order to eliminate the problem by somehow forcing away this precondition. It seems that there are only two answers available. The first is to modify the sentence in such a way that belief in ϕ is not required. Doing so is straightforward: it involves modifying the sentence with some sort of sentential operator, so that the propositional content of the sentence is no longer ϕ but something else, for instance $\neg \phi$ or $\Diamond \phi$. But this strategy won't help in the present case: we want to maintain ϕ as the asserted content of the sentence. Given this constraint, the only remaining option is to hedge

---

or that the speaker know that ϕ, both stronger than what I assume here. Extensive discussion can be found in the papers in Brown and Cappelen 2011, especially the introduction to the volume.

[4] Relevant discussion can also be found in Austin (1975).

in the sense of disclamation. However, to do this requires having some means of inducing hedging interpretations, which is precisely what we are trying to derive. So this possibility fails.

The second possibility is to eliminate one conjunct of the assertion itself. For instance, we might try to weaken it so that the content ϕ is no longer asserted, but instead merely proffered, in something like the prejacent of epistemic modals as discussed in the last chapter, or the prejacent of the hearsay evidentials which will play a large role in the latter part of the book. However, it's not at all clear how this could be done, especially in a way that preserves the intuitive force of the sentences we are interested in. I thus take this option also not to be the right one. A different strategy is required; we are left with the right conjunct, $\Diamond\neg\phi$, so that is going to have to be the locus of the operation.

Now, as we have seen, trying to directly alter the interpretation of $\phi\wedge\Diamond\neg\phi$ is a failure. Disclamation is the only possibility. However, recall that disclamation required parenthetical interpretation. This suggests that there is something special about the nature of parentheticals that allows them to be understood as hedges. Perhaps they are simply more flexible than cases of asserted conjunction with similar semantic content; in fact, they must be, given that hedging in these cases (and these cases only) functions properly at an empirical level. Following the Potts interpretation of parentheticals as acting at a separate, utterance-based meaning level, it seems plausible that they might make available some kind of pragmatically special or nonliteral reading. If this is the case, then consistency can be achieved. This is the basic idea of the semantic analysis.

Turning now to the formal analysis in the semantic style, what ingredients are needed for understanding where disclaimed interpretations come from? The requirement for parentheticality makes it seem that an analysis in terms of conventional implicature might be the way to go, and that some sort of use of dimensional shunting to work around the problem might already be sufficient. In this section I will spell out this minimalist view, but, as we will see in section 5.2, it is not enough, because the context-dependent nature of hedging means that the essentially semantic multidimensional view of conventional implicature misses out on some aspects of how interpreters arrive at hedging interpretations. There, I will propose a version of the conventional implicature view that, crucially, makes use of pragmatic operations in the hedging process. But before that it is necessary to spell out the semantic view for purposes of comparison, which will occupy the rest of this section.

Potts proposes an interpretative mechanism according to which the content of conventionally implicating expressions enters a dimension of meaning separate from that of asserted content. Thus, the interpretation of (5.17) above is $\langle WR(j), \{S(j)\}\rangle$, where the set-valued second element of the tuple contains all conventionally implicated propositional meanings carried by the sentence. Potts is not fully explicit about how these tuples are to be interpreted; we know that in general they are to be conjunctive, for conventional implicatures are entailed, but not much more than that. Now, depending on how we understand the tuple, $\langle p, \{\Diamond\neg p\}\rangle$ might not be inconsistent. Perhaps the underspecification of how this tuple is interpreted in the standard theory of CIs is just right: we understand the conventionally implicated content conjunctively if possible, but this is defeasible in bad cases, where other interpretations might be available. If so, we already have an explanation of disclamation.

There is something appealing about this view: it is simple, it makes use of existing semantic resources, and it further allows us to spell out an element of the current theory of conventional implicature in greater detail than at present. However, there are some complications which make it appear that at minimum something more has to be said. The basic problem is that it's not clear under what conditions nonconjunctive interpretations should be available. The discussion so far makes it seem that inconsistency will be enough, but this is not correct, as the following example shows.

(5.18)   # John, a good artist, is not a good artist.

So it doesn't always work; this means that we have to be a bit careful about how the claim is couched. It seems possible that the requisite defeasibility can apply only to propositions, or even utterance-level content, but not to anything "lower." If so, then some mechanism is needed to distinguish such utterance modifiers from content-level modification. But, as it turns out, such is already available in the Potts theory, even at the type level: the distinction in input types to (semantically specified) pragmatic operators. This section will try to spell out how a disclamation mechanism should look within the Potts model (or a variation of it). As I will show, the basic idea looks fairly successful, but it turns out that a straightforward implementation is not possible, and that something less direct, and more pragmatic, is needed.

Potts provides an analysis of speaker-oriented adverbials on which they modify utterances. The basic idea is to suppose that semantic parse trees are augmented with a predicate **utter**, which is true if the speaker of a sentence utters that sentence. This uttering relation between speakers and sentences can then be modified by adverbials in more or less the way one might expect: the utterance of the sentence is claimed to have certain properties, such as being frank or honest. The relevant lexical entries are reproduced below, together with an exemplar (in which an argument denoting the speaker, s, is supplied by context; note that the second argument of *frankly* is of type d, a distinguished type for declarative sentence denotations).[5]

(5.19)   a. $[\![utter]\!]= \lambda S\lambda x[utter(S)(x)] : \langle u, \langle e, t\rangle\rangle$
          b. $[\![frankly]\!]= \lambda U\lambda S\lambda x[frankly(U(S))(x)] : \langle\langle u, \langle e, t\rangle\rangle, \langle d, t\rangle\rangle$

(5.20)   a. Frankly, you're an idiot.
          b. $frankly(utter)(\text{"you're an idiot"})(s)$

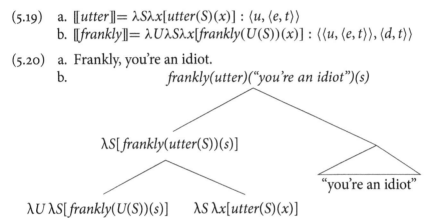

$$\lambda S[frankly(utter(S))(s)]$$

$$\lambda U\,\lambda S[frankly(U(S))(s)] \qquad \lambda S\,\lambda x[utter(S)(x)]$$

"you're an idiot"

Arguably, it is reasonable to say that this part of the Potts theory represents a genuinely pragmatic spin on questions of semantic denotation, because of its reference to utterances, rather than exclusively to composition, despite its highly conventionalized quality. This point is especially clear given that the second argument of the adverbial is a sentence denotation, meaning that it has already been interpreted; in this sense, as Potts notes, there is a sense in which *frankly* is not part of the sentence at all.

It is rather straightforward to apply this theory to hedges. Let's assume the existence of an uttering relation, following Potts, and that the effect of a hedge is to modify the uttering relation so that the utterance is disclaimed. Then a generic hedge can be given the following semantics:

(5.21)   **Compositional hedging (first attempt).**
          $[\![CH_1]\!]= \lambda U\lambda S[D(U(S))(s)] : \langle\langle u, \langle e, t\rangle\rangle, \langle d, t\rangle\rangle$

---

[5] Intensionality is ignored here and throughout insofar as it concerns the typing of predicates.

The effect of this semantics is that, while the sentence is uttered as usual and has whatever entailments we take the uttering of a sentence to have, the utterance (content) is disclaimed.

This interpretation, we can assume, is made available by the type of the parenthetical. Given the presence of comma intonation, the modifier should be of the type of utterance modifiers, $\langle\langle u, \langle e, t\rangle\rangle, \langle d, t\rangle\rangle$, meaning that it is in fact incoherent to interpret the parenthetical clause in a way that causes Moore-paradoxical interpretations to arise. We have roughly the following sort of type transformation (something Potts has no need for, since he considers only adverbials with dedicated uses as utterance modifiers). This is an operation mapping sentence denotations (i.e. the content of parenthetical clauses) to modifiers of sentences which serve to indicate that they have been disclaimed; the disclamation operation, further, happens in the dimension of meaning devoted to conventional implicature. I have left the type sorts unspecified here, for reasons detailed below.

(5.22)   **Parenthetical lifting (to be discarded).**
$COM_p = \lambda S \lambda U \lambda S[D(U(S))(s)] : \langle d, \langle\langle u, \langle e, t\rangle\rangle, \langle d, t\rangle\rangle\rangle$

The output of the first application indicated by the above denotation looks almost exactly like that of *frankly*: the only difference is that it indicates disclamation. Unfortunately, this is not going to give us precisely what we want.

An interesting thing to note about Potts's work on the topic is that he does not give a full type specification of the examples of utterance modifiers he provides. The denotation provided above for *frankly* is of type $\langle\langle u, \langle e, t\rangle\rangle, \langle d, t\rangle\rangle$, but is it of at-issue or CI type? This is not made clear. In fact, the answer is not fully obvious. If *frankly* is of at-issue type, the sentence will have, as at-issue content, that I spoke frankly; but this seems out of line with the intuition that utterance modifiers are conventionally implicated,[6] and further raises problems with the performadox (Amaral et al. 2008). Conversely, if *frankly* is given a CI type, the input content is reproduced, which is problematic if we take the adverbial to modify an externally imposed relation of uttering, given the non-resource-sensitivity of application for conventional implicatures. We end up in an uncomfortable situation, for *frankly* must modify "utters", but this results in too many predications remaining in the sentence; the tree I gave above consequently treated the two as at-issue

---

[6] They fit the profile, at least, and pass the usual tests.

types (following Potts 2005). At best, if we perform some footwork on the semantic parse trees, we can arrive at a final denotation for a frank assertion of sentence S of $\langle [\![S]\!], \{frankly(utter(S)(s))\}\rangle$, or possibly $\langle [\![S]\!], \{frankly(utter(S)(s)), utter(S)(s)\}\rangle$ if we take the **utter** relation itself to be conventionally implicated. Thus, the at-issue content is the content of the sentence, and it is conventionally implicated that the sentence is uttered frankly. It seems hard to avoid doing some damage to our intuitions here. The situation is, of course, similar for parenthetical disclamations.

I am going to suggest a simplification of the Potts analysis for the purposes of the present discussion. It seems to me that the problem with what is happening there lies in the relationship between the modifier and the postulated utterance relation. If the latter can be eliminated, many of the problems dissolve. In fact, the utterance relation is already somewhat questionable, as has been noted in the literature: Amaral et al. (2008) observe that these modifiers are different in kind from the other instances of conventional implicature that Potts discusses, in that they actually *do* modify utterances and so seem to be acting at a pragmatic, rather than a semantic, level. I think that this difference is reflected in the difficulties raised above. My suggestion therefore is to eliminate the utterance relation entirely, replacing it with an operation that shifts content to the level of speech acts. But this operation, I want to claim, *is* properly modeled in Potts's logic $\mathcal{L}_{CI}$, for it is an instance of expressivization, a move from "objective" content to expressive content.

What we need is a kind of type-lifting operation taking semantic to pragmatic content. Such an operation is easy to define, if we follow authors like Potts and Krifka (2001, 2011) and allow utterances to live in our type space. We need only introduce an operation of type $\langle t, u \rangle$ which maps propositions to utterances of those propositions. This is entirely trivial at the operational level, though it has possibly off-putting philosophical implications which will be discussed at the end of the chapter. This new operation will replace our first attempt in (5.22), with a considerable reduction in complexity. This rule, like the rule of parenthetical interpretation introduced previously, should be understood as instances of Pottsian feature semantics. Note that here I have taken the lifting operation to introduce an assertion via an operator A, rather than a bare utterance; this will become important in section 5.3.[7]

---

[7] Of course, this move limits attention to assertive speech acts, but the extension to other speech act types is entirely trivial.

(5.23)   **Utterance lifting (first attempt).**

$$\text{UL}\frac{p : t^a}{A(p) : u^c}$$

We need, of course, a corresponding alteration in the semantics of the parenthetical "feature". Parenthetical hedges can now be viewed as utterance modifiers in a much simpler sense: functions of conventionally implicated type $\langle u, u \rangle$. A nice feature of this simplification is that the semantics of utterance modifiers now have the standard form of modifying constructions in formal semantics: functions of type $\langle \sigma, \sigma \rangle$, taking objects of one type into new, changed, objects of the same type. I take this to be a positive feature. However, what type should the hedges be? They cannot be of the standard Pottsian type $\langle u, u \rangle^c$, for Potts disallows input types which aren't associated with asserted content, i.e. those which are not of an at-issue type. But utterances pretty clearly aren't of this type. We thus have to assume that utterances are of type u^s, i.e. of the "shunting type" that I proposed in McCready (2010c); for such types, which are essentially resource-sensitive types for conventionally implicated content, input types of the form $\langle \sigma^s, \tau^s \rangle$ are indeed available. We therefore need to make a minor modification to the definition in (5.23), as follows.

(5.24)   **Utterance lifting (final).**

$$\text{UL}\frac{p : t^a}{A(p) : u^s}$$

We end up with the following denotation for the hedging operation.

(5.25)   **Compositional hedging (final).**
$$[\![CH_2]\!] = \lambda U[U \wedge D(U)] : \langle u^s, u^s \rangle$$

An important feature of this account is that it makes hedges of conventionally implicating type. What this means is that, in addition to the disclaimer causing the utterance to be hedged, its resource-insensitivity will allow the utterance to be expressed as usual. This successfully models the intuition that disclaimed utterances are still processed more or less as usual by interpreters, and possibly acted on, but with the fact of the hedge providing some additional information as to whether or not it is optimal to choose to believe the uttered content.[8]

---

[8] One thing I have given up here is the explicit mention of the speaker in the uttering relation. But given the way in which the operation of utterance lifting is defined, I don't think that this is so problematic. Since all utterances are produced by speakers, the desired

However, this analysis together with other facts about shunting types does have one mildly unpalatable consequence. The application rule for shunting types in McCready (2010c) has them take an input content and yield only conventionally implicated content:

(R7) $\dfrac{\alpha : \langle \sigma^a, \tau^s \rangle, \beta : \sigma^a}{\alpha(\beta) : \tau^s}$

This means that, for (5.25), no at-issue content is left behind at all, meaning that, at the utterance level, sentences have denotations of the form $\langle \varnothing, \{A(\varphi)\} \rangle$ for a sentence with (at-issue) content φ. On the present proposal, this will turn out to be a general feature of all asserted sentences: their denotations will be empty on the at-issue side, but contain utterances in the expressive dimension. This is not wholly unreasonable, I think: utterances are expressive in the sense that they don't function as standard, deniable linguistic content. Nonetheless, they still have semantic content, something which is not captured by the present system. This is counterintuitive and further gets the facts wrong about denials on the assumption that only at-issue content can be targeted by denial (cf. e.g. Potts 2005; McCready 2004, 2010c).

In order to reintroduce semantic content, I will assume the following rule. It is reminiscent of a meaning postulate, but differs crucially in that its aim is to ensure the right kind of connection between semantic and pragmatic content. I am not sure that there are analogous rules in the literature.[9]

(5.26) **Assertion to content.**

$\text{AC} \dfrac{\langle \varnothing, \{\ldots, A(\varphi), \ldots\} \rangle}{\langle \varphi, \{\ldots, A(\varphi), \ldots\} \rangle}$

On this picture, the flow of meaning between semantics and pragmatics is as follows. We begin with a piece of content ϕ, which is ultimately to be disclaimed. Let's suppose the sentence denoting ϕ does not contain any conventionally implicated or expressive content, so we have $\langle \phi, \{\} \rangle$ as denotation. **Utterance lifting** applies to this, yielding $\langle \varnothing, \{A(\phi)\} \rangle$;

---

relativization should fall out as a byproduct of other pragmatic operations. Possible worries about overapplication should also be defused by the observation that embedding under e.g. attitudes won't be possible since the output of **Utterance lifting** is of the wrong type to be input to such predicates.

⁹ The rules proposed to overcome problems about performative embeddings are dissimilar: they go in the opposite direction, from sentence to utterance. I think the present rule is much less problematic.

then this is hedged via the compositional hedging operator *CH* in (5.25), giving $\langle \varnothing, \{A(\phi), D(A(\phi))\}\rangle$, and then semantic content is reintroduced via **Assertion to content**, ultimately giving $\langle \phi, \{A(\phi), D(A(\phi))\}\rangle$ as the final denotation.

For a more concrete example, here is an instance of the disclamation operation, together with the transformation on meanings dictated by the comma intonation. Here I redact the contrastive content of "but," as my intention is to show how the type-shifting takes place. As will be clear, the parenthetical intonation induces a change to a disclaiming interpretation (an operation in which the content of the parenthetical must also play a role), which then applies to the utterance relation, disclaiming the utterance content. But, as a result of the conventionally implicating type assigned to the parenthetical, the utterance relation also proceeds as usual, which gives the desired interpretation: the speaker lessens her commitment in the sense of disclamation, but the hearer retains the option to use the sentential content as he otherwise would.[10]

(5.27)   a. I might be wrong, but it's raining.

b.

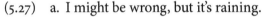

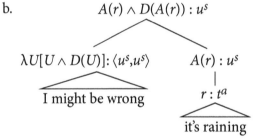

c. Sentence meaning: $\langle \varnothing, \{A(r), D(A(r))\}\rangle$
d. After **Assertion to content**: $\langle r, \{A(r), D(A(r))\}\rangle$

All this is somewhat attractive, and it seems to give more or less the right results; but we will see in the next section that the disclamation process cannot be viewed as quite this semantic in character. The evidence adduced there comes from cases in which the disclaimed content is only part of the sentence modified by the parenthetical. But the reader may have already found something fishy in the tree above: how do we go from the parenthetical clause "I might be wrong" to the interpretation $\lambda U[U \wedge D(U)]$? This is the main puzzle here, and it has essentially been papered over with what amounts to a solution involving a dubious kind of ambiguity.

---

[10] Some consequences of this lessened commitment are discussed in chapter 9 in the context of evidential update.

Intuitively, the mysterious aspect of this operation is that it must be triggered by the content of the modifier in an indirect manner; as we have seen above, without the right kind of content, the disclaiming interpretation will not arise despite the presence of the parenthetical intonation. From this perspective, the criticisms of Potts's theory as too semantic by Amaral et al. (2008) seem to apply to the proposal of this section as well. Ultimately, the theory proposed here is also too semantic in its current form; though all the operations proposed will prove to be required, some, in particular the operation of disclamation itself, will have to be pragmatically induced. The next section will carry out the necessary revisions.

Before entering into that discussion, though, we should address the final ingredient of disclamation. Disclamations usually appear with words that signal that a disclaiming is going to be performed: contrastive terms like *but*, words like *actually*, and so forth. What exactly is their function? To answer this question, we first ought to observe that some word like this appears to be necessary for a disclaimed interpretation.

(5.28)   a. I might be wrong, but John is going to come tonight.
          b. # I might be wrong, and John is going to come tonight.
          c. # I might be wrong about this. John is going to come tonight.

It does seem that the contrastive word is playing a key role here. To see what the role is, we should consider the meaning of *but*. Usually it is assumed to indicate a denial of expectation of some kind, often based on world knowledge, but sometimes at a discourse level or even the level of argumentation (Asher 1993; Umbach 2004; Winterstein 2012). In our particular case, it seems pretty obvious that the relevant denial of expectation is arising at a pragmatic level. It might be the case that, given that $\Diamond\neg\phi$, ϕ is unexpected; but it's far more likely that, given the claim that $\Diamond\neg\phi$, an immediately subsequent claim that ϕ is unexpected. I therefore think that we are dealing with contrast at the level of utterances. This perhaps does not come as a surprise given the previous discussion, which has situated the whole problem of deriving disclamations in the domain of speech acts.

The existence of utterance-oriented readings of contrastive particles seems well supported by the fact that they can appear with questions, as in (5.29); here, clearly, the question itself cannot contrast with anything at the level of semantic content, for no semantic content is at issue.

(5.29)   But how was the food?

But what exactly is the contrastive word doing? It seems to me that it's functioning to signal that the speaker is well aware of the unexpectedness of what she is doing. After all, it is strange linguistic behavior to assert something and simultaneously indicate that it might not be correct (and similarly for hedging on the other Gricean maxims). Without an explicit signal that the speaker is aware of this weirdness and is doing it knowingly and purposefully, it seems that it's just not possible to make her utterance consistent; having to do so strains the principle of charity beyond what it can reasonably bear. On this view, then, *but* serves to indicate to the hearer that there is a reason for the unexpected kind of utterance being made; it will then be natural to cast about for ways to make the utterance sensible. Given the availability of a disclaimed interpretation for a particular sentence, such an interpretation can be settled on, giving the desired result.[11]

The upshot is that there is no unavoidable relationship between disclamation and contrast, quite the contrary, which makes a semantic approach look implausible. The view gets some further support from the fact that a contrastive word isn't genuinely required; as long as the signal of intentionality is made, other kinds of terms can serve the same function. Consider again the cases of disclamation of a subpart of an utterance from the beginning of the chapter.

(5.30)   I drank the coffee, which might not *actually* have been coffee.

(5.31)   I drank the coffee, though it might not really have been coffee.

Here, the signal is made with the modal adverbs *actually* and *really*, but the disclamation remains. Note though that (5.31) contains a contrastive conjunction as well; it might turn out that contrastive terms are required when two sentences are conjoined. If this is true, the reason is not clear: it could be that it relates to contrast, and it could be that such words are needed to ensure the right kind of parenthetical interpretation, something which is required, as we will see in the next section.

---

[11] The reader might wonder why one finds disclaimers of the form $\lozenge\neg\phi$ but not of the form $\neg\phi$. For instance, we see "I might be wrong about this," but never "I am wrong about this" or "I seriously doubt this is true." The answer seems to be that, with such attempts at disclamation, we have genuine semantic contradiction, not just pragmatic (Moorean) infelicity at the level of speech act preconditions; this genuine contradiction turns out to be too strong for disclamation to work, as it cannot be made coherent.

5.2 Targeting content with disclaimers

Above, I noted that in certain cases disclaimers can target the content of nominals, nominal phrases, or predications by verbs rather than the whole sentence. This section is devoted to the exploration of cases like these and to providing a theory that can explain them. As we will see, the existence of these kinds of cases provides some support for the analysis I have given, but at the same time shows its shortcomings and reveals a possible way to rectify them by making the introduction of the disclamation mechanism more fully pragmatic.

What content is targeted by a particular instance of a disclaimer? Recall that, on the analysis sketched in section 5.1, disclaimers are introduced by parenthetical constructions and disclaim the utterances associated with some piece of content, by means of a pragmatic process. Given this picture, there appear to be two clear options for determining what is targeted by a disclaimer: a semantic view and a pragmatic view. On the semantic picture, targeting is purely compositional, involving placement of modifiers in the syntax. This was the view developed in the last section. On the pragmatic view, the content targeted depends entirely on the content of the parenthetical clause; if the parenthetical expresses uncertainty about some particular piece of content, that content would be disclaimed. So far this part of the story has only been hinted at. Which is the right way to go, or do we need some combination of both? In this section, I will argue that the semantic picture by itself is not correct, and that a combination of semantic and pragmatic factors conspires to produce disclaimed interpretations.

Situations where only one part of the content of an utterance is disclaimed seem to be good cases for trying to distinguish these views. A first observation is that, if what is targeted is determined entirely compositionally, nonlocal targeting would be unexpected. And, indeed, the most obvious cases of subutterance targeting are local, as with the examples introduced above.

(5.32)   a. I want to talk about a problem, which might not really be one.
         b. I had some coffee, which actually might not have been coffee.

Note that these examples are already problematic for the analysis of section 5.2: there, parentheticals were taken to introduce disclaimers, which applied to the entire content of their host sentences. Such a view has no way to account for partial disclamations. Further, notice that similar effects can be produced in some sense nonlocally.

(5.33) a. Though it might turn out not to really be one, I want to talk about a problem now.

   b. It actually might have been something else, but Mrs. Jones gave me some coffee when I went to her house yesterday.

Here, the disclaimed predicates are not syntactically adjacent to the parentheticals which disclaim them,[12] but, crucially, these examples contain anaphoric (in this case cataphoric) dependencies to the content that is disclaimed. I conclude that what is crucial in targeting specific content is the ability to make reference to that content within the disclaiming clause. This dovetails with the facts in the last section motivating an analysis in terms of local modification via parentheticals, but shows that the phenomenon is actually more general. It also reveals a pragmatic dimension to the case: as we saw in the previous section, a common factor in hedged interpretations is the presence of some inconsistency between the parenthetical and the asserted content. Including some anaphoric item in the parenthetical can induce inconsistency with some particular piece of content; the kind of disclamation that occurs is then partly dependent on reasoning about what content is causing the inconsistency.[13] Thus, it appears that both semantic and pragmatic elements are actually important in the picture.

   What we need, then, is a way to introduce nonasserted content, and then, after checking whether it is consistent with the content of the utterance, to apply the disclamation operation, or not. Because the consistency check is necessarily a process of reasoning carried out by the interpreter (presumably in accordance with the speaker's intentions), the content of the parenthetical, and in particular anaphoric dependencies that one might find within it, will play a role in determining what is disclaimed.

---

[12] At least on the most obvious, surface-oriented kind of syntactic analysis, which is what I will assume here; anything else seems to be semantically motivated, and perhaps better analyzed without covert operations.

[13] Grosu and Krifka (2007) discuss cases like (i), which look similar in many respects to the ones I am considering. Specifically, the relative clause appears to call into question the content of the head noun.

(i) The gifted mathematician that you claim to be would be able to solve this equation.

However, the solution they propose, that the head noun is an intensional concept dependent on the relative clause content, won't work for (all) cases considered in this chapter, because it crucially relies on the existence of an equative in the relative clause which makes available a set of worlds which satisfy the head noun content; this is precisely what we don't have for the cases of hedging under discussion here.

A theory of this form is easily achieved; all the ingredients are already in place. We merely need to assume that the content of the parenthetical is just a normal conventionally implicated clause, and not an utterance modifier at all. We therefore retain a version of the operation of parenthetical lifting, but one which does not yield a predicative object, as follows. Here, I have simply moved the content from the at-issue to the expressive dimension, in the same way as Potts (2005).

(5.34) **Parenthetical lifting (feature).**

$$\text{PL}\frac{p:t^a}{p:t^c}$$

The analysis of the previous section lifts at-issue sentence denotations to assertions via **Utterance lifting**. Something similar will be needed for not-at-issue content for reasons of symmetry. However, since not-at-issue content is not asserted, a slightly different rule will be required. I will simply assume that not-at-issue content is introduced to pragmatics via an operator U 'utter'. I leave this content underspecified except to note that the presence of $U(\varphi)$ in the expressive dimension commits the speaker to φ.

(5.35) **Not-at-issue lifting.**

$$\text{PL}\frac{p:t^{\{c,s\}}}{U(p):u^s}$$

This rule will yield content which can interact with the at-issue content of utterances in the required ways. In particular, the parenthetical content can be inconsistent with the utterance content. This inconsistency will not be acceptable to charitable speakers, resulting in a process of inference eliminating some part of the content in order to achieve consistency. The way in which this inference works will be the topic of the next section; for the remainder of the present one, I will just assume that we have a means of performing minimal revisions which gives us the desired results; the notion of minimality here is one which produces a pragmatically viable utterance while preserving as much content as possible from the original utterance content.[14]

___

[14] Before going into further details, let me consider a possible objection: could it be that this theory is still too semantic? Might tying the availability of disclamation to syntactic structure so closely be a mistake? Perhaps we should give inference a more prominent role. If one wanted to go this route, one option would be to take Asher (2000) as a starting point, assume a theory of discourse structure such as SDRT (Asher and Lascarides 2003), and let hedging parentheticals introduce discourse segments which are then attached within the

Let us consider a case or two in detail. First, take a case of standard hedging as discussed in earlier chapters. (Again, I will give a tree representing the semantic composition. This is not meant to substitute for a proper syntactic analysis.)

(5.36)   I might be wrong about this, but John came.

(5.37)

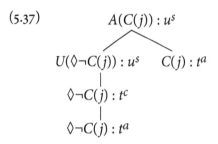

$$A(C(j)) : u^s$$
$$U(\Diamond\neg C(j)) : u^s \qquad C(j) : t^a$$
$$\Diamond\neg C(j) : t^c$$
$$\Diamond\neg C(j) : t^a$$

Here, we get the familiar kind of disclamation of the content of the whole sentence. The interesting thing to note for present purposes is the propositional anaphor *this* in the parenthetical; understood as picking up the content of the main clause as is natural and already assumed by the semantic composition in (5.37), it yields inconsistency. We arrive at this inconsistency as follows. First, the at-issue content will be shifted to its associated utterance by **Utterance lifting**, giving $A(C(j))$, which is consequently introduced into the CI dimension. $\Diamond\neg C(j)$ is also lifted to $U(\Diamond\neg C(j))$ by **Not-at-issue lifting** after its transformation to not-at-issue content triggered by the presence of the parenthetical feature. The resulting denotation for the sentence will be $\langle\varnothing, \{A(C(j)), U(\Diamond\neg C(j))\}\rangle$, which then, by **Assertion to content**, is mapped to $\langle C(j), \{A(C(j)), U(\Diamond\neg C(j))\}\rangle$. Given the inconsistency between the two pieces of content (as it's a violation of Gricean principles to simultaneously commit to $C(j)$ and $\Diamond\neg C(j)$, and by assumption $U(\Diamond\neg C(j))$ commits the speaker to the latter proposition), the assertion will be disclaimed by the parenthetical, giving the assertion of (5.37) the following denotation.

discourse structure via some kind of hedging relation. With a correction-like semantics for the hedging relation (cf. van Leusen 2004), we could get something like the required notion of minimal revision.

I think this approach is promising, but I won't pursue it here; for one thing, I think that cases of retraction or correction have a different character from hedges, despite some superficial similarities. However, a discourse-based theory would make predictions distinct from my own in some other areas. Specifically, if it turns out that (a) one can hedge multiple discourse segments simultaneously, or that (b) hedging of segments linearly distant in the discourse yet still right-frontier accessible is possible, there would appear to be good reason to explore a discourse-level analysis.

(5.38) $\langle C(j), \{A(C(j)), D(A(C(j))), U(\Diamond\neg C(j))\} \rangle$

As the reader will see, this is a less semantic version of the operation in (5.25), though in this case the semantic and pragmatic versions give basically the same results modulo the presence of the conventionally implicated $\Diamond\neg C(j)$ in the semantic representation; this is an obvious upgrade, given that the semantic operation was already fairly implausible as a lexical property. The result of this derivation is an assertion that John came, which is disclaimed though uttered, as well as an indication that the speaker takes it to be possible that John in fact did not come. This seems to capture the intuitive meaning, and also the intuitive pragmatic function, of this sentence; it also gives the hearer the resources needed to decide how to deal with this particular piece of content, as well as with the speaker and her utterances going forward.

A question that might arise at this point is why $A(C(j))$ is disclaimed, and not $U(\Diamond\neg C(j))$. I see two possible reasons. The first is, in a sense, procedural. Since the parenthetical clause is doing the disclaiming, perhaps its content just cannot be disclaimed. It does seem impossible, or even paradoxical, to simultaneously deny one's denial via the very clause performing the denial. The other possibility relates to the discussion of the disclamation of expressive content in section 4.2. As we saw there, expressive content is exempt from disclaiming operations. If this is also the case for conventionally implicated content, or even content associated directly with speech acts, then it makes sense that the parenthetical content cannot be disclaimed given that it is conventionally implicated. Both of these possibilities strike me as plausible, but I won't try to choose between them here; for my current purposes, it is enough to observe that there are plausible reasons that the content of the disclaiming clause cannot be the object of the disclamation.

Let's now turn to a case where a particular piece of content is disclaimed, rather than the entire sentence. We can take the coffee example (5.32b). Further suppose that the nonrestrictive relative is interpreted via Potts's COMMA feature as usual.[15] Then we can analyze the sentence as in Figure 5.1. (I omit the actions of **Utterance lifting** and **Not-at-issue lifting** for readability.)

---

[15] This assumption means we don't need to add the possibility of abstraction to CI-typed denotations, which is convenient (though we easily can given the work of Gutzmann 2012). See also Gutzmann and McCready (2013) on the semantics of descriptions, particularly referential ones.

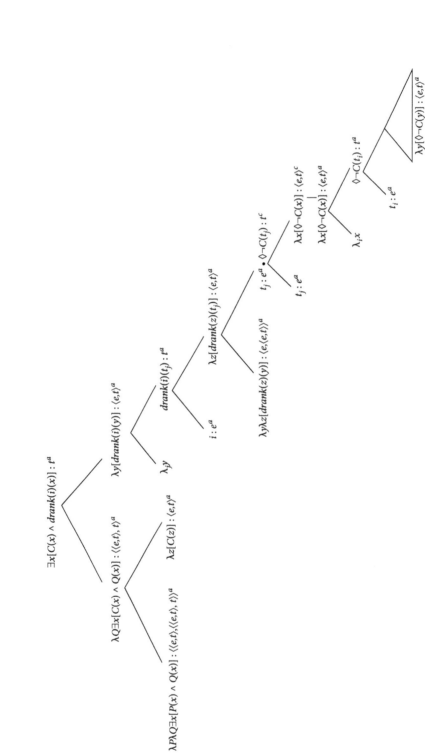

FIGURE 5.1   Analysis of sentence with partial disclaimer

The denotation of this tree will be (5.39) after the application of **Utterance lifting**, **Not-at-issue lifting**, and **Assertion to content**.[16]

(5.39) $\langle \exists x[C(x) \wedge drank(i)(x)], \{A(\exists x[C(x) \wedge drank(i)(x)]),$
        $U(\Diamond \neg C(x))\}\rangle$

But by assumption x satisfies the predicate C; this means that inconsistency results, but inconsistency only with respect to this presupposed property. Assuming that we revise minimally, just enough to maintain consistency, we thus will get (5.40).

(5.40) $\langle \exists x[C(x) \wedge drank(i)(x)], \{A(\exists x[C(x) \wedge drank(i)(x)]), D(C(x)),$
        $U(\Diamond \neg C(x))\}\rangle$

Thus, the simplest way to eliminate the difficulty in this case is to allow the bit of content $C(x)$ to be disclaimed by the parenthetical. The pragmatic story I have given here allows this, but the semantic analysis of the previous section would not; there, the parenthetical was taken to introduce a disclamation operation which (semantically) applied to the entire utterance, meaning that, without additional operations of a rather unmotivated kind, disclamation of a part of the utterance was not a possibility.

The case of (5.32a) is similar, but depends in part on what we take the proper analysis of *one*-anaphora to be; assuming a dynamic or DRT-style view along the lines that $[\![one]\!] = P(x)$ for some contextually salient property P and new discourse referent x (cf. Asher 1993 on anaphora to properties), the story will go pretty much the same way. Of course, the viability of this whole story depends on spelling out the required notion of minimal revision, which I will delay until the next section.[17]

The reader might wonder whether we need all this speech act level apparatus, or whether the analysis could work without the U and A operators. Technically, it can, of course; in fact, it is simpler and more attractive from a formal perspective. The reason I have introduced assertion and utterance operators, and the corresponding content transfer rules **Utterance lifting**, **Not-at-issue lifting**, and **Assertion to content** is

---

[16] Note that I am assuming a dynamic solution to the "binding problem" (the issue of cross-dimensional variable binding) along the lines of those proposed by Nouwen (2007); AnderBois et al. (2012).

[17] An interesting, possibly related kind of case is that of evidentials which modify subsentential content. Aikhenvald (2004) discusses a number of such cases, which I pursued to some degree in McCready (2008c). It seems at least possible that they are properly analyzed by means of some combination of compositional semantics and pragmatic interpretation. I will leave this issue for future work.

that, intuitively, what is disclaimed by a hedge is not a piece of content, but rather the act performed with that content. This intuition underlies the analysis in terms of repeated games in the previous chapters. It is not possible to have a reputation for *content*, but it is possible to have a reputation for truthfully or reliably deploying pieces of content. All this just amounts to saying that disclamation is a pragmatic, not a semantic, operation, and so it has to take place at a pragmatic level. I therefore think there is a need for the pragmatic operators I have used. Still, the operators themselves are not crucial to the core idea of the analysis of how disclaiming is introduced, which relies exclusively on charitable interpretation, speaker commitments, and minimal revisions.

A nice application of this pragmatic view involves biscuit conditionals. Chapter 4 raised the problem of determining when a conditional counts as a biscuit conditional, and when it does not. The answer I gave there was that a conditional should be understood as a hedge/biscuit just in case it doesn't make sense as a "proper" conditional. Of course, ordinarily conditionals have interpretations involving causal or conceptual dependence; but if there is no such dependence, for instance in cases of genuine conditional independence (cf. Franke 2007), conditional interpretations don't make sense. In such cases, they should be reanalyzed as hedges. We can think of this as another kind of charitable interpretation: When a conditional cannot be properly interpreted with the usual kind of conditional meaning, it should be understood as a pragmatic hedge of some kind.

For these cases, we need a different notion of inconsistency than before. There is nothing strictly inconsistent about interpreting biscuit conditionals as ordinary conditionals, but doing so results in nonsense, in the sense that such conditionals violate our knowledge about the world. We know that one's hunger does not determine whether there is pizza in the fridge. Understanding a speaker as indicating such a conditional relation violates the principle of charity in a way different from what we find with the Moore-paradox-like cases discussed so far in this chapter. There, we saw utterances which could not be interpreted consistently without taking the speaker to be violating norms of communication. Here, we have conditionals which cannot be interpreted "conditionally" without assuming the speaker is terminally confused about the world. Presumably, taking your interlocutor to be saying something bizarre and confused is uncharitable, given that other ways of understanding her utterance are available; the fact of hedged interpretations allows an application of the principle of charity, which in turn leads to the phenomenon of biscuit conditionals.

For another case which shows a further level of complexity, consider the following example.[18]

(5.41)   If you walk another 20 meters, there is a bench you can sit on.

Plainly this is not an ordinary indicative conditional. My walking 20 meters will not cause a bench to come into existence. But equally obviously it's not a pure hedge. There is no question about the truth of the consequent or its relevance (on the assumption, say, that the addressee of the utterance is looking for somewhere to rest). It seems to me that what we have here is a conditional construction which is given a temporal interpretation: $A \Rightarrow B$ is interpreted as "given A, then, afterward, B." Such interpretations for conditionals are known to exist in the world's languages. For instance, one of the conditional markers in Japanese, a verbal suffix *-tara*, is well known to have a *when*-clause interpretation in addition to its conditional meaning (e.g. Masuoka and Takubo 1989).

Supposing that this kind of interpretation is made available, the example (5.41) can be assigned temporal content: "after you walk 20 meters, there is a bench." Given a path-based semantics for motion verbs (e.g. Denis et al. 2003), the sentence will then indicate roughly that at the end of a path with length 20 meters, there is a bench, and after traversing that path, the bench will be accessible. Here, then, we arguably have a case in which there is no disclamation at all, but instead a construction with two interpretations, one temporal and one conditional; since the conditional interpretation is not coherent, the temporal one must be selected. Thus the problem is just an instance of the general problem of interpretation selection, one fairly well understood within game-theoretic pragmatics and discussed further in the next section. Of course, this analysis depends on the existence of a temporal interpretation. If the existence of such an interpretation cannot be supported, the analysis becomes more difficult. The key issue then is that the disclamation must work simultaneously with the introduction of semantic content in the conditional antecedent. This makes the analysis somewhat nontrivial: it's necessary to explore the interaction between disclamation and ordinary content in a deep way, which I will not attempt to do in this work, especially as it is not clearly required on the basis of (5.41).

---

[18] I thank an anonymous reviewer for providing this case and relevant discussion.

5.3 Minimal revisions and the principle of charity

In the past sections, we have seen a complex pragmatic mechanism at work in two distinct kinds of case. First, I claimed that, when a particular sentence cannot be interpreted without assuming some pragmatic deficiency on the part of the speaker, a charitable hearer would search for other, more sensible, interpretations, and assume that those were the aim of the speaker. Second, we saw that in cases where there were multiple possible such interpretations, the speaker would select the one which maintained the most of the sentence's original content, or modified it in the simplest possible way. Both of these cases involve charitable interpretation, but its manifestation is different in each case, which seems to involve different kinds of processes. This book is not the place to spell out what is happening here in technical detail but I want to say a bit about what appears to me to be going on.

Let's first consider the case of searching for a sensible interpretation. This situation is analogous to many other cases we find in linguistic interaction, which are (relatively) well studied in formal pragmatics. Consider the case of pronoun resolution.[19] What is the referent of *he* in the following example?

(5.42)   John had a drink of Bill's tea. He was thirsty.

Working solely from gender features of the pronoun and accessibility considerations, the pronoun could be referring to either John or Bill or to some third party. Still, resolution to John is highly preferred, for various reasons: structural considerations, since subjects tend to be prominent, or parallelism, since both pronoun and antecedent are subjects. We also have considerations of coherence: resolving the pronoun to Bill makes the connection between the two sentences unclear. Sometimes the features conflict, as in (5.43).

(5.43)   John had a drink of Bill's tea. He didn't have much left afterward.

In (5.43), structural factors invite us to resolve *he* to John; but doing so leaves a fairly incoherent discourse compared to the resolution of *he* to Bill. It seems that both interpretations are possible here, but the latter is preferred.

Beaver (2004) analyzes the pronominal resolution case in optimality theory, a system using interlocking weighted constraints. No individual

---

[19] See, for example, Ariel (1990); Kehler (2001); Beaver (2004) for various approaches to pronominal resolution.

constraint is in principle inviolable (though the one with the highest weight is in practice), but taking the constraints together gives what amounts to a system of defaults, which together determine the "best" resolution. Something similar is used by the theory of discourse structure SDRT to analyze discourse connections (Asher and Lascarides 2003), where a default logic and reasoning about speaker intention helps to determine discourse attachments, for example with the kinds of relations between discourse segments seen in (5.42) and (5.43). McCready (2012a) proposes a similar mechanism in order to select the optimal interpretation of expressions which introduce underspecified emotive content, such as that in (5.44), which context can bias toward a positive or negative interpretation when conventions of language use are taken into account; here, the key feature of the account is interpretation selection on the basis of probabilities derived from knowledge about the world and normal linguistic behavior.

(5.44)   Damn!

What is the relationship of this data to hedged interpretations? For hedging, also, multiple interpretations are possible, but one is much more sensible than the other(s) from a pragmatic perspective. It seems that the same kind of process is at work in selecting the hedged interpretation: the sentence makes available a number of different interpretations, and the hearer must select from them one that seems to most closely match what the speaker's intentions are likely to be. The present case is much simpler than pronoun resolution, though: the literal interpretation is so pragmatically deficient that it's not hard to pick the disclaiming interpretation as the intended one.

The second mechanism at work in these cases is closely related to the last, but is more complex. For examples like (5.32), there are multiple disclamations available, each of which will eliminate the inconsistency: one can disclaim the entirety of the non-parenthetical content, or merely the presuppositional part. In general, disclaiming all of the sentential content will serve to induce consistency. So why is it then that we find partial disclamations? One might think that the reason is structural, but the availability of examples like (5.33) shows that structure cannot be the whole story, because the connection between disclaiming clause and local disclamation there was purely semantic. I propose to view this phenomenon as another instance of charitable interpretation; a charitable hearer will try to understand the speaker as maximally cooperative, and so try to eliminate the fewest speaker commitments she can, on the assumption that the speaker intended to convey what she indeed conveys. The most cooperative speaker will make the strongest relevant commitment, as we know from Grice; the same should hold for the repeated game setting, where cooperative speakers strive to go on the record to the maximal possible degree.

This strategy is familiar from the literature on Quantity implicatures, especially that concerned with alternative semantics and nonmonotonic interpretation (van Rooij and Schulz 2010). What is required is an information-based ordering on alternative interpretations of the original sentence, together with attention to the content of the disclaiming parenthetical.

With this, and the logical form associated with the locally disclaimed sentence, it becomes possible to derive a strongest disclaimed interpretation. For concreteness, consider again (5.32b). The interpretation of this sentence is, before disclamation,

$$\langle \exists x[C(x) \wedge drank(i)(x)], \{A(\exists x[C(x) \wedge drank(i)(x)]), U(\Diamond \neg C(x))\} \rangle.$$

Supposing that disclamation is pragmatically introduced and can apply to any part of the asserted content of the sentence, we have multiple possible disclamations: (a) it could be that $C(x)$ is disclaimed, (b) it could be that $drank(i)(x)$ is disclaimed, and (c) it could be that the conjunction of the two is disclaimed, which also means denying the existential quantification.[20] Note that in terms of information we have the following ordering of possible disclamations: (a) and (b) are both more informative from the perspective of assertion than (c), for, in (c), all the content of the sentence is disclaimed. This means that, given a preference for stronger meanings, both (a) and (b) will be preferred to (c).

We now must choose between (a) and (b). Considerations of strength don't allow a choice between them, as neither entails the other. But when the content of the parenthetical is taken into account, it becomes clear that the intended target is (a), the proposition that what the speaker drank was coffee. The parenthetical indicates that the speaker takes it to be possible that what was drunk was not in fact coffee. This means that the "main" predication coming from the verbal complex is not in conflict with the parenthetical, so disclaiming it won't help in making

---

[20] I won't consider the disjunction, but it might be that it's not available: according to Krifka (2001), speech acts don't admit disjunction, and if it's correct that (as some have it) sentences carrying conventional implicatures introduce multiple speech acts, there is no possible disjunction to be disclaimed.

the utterance coherent—given that (c) has already been eliminated as an option on the basis of Quantity. We are left with (b), as desired. I take this to be the proper notion of minimal revision.

It is interesting to consider the relationship between this notion and models of belief revision or the "Quinean web" (cf. Gärdenfors 1988). There, the issue involves update with new information that contradicts the information an agent already has. The goal is to find a way to add the new information while retaining the maximum possible amount of information the agent already has. The connection here looks quite deep; indeed, it seems likely that, for the linguistic case, the connection between belief revision and charitable interpretation goes deep. But I will not pursue this line further here.

5.4 Conceptual implications

Finally, I want to briefly discuss some implications of the analysis for the semantics/pragmatics interface.

Consider the way I have framed the analysis above. I claimed that there is an operation of utterance lifting which transforms the denotation of a sentence into a statement of the act of uttering that sentence; the latter object was then available for further modification, for example by utterance modifiers and by shield hedges. A natural question to ask at this point is the way in which this operation should be viewed. Is it a pragmatically induced operation or a semantic one? I've already considered this issue in some detail, concluding that the hedging operation lies somewhere in between, but I would like to make my conclusions fully explicit before moving on. Further, what is the conceptual basis of modifiers which alter the status of the utterances in which they appear? How can something *in* a sentence change the *act* which the sentence is used to perform?

On the semantics I have given, hedges are utterance modifiers: they denote functions which take inputs of type u. This means that, without application of (5.24), composition will fail: the sentence denotation is of type t, and consequently cannot serve as input to the modifier. From this perspective, (5.24) is nothing more than a special kind of type-shifting operation: it differs from more familiar ones only in outputting an object of utterance type. In some sense, then, this is a purely semantic operation, and therefore a semantic view of what one might, given that it involves speech acts rather than denotational content as standardly construed, prefer to understand as a pragmatic process. Here we can make a connection to criticisms of the theory of Potts (2005), which also has a highly semantic character (cf. Amaral et al. 2008).

In general, the boundary between semantics and pragmatics in my proposal is rather hazy. Elements of sentences are allowed to modify the utterances of which the sentences are the objects, and utterances are the objects of update rather than simple semantic contents as in traditional dynamic semantics. In the second part of the book, I will analyze update on the basis of evidence using histories like those I have used here to derive trustworthiness and reliability. There I will take the use of evidentials to correspond closely to the experience with particular evidence sources of the conversational participants: there we will find histories related to evidence and histories related to evidentials, both with very similar forms. Semantic and pragmatic analysis will overlap even further. I am quite willing to bite this bullet. I think this style of analysis, while perhaps not fitting neatly into the traditional boxes, is useful; I hope my discussion of disclamation here has shown that already. There seems to be a space between "pure" semantics and "pure" pragmatics which has partly evaded the standard toolkit. An entry into this space is gained by allowing the semantics/pragmatics boundary to relax; where the usual categories don't apply, we are well served to not pay too much attention to them.

Returning to issues more directly connected to the empirical aims of this book, it is time to reconsider the status of minimal revisions, cooperativity, and the elimination of incoherent discourse moves. I have claimed that disclaimed interpretations are arrived at by a combination of compositional operations running at the semantics/pragmatics interface and purely pragmatic reasoning working to assist in charitable interpretation. A natural question is how far this kind of interpretation can be pushed. We have seen that disclaimed interpretations can be arrived at, but other situations exist in which this reasoning could apply. For example, is it possible to cancel incoherent presuppositions or conventional implicatures? Perhaps, but it is definitely not automatic. We have already seen, in example (5.18), that the strategy does not always work. The key difference between that case and the good examples of disclamation under discussion seems to be the presence of an epistemic modal in the disclaiming clause. The speaker in the good cases indicates that she has some degree of uncertainty about the asserted content, but in cases like (5.18), the speaker appears completely certain of a contradiction (taking the asserted content together with the content otherwise expressed). It seems hard to make this coherent. On a pragmatic view, then, the infelicity of (5.18) is expected. Still, there are other kinds of cases, such as the following.

(5.45)   #! There might not actually be a king of France, but the king of France is bald.

(5.46)   #? It might not actually have been raining before, but it's (definitely) still raining now.

The example (5.45) strikes me as much worse than (5.46). Intuitively, this makes sense: (5.45) cannot be sensible at all if there is no king of France, but something reasonable can be recovered from (5.46) even if the presupposition of *still* is not satisfied, namely that it is raining now. I will not delve deeper into these contrasts here, but they do seem to fall out from a pragmatic view on which charitable interpretation is the engine driving the derivation of hedged interpretations.

   I have taken cooperativity to be the result of interaction between semantics, pragmatics, and general considerations about human behavior. However, the analysis has a somewhat counterintuitive consequence. The claim has been that we can get disclaimed interpretations due to pragmatic (Moorean) inconsistency and speaker reasoning about that inconsistency. Of course this isn't universal; it depends on some special properties of the constructions, i.e. the availability of utterance modification. Still, though, pragmatic reasoning—charitable interpretation—gives the effect of disclamation. It follows from charity that hearers must assume that a speaker wouldn't purposefully say something incoherent, which leads to disclaimed interpretations, as extensively discussed in this chapter.

   But charitable interpretation is only a sensible strategy if the speaker is cooperative; if the speaker is not cooperative, and is judged not to be cooperative, no hearer will interpret them in a charitable way, since they might be speaking nonsense or simply lying. Further, charity will only arise if the hearer is also cooperative, for otherwise coherence won't be in question – the hearer simply won't care if a reasonable interpretation is derived or not. But this means that disclamation requires cooperativity! I find this an unexpected result in some respects. Disclaimers, in their guise as reputation protectors, are most naturally thought of as uncooperative moves; consider the case of disclaimers in advertising, where the disclaimer has a genuinely anticooperative quality. But disclaiming itself requires cooperativity, as we've seen. There is an ironic quality to this result, but perhaps it's in the end sensible. Given the Propriety Principle, outrageous disclaimers will be taken to be uncooperative after all. The avoidance of this situation is up to the speaker, as she attempts to protect her reputation. The care this requires is a kind of converse of Sperber et al.'s (2010) epistemic vigilance, where the speaker self-polices in order to avoid censure. And it does seem that hedging in ordinary language does not feel nearly as aggressively reputation-protecting, and consequently noncooperative, as do advertising disclaimers. It may be that, in the end, the apparent paradox of uncooperative moves requiring cooperativity is nothing more than the result of a disconnect between the judgements of normal agents and courts of law about what counts as an outrageous disclaimer.

Part II
Evidentials and Reliability

6

The nature of evidentials

Our understanding of evidentials and their semantics has advanced greatly in the past ten years or so. Starting with the work of Garrett (2001) and Faller (2002b), researchers have isolated distinct kinds of evidential systems (McCready and Ogata 2007b; Matthewson et al. 2007; McCready 2008c; Murray 2010) and proposed some universal traits of evidential meanings (McCready 2010a, 2014). Specific evidential constructions have been given formal analyses in many languages: Quechua, Japanese, German, St'at'imcets, Cheyenne, Korean, and others. It is fair to say that a great deal of progress has been made. This chapter will survey some of this work with an eye to three points: first, giving a sense of what evidentials are and their linguistic (or epistemological) function; second, showing and evaluating existing results about evidential typologies and systems that have been used for analyzing them; and, most importantly, third, indicating what I take to be gaps in the literature. One of the most important of these, which might be called the problem of evidential update, will be the topic of the following chapters. It can be put simply and informally as follows: what should a hearer do with the content of an evidentially marked sentence? The nature and force of this question will become clear as the chapter proceeds.

To briefly preview, we can ask whether or not the content of an evidentially marked sentence is asserted. It is known that evidentials have different force in different languages: in some, they are closely related to epistemic modals from a semantic perspective, and in others, they seem to simply add extra content to assertions at the level of speech acts. This fact results in complications when trying to give a unitary model of "evidential update." The problem is compounded by the fact that not all evidentials, even within individual languages, are created equal with respect to whether the content of their complements is entailed. The result is difficulties in modeling how update should work; further, well-known problems with modeling inconsistent information are brought to the fore when evidentiality enters the picture.

6.1 What are evidentials?

Evidentials can be roughly defined as expressions indicating something about the speaker's basis for the speech act performed with the sentence.[1] In the case of assertions, they indicate the source of information, or the evidence, on which the speaker bases her assertion. The following examples give the flavor of the phenomenon.

(6.1)   a. Para-sha-n-mi
           rain-Prog-3-MI
           'It is raining. + speaker sees that it is raining'   (Quechua)

        b. It must be raining.   (seeing a dripping umbrella)

        c. Ame-ga   futteiru soo   desu
           rain-Nom falling   HEARSAY Cop
           'It is raining (I heard).'   (Japanese)

Evidentials have seen extensive attention from typologists (e.g. Chafe and Nichols 1986; Mithun 1986; de Haan 1999; Aikhenvald 2003, 2004). This research has yielded many interesting typological generalizations, and a great deal has been learned about patterns of grammaticalization leading to purely evidential lexical items or evidential interpretations of other terms. However, the typological literature leaves the nature of evidential meaning quite inexplicit: it is difficult to see, except on a very abstract level, what evidentiality *is* or *does*.

Aikhenvald (2004) provides the following criteria for evidentials:

1. Evidentials indicate the source of justification for factual claims.
2. Indication of evidence source is the primary meaning of evidentials (i.e. it does not follow pragmatically).
3. Evidentials are usually not used when the fact in question is known directly to both speaker and hearer (and, if used, have a special pragmatic significance).

Criterion 3 appears to me likely to be a special case of more usual restrictions on assertion, as spelled out by Searle (1969) and others; I think it can be disregarded as a criterion for evidentiality. However, the other conditions are cogent, though there are caveats to be made. Criterion 1 just states that evidentials present the evidence the speaker has for what she says. It is correct as far as it goes, but it does not

---

[1] The reader wishing more detail on how evidentials should be defined is referred to the semantically sophisticated discussion in Murray (2010).

cover the case of evidentials used outside of speech acts which make factual claims; as has been shown (Aikhenvald's book itself has extensive data and discussion), evidentials are commonly used in questions, and indeed can be used in intensional contexts where no factual claims are made at all (see McCready and Ogata 2007b).

Criterion 2 limits the domain of evidentiality to expressions which contain specification of evidence source as part of their "primary meaning." Here, I believe that "primary meaning" should be understood as: "part of literal content." This understanding of the definition excludes cases where the evidence source is inferred by pragmatic means, for instance as a (conversational) implicature in the Gricean manner. For instance, supposing that the English attitude verb *believe* often indicates a lack of perfect confidence, and that lack of perfect confidence about observable sensory facts often means a lack of such facts, we would not want to understand *John believes that this apple is red* as carrying the *evidential* content that John has not seen whether or not this apple is red, although such an implicature might be drawn in the right context. It seems fair to include presupposition, conventional implicature, etc., under this rubric, and indeed this is the standard usage in the (semantic) literature (see e.g. Matthewson et al. 2007 for a case where presuppositional content is spoken of as evidential). A possibly nontrivial factor is that it may not be easy to determine what counts as literal content (e.g. Cappelen and Lepore 2005); I will basically rely on an intuitive understanding here. It's not easy to make things fully precise, but, intuitively, the evidential content should be at least as "important" as any other part of the content of the expression.

What then counts as an evidential? Lots of things do: certain modals, such as the English *must* or the German *sollen*, words that appear to have both modal and clearly specifiable evidential content (Japanese, St'at'imcets), and even certain attitudes, such as verbs of perception taking clausal complements. In addition, of course, there are "pure" evidential items, such as certain affixes (e.g. those in Quechua) or particle-like items in languages like Khalkha (Street 1963).

But the above does not exhaust the content of Aikhenvald's criteria. An important point concerns the exegesis of "for factual claims." What do we mean by "factual claim" here? Suppose I assert $\phi + Evid$. Then my claim could be: ϕ or $Op\phi$, where Op is some operator which is part of the content of the evidential. For instance, supposing that English *must* is an evidential with a claim of epistemic necessity in addition to its evidential meaning, the claim made by the sentence *Must p* could be either p or $\Box p$, depending on whether one takes the operator to be part of the claim for which the speaker indicates herself to have evidence.[2] The answer we choose determines something important about the semantic status of the evidential contribution: if the claim is "ϕ," then the evidential contribution is not part of asserted content, and if we choose "$Op\phi$," then it is part of asserted content. This choice marks a major split between definitions and between accounts, as we will see, and a principled one stemming from a split in types of languages and evidentials.

6.2 Examples and analyses

To get a better sense of what evidentials are, I will now introduce some specific examples and analyses. The first will be that of Cuzco Quechua, as analyzed by Faller (2002b), who takes them to be speech act modifiers, for reasons closely related to their semantic behavior and interactions with operators. Cheyenne exhibits some similar traits, but is analyzed in a rather different way by Murray (2010), who treats them as introducing "not-at-issue updates," a kind of dynamic update which does not allow rejection by the interpreter; this analysis is examined second. A quite different kind of case, that of Japanese, is explored by McCready and Ogata (2007b), according to whom evidentials are literally epistemic modals with (what amounts to) a presupposition of "sufficiently strong" evidence of a certain kind. The difference between the former accounts and the latter points up a difference in kind between evidential systems, closely aligned with the difference in what is asserted pointed out in the last section. Of course, the examples picked up here are far from exhausting even the formal literature on evidentiality, but they will be sufficient for my purposes, which are to give a feel for the relevant phenomena.

6.2.1 Cuzco Quechua

Cuzco Quechua has several enclitic suffixes that mark evidentiality, of which several are analyzed in detail by Faller (2002b). Faller mainly examines three affixes. The first, -*mi*, is what is generally referred to as a direct evidential; it indicates that the speaker has direct evidence

---

[2] Abstracting away from (here) irrelevant worries about the truth-evaluability of modal claims, of course.

for the claim made. This should be understood as, roughly, the best possible grounds available for the assertion. Such evidence is usually perceptual, but not always. For example, given a claim that John is at his house, the most direct available evidence would indeed be perceptual—for example, I might have seen John answering his door—but in the case of a claim that John is going to Quito tomorrow, a claim about the future, no perceptual evidence is available. Here, the best possible grounds might be a statement by John about his plans. The issue of best possible grounds will be extensively discussed in section 8.3. The next affix, -si, is a reportative evidential; it indicates that the speaker heard the information expressed in the claim from someone else. Finally, -chá, an indirect or inferential evidential, indicates that the speaker's background knowledge, plus inferencing, leads him to believe the information in the claim to be true. (6.2) roughly exemplifies the behavior of each affix.

(6.2)   a. Para-sha-n-mi
            rain-Prog-3-MI
            'It is raining.' + speaker sees that it is raining

        b. Para-sha-n-si
            rain-Prog-3-SI
            'It is raining.' + speaker was told that it is raining

        c. Para-sha-n-chá
            rain-Prog-3-CHÁ
            'It may/must be raining.' + speaker conjectures that it is raining based on some sort of inferential evidence

Notice that the meaning contributed by the evidentials is left outside the literal paraphrase. The reason is that the evidential meanings do not appear to be "at-issue" in the sense of Potts (2005) or Simons et al. (2011); they are not part of the asserted content, and do not play a direct role in information transfer. This point is key in understanding Faller's analysis of the Quechua evidentials, which is stated in terms of speech acts.

What is the proper analysis of these terms? From the above observation, we see at least one criterion: the analysis must derive the apparent fact that the evidential content is not part of literal content, in the sense of the content which is manipulated by the speech act. In order to achieve this, Faller uses Vanderveken's (1990) speech act theory for her analysis. Another main reason for using a speech act-based analysis is that the Cuzco Quechua evidentials do not embed semantically. "At-issue" operators cannot apply to them; they thus either always take widest scope, or else remain scopeless entirely.

(6.3)   Ines-qa   **mana-n/-chá/-s** qaynunchaw ñaña-n-ta-chu
        Ines-Top not-MI/CHÁ/SI yesterday   sister-3-Acc-CHU
        watuku-rqa-n
        visit-Pst1-3
        'Ines didn't visit her sister yesterday.' (and speaker has evidence
        for this) NOT 'Ines visited her sister yesterday' (and speaker
        doesn't have evidence for this)

They also cannot be "bound" in the way that presuppositions can
(van der Sandt 1992). Consequently, a speech act analysis is quite natural:
speech acts cannot in general be scoped over (though see e.g. Krifka
2001 for a differing view, which may not be incompatible with Faller's
analysis) and obviously cannot be bound.[3]

In Vanderveken's speech act theory, like any other, speech acts have
preconditions for successful performance. These are formalized as a set
of (propositional) "sincerity conditions," written SINC. For assertions,
one of the relevant conditions is that $Bel(s, p)$ holds—that the speaker
believes the content of the assertion. An assertion is plainly not proper
if the speaker does not believe its content; in Gricean terms, it violates
Quality, and is therefore uncooperative. There are interesting questions
here involving the proper division of labor between Gricean implicature
and speech act precondition. The latter is far more conventionalized
than the former. Is it genuinely the case that an assertion is not properly
performed if the precondition is not satisfied? Or is it merely a violation of norms of assertion, but one which can still result in a proper
assertion? The implicit answer given in this book is that assertions can
be performed even when their preconditions are not satisfied, but that
such assertions can, if the result turns out badly (here, if the content
of the assertion is false, and that falsity is detected), have negative
consequences for the speaker's reputation.

Turning back to the evidentials, the focus of Faller's analysis is largely
on the sincerity conditions for the assertion. The direct evidential
-mi adds an additional sincerity condition: that $Bpg(s, p)$. The formula
$Bpg(s, p)$ means that the speaker has the best possible grounds for
asserting p. What are "best possible grounds"? This is just the notion
introduced above; the best possible grounds for the assertion is the best

---

[3] McCready (2010c) proposes to capture these facts in terms of conventional implicature
or expressive meaning in the Pottsian sense (Potts 2005). I will not consider this analysis in
much detail in the present context.

available evidence for the asserted proposition. This notion is already difficult; Faller does not analyze it in more detail. Two obvious questions are (i) what the best evidence is, and (ii) whether the best possible grounds are the best evidence actually available, or the best possible kind of evidence. As for question (i), I believe that the notion should be understood as picking out the most *reliable* kind of evidence for the kind of proposition being asserted; my analysis in section 8.3 will be built on this idea. For question (ii), clearly, the notion of best possible grounds must be understood modally. If $Bpg(s, p)$ merely states that the speaker has the best grounds currently available for asserting p, it is always satisfied, and thus ineffectual. But if the notion of best possible grounds is a modal one, we must say what it is for something to be the best *possible* evidence. My answer to this question, again, will be that the best possible evidence is evidence coming from a source which, with respect to propositions of the kind being asserted, is as reliable as one can get.

What about the other evidentials? Faller analyzes the inferential evidential *-chá* as being simultaneously modal and evidential: the asserted proposition p is mapped to $\Diamond p$. The corresponding belief object $Bel(s, p)$ in SINC is changed in the same way, yielding $Bel(s, \Diamond p)$. The condition *Reasoning*$(s, Bel(s, \Diamond p))$ is also added to SINC; this is supposed to indicate that the conclusion $\Diamond p$ is arrived at by the speaker via a process of reasoning. The result is that the speaker does not assert p, but instead $\Diamond p$, and the normative requirement on belief is that the speaker believe p possible (on the basis of some inferential process).

Finally, the hearsay evidential *-si*. This evidential has a special complication, which is not reflected in the glossing in (6.2b): the content in the scope of *-si* is not entailed to be true by assertion of the *-si*-marked sentence. This fact is cross-linguistically quite robust for reportative evidentials. Some further examples will be introduced below. As a consequence of this, the analysis of *-si* is also complex. On Faller's picture, the propositional content p is not asserted at all when this hearsay evidential is used. In order to achieve this, Faller posits a special speech act PRESENT for this situation, on which the speaker simply presents a proposition without making claims about its truth. Exactly what this amounts to is not discussed in much detail by Faller; presumably it involves making the proposition salient, and, as such, it relates closely to the discussion of modals in chapter 4. Formally, the nonentailed nature of the embedded proposition is derived by eliminating $Bel(s, p)$ from

SINC (this itself is what the new speech act PRESENT amounts to), and adding the condition $\exists s_2[Assert(s_2, p) \wedge s_2 \notin \{h, s\}]$, that there exists an act of assertion of p by some third party, to the set of sincerity conditions.

An interesting question that arises involves the following specific case of the question raised at the beginning of the chapter: what is the status of ϕ-si with respect to information transfer? Here, ϕ is not asserted, only "presented," much like the proffering of modal prejacents in chapter 4. Presentation is, presumably, something semantically/pragmatically inert; plainly, this is Faller's intention. It therefore won't feed into dynamic semantic mechanisms of update in the way that asserted content will (though, even there, the exact means by which assertion results in update is left quite underspecified, as I will show later). As a result the problem of what to do with the presented information is left up to the hearer. But what is the hearer supposed to do with it? There are several options. The hearer can accept it (so, where σ is an information state and '+' denotes an information update mechanism, the information state σ' obtaining after processing an example like (6.2b) will be $\sigma + \phi$), or else ignore it (giving $\sigma' = \sigma$). There is also a third possibility, to update with some kind of derived content (so that σ' is, for example, $\sigma + Heard(s, \phi)$; here there are no entailments about whether ϕ, but some information is still obtained). What should happen is left rather underspecified by the theory; all possibilities seem non-universally applicable. Situations like these are a major motivation for the theory I will develop in chapter 8, while chapter 9 is concerned with exactly what the hearer should do with both the content of testimony and (in a derived way) content in the scope of reportative evidentials.

6.2.2 Cheyenne

The Cheyenne evidential system has much in common with the Quechua case; the two can (along with many others) be viewed as falling into a natural class of evidential systems, which Murray (2010) dubs *illocutionary evidentials*. Murray 2010 is an extensive presentation and analysis of this system, which, in contrast to Quechua, exhibits a four-way evidential distinction, with a direct evidential, a reportative, a "narrative" evidential used for knowledge common to a group or general information, and finally an inferential evidential. This distinction is exemplified in (6.4).

(6.4)   a. É-hoo'koho-∅
             3-rain-DIR
             'It's raining, I am sure.'

        b. É-hoo'kȯhó-nėse
             3-rain-RPT.SG.B
             'It's raining, I hear.'

        c. É-hoo'kȯ'hó-neho
             3-rain-NAR.SG.B
             'It rained, it is said.'

        d. Mó-hoo'kȯhó-hane-he
             CNJ-rain-Mod$_B$-Y/N
             'It's raining, I gather.'

The Cheyenne system, although it shows more distinctions than the part of Quechua analyzed in detail by Faller, shows closely related semantic behavior: the content of its evidentials is also not challengeable or deniable, just as in Quechua, and further the evidential content cannot be embedded. In short, the contribution of the evidentials is not at issue. In (6.4) I make use of Murray's glosses; according to her, the parentheticals in those glosses capture quite closely the semantic sense of the evidential contribution. Using parentheticals for the paraphrase, again, shows that evidentials in Quechua–Cheyenne-type languages behave much like conventional implicatures.

Murray's proposal for capturing this fact is formally more sophisticated than Faller's. She distinguishes two kinds of assertion. The first kind is at-issue assertion, which introduces "standard" or negotiable content; in general, this is new information, which is first proffered to the hearer, and then, if accepted, induces an update. The second type is not-at-issue assertion. Content introduced via not-at-issue assertion is added to the common ground via a "direct" update; the hearer has no choice about whether or not to accept the content, for it is "imposed" directly on the interpreter. Still, new information is introduced. As one would expect, this analysis looks much like what one might want for conventional implicatures or expressives, and, consequently, the proposal that Cheyenne evidentials introduce content which enters the common ground via not-at-issue assertion seems a quite natural one.

On Murray's proposal, informational update takes place in three steps (in general). First, the at-issue proposition is presented; this is, in some sense, similar to the action of Faller's PRESENT speech act, but, because of the formal implementation it is given and its embedding in a dynamic model, it does not come with the puzzles associated with PRESENT; it is quite clear what presentation is here, merely the introduction of a proposition. Second, there is a "non-negotiable" update; conceptualizing the common ground model in terms of a set of worlds, this is a direct restriction to those worlds satisfying the condition(s) imposed by the not-at-issue content. In Murray's system evidentials act at this level. For instance, a direct evidential indicates, non-negotiably, the existence of direct evidence for the presented proposition. At this point in the update process, the common ground may contain worlds that do not satisfy the presented proposition. Consequently, the last update step involves a "negotiable" update, implemented as the imposition of a preference ordering on the remaining worlds which ranks those worlds satisfying the presented content above those that don't. The remaining preference-maximal worlds comprise the new common ground. We will see this operation again in the next chapter, where it will play a key role in the analysis of evidential update that I will propose. This second update is introduced by a mood operator (null in languages like English). The update operation is complete at this point, though one step remains: a discourse referent is introduced for the new common ground, which is available for later anaphoric reference. The whole is implemented in the system of Bittner 2011.

This analysis is quite satisfying. It makes the right predictions. For one, since the evidential content introduces a not-at-issue update, it is not challengeable, by definition. The update takes place before challenges are even available. It also gets right the availability of certain kinds of interactions with speech acts, for instance questions, because of the later presence of mood operators (closely related to speech acts) which can modify what happens with the evidential itself. Some of the mystery of the reportative evidential also vanishes; since the restriction to the "presented" content happens at a later stage, it is possible to eliminate this restriction in the case of hearsay evidentials, avoiding the need to disable mechanisms that would otherwise be expected to function. These are nice consequences.

Still, some puzzles remain. Murray gives an admirably clear answer to the question of how evidential update might proceed, but questions about (as it were) *when* it should proceed remain unaddressed. For instance, the key question of when a hearer ought to simply accept the content in the scope of a reportative evidential is not discussed, and neither is the case of conflicting evidential information. This is not meant as an attack on Murray's proposal, which is semantic in nature and thus orthogonal to pragmatic considerations of the kind mentioned here. For her, the asserted content is presented as a proposal for update. The question of whether this proposal should be accepted or not is taken to be quite distinct from the evidential itself; but this leaves aside the influence of the evidential content on the pragmatic process involved in information uptake. I think it is fair to say that the analysis in Murray (2010) can be viewed as a satisfying way to understand the semantics of evidentials of the Quechua–Cheyenne type without making recourse (directly) to speech acts, but one which remains silent on the more purely pragmatic issues involving evidentials that are the focus of the second half of this book.[4]

6.2.3 Japanese

The evidential system of Japanese exemplifies a different class, which Murray calls the "epistemic evidentials." Unlike the examples we have looked at up to now, evidentials like these have a strongly epistemic modal-like flavor, consequently inducing weakened assertions together with implicatures about the speaker's confidence in the proposition in the scope of the evidential. Evidentials in this class also show behavior quite distinct from the illocutionary evidentials with phenomena like embedding and denial, as we will see below.

Japanese has a number of evidential expressions: the inferential evidentials *mitai*, *yoo*, *rashii*, and *(inf-)soo* (a version of the affix *soo* which takes an infinitive complement), and the hearsay evidential *S-soo* (a different *soo* which looks for a sentential complement), though *rashii* also has a use as a reportative evidential (McCready and Ogata 2007b).[5]

---

[4] It's worth observing that Murray's picture has some similarities to the proposal of McCready (2010c), which treats evidentials as introducing conventional implicature. The reason is that some of the special properties of evidentials are derived by treating them as inducing not-at-issue updates; as Murray herself notes, a similar analysis could be applied to conventional implicatures, and indeed this has been carried out by AnderBois et al. (2012). Murray herself does not support this view, but her arguments are either quite indirect, or else apply only to a particular version of the analysis (2010:139); they do not apply to the implementation in $\mathcal{L}_{CI}^+$ in McCready (2010c).

[5] People often also talk about the marking of particular content as having a "first-person" source, as with the so-called experiential predicates in Japanese (cf. Aoki 1986; McCready 2007). In these cases, a different form is used for statements about the self than is used for statements about others for certain kinds of predications (such as some predicates of personal taste or those relating to sensory phenomena). Since these expressions do not mark

(6.5) a. Jon-wa   konya-no   paatii ni kuru
          John-Top tonight-Gen party to come
          rashii/mitai/yoo
          RASHII/MITAI/YOO
          'It seems that John will come to the party tonight.'
       b. Jon-wa   konya-no   paatii ni ki-soo   da
          John-Top tonight-Gen party to come-SOO$_{Inf}$ Cop.pres
          'It seems that John is coming to the party tonight.'
       c. Jon-wa   konya-no   paatii ni kuru soo   da
          John-Top tonight-Gen party to come SOO$_{Rep}$ Cop.pres
          'I heard that John will come to the party tonight.'

Despite the identical glossing above, there are substantial differences
between the inferential evidentials. A relevant difference in the present
context is that they vary in the kind of evidence they allow: for example,
inferential *soo* is good with olfactory evidence, meaning that (6.6) could
be asserted after the speaker smells ozone, but *mitai* requires that the
evidence it references be of a different type, and so could not be used
felicitously in such a context.[6]

(6.6) Ame-ga   furi-soo da
       rain-Nom fall-SOO Cop
       'It seems as if it will rain.'

What is the proper analysis of the Japanese evidentials? According
to McCready and Ogata (2007b), dynamic semantics is needed. The
reasons for this move, though, are different from Murray's. For Murray,
dynamics allowed the modeling of two distinct kinds of assertion, so
that the evidentials could contribute to asserted content in some sense,
but at a different "level of content" than that of "standard" assertions. But
this sort of argument is not really relevant to the Japanese case: there,
evidentials seem to contribute content in the same way as epistemic

the information as following from a particular source specifically, I will leave them out of
this book, though nothing deep hangs on this choice. See Garrett (2001) for related facts in
Tibetan.

   [6] Another difference between the inferential evidentials involves aspect. When a nonsta-
tive verb phrase is the complement of the inferential *soo*, it is interpreted as meaning that the
event described by the verb phrase will happen very soon or immediately; conversely, when
the verb phrase denotes something of stative aspect, it is indicated to hold at the present time.
This difference is probably closely related to the aspectual differences found with modals and
explored by Condoravdi (2002); a similar explanation should account for the facts here. See
McCready and Ogata (2007b) for discussion.

modals, and thus in a way essentially part of normal assertion. One motivation for this view is the fact that Japanese evidentials can easily be embedded under operators: (6.7) shows examples in which inferential evidentials appear under conditionals, for instance, and (6.8) a case where a reportative evidential is in the scope of an epistemic modal. (The latter is naturally used in a context in which, for instance, our friend Mika consistently follows Taro around, and we are using this fact as an explanation for her having appeared at the party tonight, where we otherwise would not have expected to find her.)

(6.7)   a. Taro-ga   kuru yoo   da-ttara   oshiete kudasai
           Taro-Nom come YOO Cop.Pres-COND teach   please
           'If it looks like Taro will come, please tell me.'

        b. Taro-ga   kuru soo   da-ttara   oshiete kudasai
           Taro-Nom come SOO Cop.Pres-COND teach   please
           'If you hear that Taro will come, please tell me.'

(6.8)   Mosikashitara Taro-ga   kuru   yoo   datta   kamoshirenai
        maybe   Taro-Nom come YOO cop.Pst possibly
        'Maybe it looked like Taro would come.'

In this respect, Japanese exemplifies a larger class of "epistemic evidential" systems; for instance, Matthewson et al. (2007) show that St'at'imcets evidentials also embed, and that their semantics has modal-like qualities. For another example (not yet examined in the formal literature, to my knowledge), Warlpiri also proves to be similar to Japanese in terms of embeddability; in the following example from Aikhenvald (2004: 97), the evidential clearly scopes under the propositional attitude in the answer to the question.

(6.9)   a. Ngana-nku nganta paka-rnu
           who-ERG   REP   hit-PAST
           'Who do they say hit him/her?'

        b. Ngana-nku mayi   nganta paka-rnu
           who-ERG   don't.know REP   hit-PAST
           'I do not know who they reckon hit her.'

A second key observation about Japanese is that the inferential evidentials support modal subordination. Modal subordination names a phenomenon in which, intuitively, a modal "accesses" content in the scope of another modal. The rough idea is that a first modal sets up a context, a set of salient possibilities or the like, which a subsequent modal can "find" and modify. When anaphoric relations are present, it is easy to see this situation arise. A first observation, familiar from the early dynamic semantics literature (Karttunen 1976; Kamp 1981; Heim 1988), is that nonveridical operators (with respect to existential entailments) normally block anaphora. This is well known for the case of negation and universals but it also holds for modals; for instance, if the first sentence is read *de dicto* so that the existence of the wolf is not entailed outside the modal context, anaphora is infelicitous.

(6.10)   A wolf might come in. # It is very big.

But if the second sentence also contains a modal, anaphora is enabled, as in the following example.

(6.11)   A wolf might come in. It would/might eat you first.

Here the idea is that the second modal is able to "pick up" the content of the first. Very informally, suppose that the *might*-sentence makes salient a set of worlds verifying the prejacent proposition. If a world makes the prejacent true, it will contain an object in the extension of *wolf* at that world. Then, supposing that the modal in the second sentence can access this salient set of worlds, this truthmaking object can serve as antecedent to *it* in the second sentence. This is the basic intuition, which has been spelled out in varying ways by many people (Roberts 1989; Frank 1997; van Rooij 2005; Asher and McCready 2007; Brasoveanu 2007, among many others).

   For modal subordination to occur, obviously, a modal must be present. If we find modal subordination occurring with evidentials, then, there must be a modal in the at-issue content of that evidential, for without one, modal subordination is not possible.[7] As it turns out, in Japanese, modal subordination is possible following evidential sentences, both with modals in the subsequent sentence and with other evidentials.[8]

----

   [7] At least, this appears to be the case in general; one puzzling case is that of the modal subordination licensed by the Japanese sentence-final particle *yo*, though even this particle has been analyzed as having a modal meaning in modal subordination contexts, where such a meaning is needed to maintain discourse coherence (cf. McCready 2008b).

   [8] However, if an inferential evidential follows a modal, modal subordination is not enabled. Why is this? Likely it has to do with the required evidence for the prejacent of the evidential (see below in the main text). For instance, in the case of the Roberts-inspired wolf examples in the main text, how could one have evidence for what a hypothetical individual will do, given a hypothetical situation in which the individual appears? Getting clear about this requires being more specific about the interaction between modals and evidentials, and about the nature of evidence itself; see McCready and Asher (2006); McCready and Ogata (2007b); McCready (2014) for relevant discussion.

(6.12)   a. Ookami-ga kuru mitai   da
             wolf-Nom come MITAI Cop.Pres
             'A wolf will come in, it seems.'

         b. Anta-o   taberu kamoshirenai
             you-Acc eat   might
             'It might eat you.'

(6.13)   a. Ookami-ga kita   mitai/yoo   da
             wolf-Nom   came MITAI/YOO Cop.Pres
             'A wolf/Some wolves has/have come, it seems.'

         b. Yatsu(ra)-wa totemo onaka-o   sukaseteiru
             it(they)-Top very   stomach-Acc emptied
             mitai/yoo   da
             MITAI/YOO Cop.Pres
             'It/they seems/seem to be very hungry.'

However, this phenomenon doesn't arise with hearsay evidentials. This fact makes sense: intuitively, reportative evidentials don't have a modal component, but simply indicate that the information the speaker proffers was obtained via testimony of some kind.

In view of the data above, McCready and Ogata (2007b) gave an analysis which modeled the Japanese evidentials within a dynamic semantics augmented with probabilities. The reason for using dynamics, as may be clear from the above, was partly to enable the analysis of the modal subordination phenomena; the second reason was to show the interaction of the evidentials and discourse-introduced evidence sources, observation sentences in the sense of Quine (1960). In this dynamic framework, inferential evidentials were modeled via an operator $\triangle_a^i$, where i indexes an evidence source and a is an agent. Informally, this operator has the following semantics:

(6.14) $\triangle_a^i \phi$ is true given a world w, time s, and probability function P iff

         a. ϕ was less likely according to a at some time preceding s (before introduction of a piece of evidence i);

         b. ϕ is still not completely certain for a at s (given i);

         c. the probability of ϕ for a never decreased between the time a became aware of the evidence i and s as a result of the same piece of evidence i (convexity).

There are several things worth noting about this definition. The most important for my purposes in this book is the presence of the index i on the $\triangle$ operator. This index is dependent on a source of evidence, which can be introduced explicitly in the previous discourse, or can be made available by the nonlinguistic context, in the usual way of variables in dynamic theories. Evidentials are viewed in this theory as containing variables which must be bound by evidence source indices. The existence of an evidence source, then, is effectively presupposed by use of an evidential, in just the way an antecedent is for anaphoric pronouns (Geurts 1999).

As with pronouns, we can distinguish here between free and bound evidence variables. Free variables will depend on objects in the extralinguistic context, as usual. Bound variables depend on evidence binders. Where do these evidence sources come from? As mentioned above, they are introduced by Quinean observation sentences. The logical form of such sentences contains a predicate E, which is essentially an existential quantifier over evidence sources. In addition to introducing an evidence source index which can serve to bind later variables, this predicate also has a complex semantic function. Informally, it works as follows:

(6.15) $E_a^i \varphi \ldots$

       a. changes the probabilities assigned to every proposition ψ (excluding φ itself) in the current information state σ by replacing them with the conditional probability of ψ given φ, if defined;

       b. replaces the modal accessibility relation with one restricted to worlds in which φ holds.

This account is meant as a treatment of what evidence does in a context; it changes the probability of other propositions that are related to it conditionally (6.15a),[9] and revises the set of accessible possibilities to one containing only those possibilities that make the content of the evidence true (6.15b). The latter just amounts to a particular implementation of what happens when learning new information.

What about the reportative evidential *soo(da)*? Unlike the inferential evidential, here the $\triangle$ operator is inappropriate, for there is no require-

---

[9] Conditional probability is defined as

$$P(A|B) = \frac{P(A, B)}{P(B)},$$

where $P(A|B)$ is not defined if $P(B) = 0$, in the usual way.

ment about probabilities, and indeed no modal content at all, as shown by the modal subordination facts. Consequently McCready and Ogata (2007b) gave it a rather different semantics; it was modeled with an operator H_a, a dynamic test, understood as follows.

(6.16) $H_a\varphi$ indicates that a has experienced an event of acquiring hearsay knowledge $E_a^h\varphi$, at some past time.

The hearsay evidential just tests for the existence of an evidence acquisition event of type *hearsay*. Japanese evidentials, then, simply introduce semantic operators, which can scope over and under other bits of content as usual, unlike what would happen if they were tied to speech acts or other kinds of scopeless content such as conventional implicature or not-at-issue update.

A key point for the project of this book is the existence of distinct classes of evidence sources. Plainly, one can learn about an event, or gain evidence for some event having happened, in a variety of ways. One can hear that something happened from another person by testimony; one can see it happening; one can observe other sorts of sensory clues to the event, such as the sound of engines or the smell of brewing coffee. Other, more indirect, kinds of clues are also available. All these things are distinguished in the McCready–Ogata framework by assuming the existence of different classes of evidence sources into which each instance of an evidence index can be classified. The particular implementation involves a function *Sort* which maps indices to evidence sources; the exact classes available include at least the members of the set of 'source sorts' Σ postulated in McCready and Ogata (2007b), which includes {*tactile, auditory, internal_sensory, hearsay, visual, secondary*}. These source types will be crucial to the theory to be developed in the next chapter for evaluating the likely reliability of a given piece of evidence, and thus in determining hearer actions in the process of evidential update.

This analysis instantiates an observation that will be important going forward: the range of evidence types that natural language evidentials "select for" is limited. Aikhenvald (2004, chapter 2, especially pp. 63–66) indicates that languages make use of the evidence types in Table 6.1.

Evidentials in different languages can select for any of these information sources. Presumably the information sources can be taken to have properties of their own, for instance specifications of reliability or

TABLE 6.1   Evidence types (after Aikhenvald 2004).

Visual	Information acquired through sight
Non-visual sensory	Information acquired through other four senses
Inference	Information based on "visual or tangible" evidence, or result state
Assumption	Other inferentially based information: reasoning, assumption, general knowledge
Hearsay	Testimony by nonspecific individual
Quotative	Testimony by specific, referenced individual

trustworthiness, possibly dependent on the particular individual using the evidential. We will return to this issue extensively below and in the following chapter.

6.2.4 Summing up

In this section we have examined three evidential systems, those of Quechua, Cheyenne, and Japanese. I hope the reader has got a sense of the phenomena. As we saw, there appear to be two basic kinds of evidential systems in the world's languages: in one, evidentials are more or less scopeless, interacting only with content at the level of mood or speech acts, and in the other, they behave more or less like epistemic modals in this respect. We also saw that the two systems lead naturally to different kinds of analyses.[10] We have also seen an issue which is left open by the theories of evidentials I have presented so far, at least to some degree: the question of how the information state of a processor should change after update with an evidentially marked sentence. The answer presumably depends on the particular evidential used, and by extension on the type of evidence the speaker indicates she has for her assertion. But this is, at least in part, a pragmatic issue; we should examine theories of evidential pragmatics. I will turn to this task in the next section.

---

[10] A question that might arise here is whether the kind of analysis developed for one type of system can naturally be extended to the other; presumably it is possible (at least for the case of epistemic evidentials; the other direction looks rather difficult), but perhaps the question itself is not very interesting at the end of the day. The difference in the two kinds of system amounts to a lexical difference; whether or not a single theory can accommodate the two systems, the differences between particular evidentials will have to be lexically stipulated in any case (see McCready 2008c, 2010a for some relevant discussion). A more interesting issue is whether the difference in systems can be tied to other facts about the languages in question. At present, I do not know whether such connections exist, and this is not the place to explore the issue.

6.3 Pragmatics of evidentials

As the last section showed, evidentials vary widely in their effect on the content of the sentences they appear in.[11] Epistemic evidentials function much in the manner of epistemic modals, as do inferential evidentials in at least some languages (e.g. Quechua). Consequently, they have clearly defined effects on assertion; the asserted content is no longer p, the content of the prejacent, but instead $\Diamond p$, the prejacent modified by an epistemic modality. Illocutionary evidentials (excluding the inferential), on the other hand, do not have effects quite so easily defined. Direct evidentials indicate a certain kind of evidence, and continue to assert the evidential prejacent; reportative evidentials no longer assert the prejacent at all. As noted above, a result of this complexity is that problems arise for the hearer with respect to how the prejacent should be treated during the process of information transfer. This section will explore one model that provides an answer to this question. After examining it, in the next section, I will indicate the issues that arise in the particularly complex case of hearsay evidentials.

Considering the process of conversation yields two perspectives on the question of evidential use. From the speaker side, there are questions about evidential production. For example, when should one use an evidential? One might think that this question is not very cogent, in that in many languages which have grammaticalized evidentiality, the use of evidentials is obligatory in every sentence.[12] But this is not so. It is often the case that one will have more than a single kind of evidence for some putative fact. For instance, if I watch James buy a giant peach, and Harry later tells me that James bought a giant peach, then I have at least the options of using a direct or reportative evidential in languages where both are available. Which one, then, should I use? One would like one's

---

[11] Aikhenvald (2004) discusses constructions in which evidentials appear to take subsentential scope, for instance where they are found in relative clauses and indicate the speaker's evidence for the content of the relative clause, but not that of the rest of the sentence. It is interesting to speculate about how these interpretations are derived. A natural idea is that the scope of the evidential is set during the process of relative clause derivation, much as happens in the case of modals: but it is not obvious how this sort of thing could be handled under a speech act analysis of (illocutionary) evidentials. However, the analysis of partial hedging in chapter 5 might well be applicable here as well. I will not discuss these cases further here.

[12] At least this is the folk wisdom; in practice, it appears that many or most such languages admit cases where no overt evidential is used. In such contexts, the unmarked sentence is usually taken as having the force of direct evidential marking. (Though see Miyara 2002 for a possible counterexample; Miyara claims that, in some dialects of Ryukyuan, unmarked sentences are interpreted as, effectively, being modified by an inferential evidential.)

theory to have something to say about this issue. Perhaps more generally, we can ask whether evidentials change the circumstances under which one can perform this or that speech act.

From the hearer's perspective, obviously, the key question is what to do with an evidentially marked sentence in terms of update. I will focus on this question in the next chapter; as we will see, the situation is not at all simple. But one can also ask the related question: What can the use of an evidential allow one to conclude about the speaker's state? Presumably at least that the speaker has evidence of the relevant kind. But there may be more to find; for instance, one might be able to derive implicatures from the speaker's use of one evidential and not another, or even implicatures which let one draw conclusions about how to update with the content of the prejacent.

In fact, the literature addresses (some of) these questions but not very systematically. For instance, consider the question of the effect of evidentials on speech acts. Clearly, Faller's theory provides an answer to this question: evidentials shift the speech acts performed with the sentences they appear in to *different* speech acts, in operator-like fashion. Two questions immediately arise here. First, one could ask whether the analysis is conceptually sensible on its most obvious interpretation. How can it be that sentence-internal operators directly affect what is done with the sentence that contains them? The idea just seems bizarre, like saying that a weight on the handle of a hammer could affect, not the way in which it is swung, but *whether or not* what is done with it *counts* as a swing.[13] The analysis could, however, be understood as indicating that the speech acts performed with sentences containing the evidentials are simply speech acts of a different kind. On this understanding, the view of "evidentials as illocutionary operators" is lost. But a second question can be asked here. Faller's analysis is quite direct (as is Murray's). Can the change in speech act type be derived in some way? And could such a derivation help illuminate the change in normative behavior with respect to update?

Davis et al. (2007) provide an interesting attempt. The basic idea is that evidentials induce shifts in how requirements on speech acts are *satisfied*. Note the difference with the Faller picture: on this view, the speech acts themselves remain the same, preconditions and all; but the evidential(s) present in the sentence affect what is actually needed to

---

[13] Note the similarity here to Potts's (2005) analysis of utterance modifiers, which, as discussed in chapter 5, are taken to be external to the sentence proper.

satisfy the preconditions. This view is yet a different possibility from that suggested in the last paragraph. The three could be sloganized as follows: on the Faller analysis, evidentials are genuine operators on speech acts; on the variant of the Faller view of the last paragraph, the presence of an evidential in a sentence used to perform a speech act simply means that a different speech act is being performed; and on the Davis et al. picture, the speech acts do not change, but the context does, in such a way as to weaken or strengthen the preconditions. Let us see how this idea is spelled out.

The theory is couched in probabilistic terms. As usual, the probability function P it assumes satisfies the standard conditions described in chapter 2, in (2.1). Slightly less standardly, Davis et al. (2007) also require probabilistic *uniformity* with respect to propositions: the following condition says that the probability of all the worlds that comprise a proposition is equal, so the probability distributes equally over all the worlds in the proposition.

(6.17) $P(\{w\}) = P(\{w'\})$ for all $w, w' \in \varphi$ for all propositions φ

This condition is puzzling: how could it be true? Intuitively, the probability that it rains tomorrow and my hair abruptly turns blue at 3:03 pm is lower than the probability that it rains and my hair color remains the same. Stated slightly more formally, there seems no sense in which one could require that the probability of a world in $\varphi \wedge \psi$ be identical to the probability of $\varphi \wedge \chi$ for arbitrary φ, ψ, and χ; but this is just what the condition in (6.17) requires, for it says that all worlds in φ must have the same probability. Fortunately, this point will not affect our discussion much.

The idea on which the theory is founded comes from Lewis (1976): "assertability goes by subjective probability." This amounts to a normative condition on assertions, in fact the so-called belief norm for assertion (Brown and Cappelen 2011), which has it that A is assertable only if $P(A)$ is sufficiently close to 1.[14] On the basis of this, one can define a notion of a *quality threshold* (written q_τ), as done by Potts (2006), a point on a scale based on subjective probabilities (so $q_\tau \in [0,1]$ for all quality thresholds) above which an assertion does not violate Gricean Quality. As one would expect from the proposed norm, quality

---

[14] This condition competes with others, for instance a knowledge-based norm or even one based on utilities or practical interest. See the papers in Brown and Cappelen (2011) for extensive discussion, and the introduction to the volume for a useful summary of the debate.

thresholds can usually be assumed to be quite high, indeed ≈ 1. Still, they are somewhat variable. In the right context, one need not be completely certain about a proposition in order to assert it felicitously. This is the key observation behind the theory of Davis et al. (2007).

What do evidentials do, on the Davis et al. theory? Suppose first that each evidential is associated with a quality threshold q_τ. The exact location of q_τ is to be determined by context in an unspecified way, as usual with theories making use of thresholds and scales (Kennedy 2007). This process might be specified as "black magic" (though I will briefly consider some ways of demystifying the magical process below). Let us call this black magic a function and name it μ_c. With these pieces, evidentials can be specified as having the following function.

(6.18)   If S[ev] is uttered by agent A in context c, then
     1. A assumes a commitment to having ev-type evidence for [S],
     2. q_τ becomes $\mu_c(ev)$, and then
     3. A performs a speech act with $[\![S]\!]$ (probably an assertion if S is a declarative, probably a question if S is interrogative, etc.).

On this view, three things happen on utterance of a sentence containing an evidential. First, the speaker commits to having evidence of whatever kind the evidential specifies. What is it to have such evidence? This is not specified by the Davis et al. theory; in fact, the nature of the evidence which is indicated by evidentials is a weak point of nearly all theories of evidentials at the present time. McCready and Ogata come the closest to integrating a view of what evidence is into their theory, by the use of their E predicate. I will return to this issue in section 6.5. Second, using an evidential shifts the quality threshold to whatever is indicated by μ_c, the contextually specified threshold associated with the evidential. Again, exactly where this threshold lies is not set, but is left up to context. Davis et al. present this as a virtue of the theory, and in some sense it is. The location of the threshold should track reliability, and, as Faller (2002a) has shown, the reliability given to a particular evidence source is variable due to contextual factors (a point which will be returned to in chapters 7 and 8). However, one would presumably like some way to specify what this variability amounts to, something not provided by Davis et al. (2007). Third and finally, the usual speech act associated with the utterance is performed.

Crucially, these effects are sequential. Because they are, the utterance becomes felicitous even when the speaker lacks a high degree of confidence in the asserted proposition (putting other speech acts aside). The reason is as follows. Take an utterance of p decorated with a reportative evidential. In the general case, testimony is less reliable than direct evidence. One may lack full confidence in testimony. But if the evidential drives the quality threshold down far enough, assertion can still felicitously take place despite that low level of confidence. Evidentials, then, are essentially taken to be operators on other, pragmatic, aspects of the context model.

Two questions immediately arise about this model. First, what determines q_τ? As I said above, this is not an issue which is exclusive to the analysis currently under consideration, as it must be answered by any theory employing thresholds such as standard theories of adjectival predication (cf. chapter 3). However, the present case seems to present a problem of a different order than deciding (for example) thresholds for vague predicates, though it must be said that this problem itself is one that gets surprisingly little attention even from those who espouse threshold-type theories. For predicates of that kind, it seems reasonable to think of threshold-setting as essentially a kind of coordination over possible thresholds. The manner in which this might be done could be based on a number of factors. For instance, one might take the discourse goals of the speaker and hearer in the utterance context to fix a particular point, an idea I explored briefly in McCready (2010b), or, similarly, make the threshold dependent on the question under discussion. One might also try to use a more direct notion of coordination in the way suggested in McCready (2012b), so that the threshold depends on the hearer's guesses about what the speaker has in mind, and conversely the speaker's guesses about what the hearer is likely to guess, and so on.

But there are disanalogies with all these cases. As noted by Matthewson (forthcoming), only the speaker has access to the source and consequent reliability of evidence. Furthermore, no evidential can always be associated with the same level of reliability, as shown by Faller (2002a). So how is one to set the threshold across speaker and hearer? It does not seem that there is any universally reasonable basis for the hearer to use in making guesses about what the quality threshold might be, or about how the speaker might be setting it. If this is correct, then the basis of the threshold can only be speaker judgements about what counts as assertable. But if so, what need is there to change the threshold? Otherwise stated, what is the real content of Gricean Quality at this point? If the speaker can unilaterally reset what counts as assertable, and the hearer has no access to the quality threshold, the whole idea of

Quality seems to become empty, which strikes me as a highly undesirable result.

Given the above, the second question is clear. What is the hearer supposed to do with the "asserted" content? This question is the same that has arisen a number of times in this chapter, but Davis et al. (2007) address it explicitly, as one would expect given their pragmatic focus. They indicate that we should expect inferences about reliability to arise, via comparisons made in the manner of Quantity implicatures: "S asserted 'A-hearsay' not 'A-direct', so she is probably not so confident about A" (or the opposite, in context). There is an obvious tension here between Quantity-style inferencing about reliability and the observation that any given evidential is not associated with a constant level of reliability, but in any case, the result is that update mechanisms are left highly indeterminate. However, it does appear that the model always predicts update with p; although the update may be made with some reduced degree of confidence, something which is not reflected in the way update proceeds in the model as constructed by Davis et al.

The above considerations lead to a clear conclusion: for the proper understanding of the pragmatics of evidentials in the context of information transmission, a full account of update with evidentials is needed. Such an account should incorporate a means of judging the reliability of a given use of an evidential, and of integrating that judgement into a theory of (dynamic) update for assertive content. No such theory is currently on the market. The task is nontrivial: one needs a theory of ranking for evidence sources, and then a way to incorporate the resulting picture of confidence in testimonial evidence, with its complex shades and gradations of reliability, into a theory of update. Providing such a theory and exploring its consequences is the task of the remainder of this book, on the basis of some suggestive recent work in dynamic epistemic logic (Baltag and Smets 2008; Holliday 2010; van Benthem and Pacuit 2011).

6.4 What to do with hearsay evidentials

In this chapter, I have pressed the necessity for an analysis of how update should proceed with evidentials. But the discussion has been abstract. I have not considered any cases in detail. Let me now briefly present an example to allow the reader to see the complexity of the issue. In essence, this section states a problem that will be considered extensively in chapter 9.

The particular case I would like to investigate is that of hearsay evidentials (McCready forthcoming, a). Let us begin with the view of Davis et al. (2007) on evidential implicatures. According to their analysis, when observing an utterance of $\phi + Dir$ (for a direct evidential Dir), a hearer ought to feel justified updating with ϕ. The reason is twofold: first, for them, *all* instances of evidential "assertions" should induce update of stronger or weaker quality; second, in general, since perceptual evidence ("best possible grounds") is highly reliable, being told that $\phi + Dir$ is a pretty good reason to believe ϕ. But observing $H\phi$ should in general be the opposite. The following implicature-style chain of reasoning can be applied:

(6.19)   Speaker could have said $\{\phi, \phi + Dir\}$
         speaker said $H\phi$
         reliability of testimonial evidence varies but is typically low
         ───
         $\approx$ speaker must not feel confident in ϕ

Plainly, this is the kind of evidential-based Quantity implicature that Davis et al. (2007) have in mind.

However, there is a competing line of reasoning. Consider the philosophical work of Burge (1993) on the epistemological status of testimony. He proposes what he calls the "Acceptance Principle": speakers are "entitled," in the absence of overriding reasons not to do so, to believe proffered content (if that content can be understood). This is, of course, a normative principle and can easily be overridden. As Burge says, it may not be the final word in justification for anyone over the age of 11. This is basically a Reidian view on testimony; the opposing Humean picture has it that trust depends on experience with particular individuals (e.g. Graham 2006a). These views and their consequences will also be discussed in detail in chapter 9. As will be made clear, there are certainly appealing aspects to the Reidian picture as well as to the more skeptical Humean one.

How does all this apply to update with $H\phi$? Consider the following chain of reasoning. Suppose that I have observed $H\phi$. By the Acceptance Principle, I should believe $H\phi$. But $H\phi$ implies that the speaker has testimonial evidence for ϕ. Then by the Acceptance Principle I should be entitled to believe ϕ as well, since, given that principle, testimonial evidence is reliable. This reasoning competes with the previous Quantity implicature, which indicates that we should not believe ϕ. Which is correct? The question is empirical and situation-dependent. But it should already be clear that the issues surrounding evidential update are not at all simple, even in what may look like relatively straightforward cases. This particular case will be returned to in chapter 9 after I have developed my theory of testimony and of evidential update; there it will be shown that the apparent problem is mostly a consequence of insufficiently appreciating the complexity of how update with testimony works. Chapters 7 and 8 will consider some other cases of interest.

6.5 Evidence

Before turning to the main topic of this second half of the book, the relationship between judgements about reliability and update with evidentials, I want to briefly address one last issue in the semantics of evidentials. What is the nature of the evidence that is required for the proper use of evidentials? In the literature, the existence of a well-defined notion of evidence is often taken for granted. Here I wish to establish the assumptions I will make in the rest of the book about the nature of "evidence for evidentials"; since I will make extensive use of the idea that information derives from this or that evidence source, I first should make clear exactly what evidence is meant to be.

Evidence, intuitively, provides justification for certain beliefs. One way to think about this justification is by means of changes in the probabilities assigned to the content of those beliefs, a notion implemented in the semantics of McCready and Ogata (2007b), as we have seen. But what kind of probability is at issue? Here, we have several options. First, there is the objective, or classical, probability of φ, defined roughly as the fraction of total possible outcomes in which φ is true:

$$OP(\varphi) = \frac{|\{w|\varphi(w)\}|}{|W|}.$$

Alternatively, we may follow McCready and Ogata (2007b) and Davis et al. (2007) and make use of subjective probabilities: the degree of belief in φ an agent a has, again definable as, where Dox_a is the set of worlds compatible with a's beliefs,

$$SP_a(\varphi) = \frac{|\{w|w \in Dox_a \wedge \varphi(w)\}|}{|Dox_a|}.$$

In a sense, these are externalist and internalist notions of probability. The first is defined purely with respect to the external facts, and the second, with respect to the judgements the speaker has made with respect to belief about those facts (indeed, normatively, on their basis).

It is far from clear that everything that raises subjective probabilities can objectively be considered evidence, because belief does not track truth in all cases. Consequently, in McCready (2010a) I took evidence at a minimum to be knowledge, following authors like Williamson (2000). However, even here questions remain, given the diversity of theories of knowledge. A basic line of demarcation involves internalist and externalist theories. Internalist theories, roughly speaking, are those which take justification to depend exclusively on the state of the agent, i.e. on her mental states; externalist theories conversely put some part of the responsibility for justifying in the external environment. Which kind of theory looks preferable for natural language evidentials? The above observation about subjective probability makes it appear that some sort of externalism, perhaps a very weak one, is warranted, as do observations about the use of evidentials in Gettier-type scenarios (McCready 2008a, 2010a, 2014). In McCready (2014) I argued that the proper notion is a variant of so-called knowledge-level justification (Fantl and McGrath 2009:97). Here, knowledge is defined as (justified) belief that you are justified enough to know, though you may in fact be mistaken. These amount to higher-order beliefs about the reliability of one's own justification.

In light of the above considerations about justification, McCready (2014) proposes that the required notion of evidence involves self-ascription of a rise in objective probability. On this conception, evidence induces an increase in probability via conditionalization in the usual manner, where the relevant probabilities are construed objectively; the epistemic then self-ascribes the property of being in a world in which the required increase occurs. This proposal is meant to be a way to spell out the notion of knowledge-level justification. It accounts for evidential use in a variety of scenarios, involving clear cases of genuine evidence and also cases where the speaker is confused about the status of the putative evidence she has, either for reasons of its truth, its status as a probability-changer, or because of the speaker's lack of awareness of its status as actual evidence. I will assume this notion of evidence in what follows.

Before moving on, it is worth noting one strange possible counterexample. This is the case of Japanese *rashii*. This evidential is a bit special in the context of the Japanese evidential system. Unlike the other Japanese evidentials, *rashii* does not like to embed; it is extremely difficult, if not impossible, to place it in the scope of other operators. The reason is not at all obvious. It does not seem likely that it is based on the kind of evidence sources at issue: those available for *rashii* are pretty much the same as those available for other evidentials, either inferential or reportative. It also does not easily enable modal subordination (for most speakers, though a few do seem to accept it).

(6.20) a. Ookami-ga kita   mitai/yoo   da
        wolf-Nom came MITAI/YOO Cop.Pres
        'A wolf/Some wolves has/have come, it seems.'

  b. # Yatsu(ra)-wa totemo onaka-o   sukaseteiru
     it(they)-Top very   stomach-Acc emptied
     rashii
     RASHII
     'It/they seems/seem to be very hungry.'

A possible explanation for this situation comes from considering the following examples, uttered in a normal situation. These sentences essentially deny skepticism about the speaker's external surroundings, stating that it appears that what the speaker is currently experiencing is (not likely to be) a dream.

(6.21) a. Yume janai   yoo da
        dream Cop.Neg YOO Cop.Pres
        'This seems not to be a dream.'

  b. ?? Yume janai   rashii
        dream Cop.Neg RASHII
        [As above; impossible when read as inferential evidential.]

What is interesting here is that *rashii* is impossible, while the other inferential evidentials are fine (exemplified here by *yoo-da*). Why should this be? Surely we have enough evidence to make the inference to the actuality of the current situation, at least to the degree specified by the Japanese inferential evidentials ($\approx$ 75%), which for present purposes is not high at all. Also, we can take our pick of information sources. So it does not seem that any of the ingredients in the McCready and Ogata (2007b) analysis can be of much help here.

  But the present discussion makes another kind of account available. I have proposed that evidentials require self-ascription of the property of being in a world in which something is true that raises the objective probability of the truth of the evidential prejacent above some particular level. As mentioned, this is a kind of implementation of Fantl and McGrath's knowledge-level justification. In my previous research on this topic (cited above), I assumed that all evidentials use the same notion of justification; this seems prima facie plausible, and is also the strongest available assumption. But what if this assumption is not correct? Abandoning it gives the possibility that different evidentials use different notions of justification: some might require only knowledge-level justification, others something stronger, possibly even much stronger. In particular, some evidential might require (what might be called) *true knowledge*: completely error-free belief in some external fact, so even the possibility of fallible belief is not allowed. Now, supposing that different evidentials can make use of different metasemantic interpretations of knowledge even within a single language, we have an explanation for the impossibility of *rashii* in both of the contexts discussed above.

Suppose that *rashii* requires an extremely strong conception of infallible knowledge. Then, since skeptical scenarios by definition call into question all the speaker's available evidence, there can be no infallible evidence for the falsity of a skeptical scenario, and so the use of *rashii* in antiskeptical cases like (6.21) is ruled out. Similarly, modal subordination depends on the statement of a possibility on the basis of another possibility; perhaps the kind of evidence needed by *rashii* just disallows modal evidence, in that such evidence is too prone to error and subjective judgement. There are many avenues to be explored here, but before going down them additional empirical work is certainly needed to see if the rather drastic step outlined here is actually necessary. This is an interesting project for the future.

6.6 Summary

This chapter has had two purposes. First, it introduced the essential phenomena relating to evidentials as they relate to information transfer (as well as indicating some assumptions about evidence and a few interesting loose ends). In particular, I took the key elements to be the kinds of meaning types evidentials can have and the range of evidence which evidentials can pick out. In the process I introduced several current theories of evidentiality from a pragmatic perspective; the main goal here was to see what current views suggest about information transfer with evidential sentences. The result of this investigation was, first, that any theory of dynamic update with evidentials ought to give a way for processors to assign different levels of confidence to content marked with distinct evidential types, and, second, that those confidence levels should be allowed to shift with changes in context. The next chapter provides a theory which takes these criteria into account.

7

Updating with reliability

The preceding chapter described recent work in formal semantics on evidentials. As I said there, the focus on the typology of evidential systems and the semantics of particular evidentials has resulted in the neglect of some fundamental issues surrounding evidential constructions. The focus of the present chapter is the changes learning evidential sentences induce in the epistemic state of the processor, and how the information conveyed by them is stored and used in information states. Standard theories of information transmission in discourse tell us that asserted content yields a change in common ground via a change in the (public) beliefs of the hearer, though opinions differ when it comes to the precise nature of the belief change mechanism (Groenendijk and Stokhof 1991; Stalnaker 1999; Gunlogson 2003). We also know that update with sentences containing operators like epistemic modals do not change beliefs in the same way: an update with *mightϕ* is not the same as an update with ϕ (Veltman 1996). It is therefore to be expected that evidentially modified sentences would differ in their updating behavior from sentences without evidentials, as already discussed in the last chapter. We have already seen in the last chapter a sophisticated model of how update with evidentials proceeds, which makes the evidential content into a not-at-issue update (Murray 2010). In this chapter I will provide a theory intended to directly address pragmatic aspects of update. Let me begin by briefly reviewing some of the empirical problems at issue.

Consider an update with an instance of *Direct(ϕ)*, where *Direct* is a direct evidential, for example the Cuzco Quechua sentence (7.1) from Faller (2002b). Here the gloss reflects the nonasserted status of the content of the direct evidential.

(7.1)   Para-sha-n-mi
        rain-Prog-3-MI
        'It is raining.' + speaker sees that it is raining

Presumably use of the direct evidential signals a high confidence of the speaker in ϕ, due to its implication of the existence of perceptual evidence (in the present case), which is highly reliable under ordinary circumstances. Given this confidence and general reliability, the hearer ought to feel justified in updating with ϕ, plus whatever the content of the evidential might be. But what about an update with $H(\phi)$, where H is a hearsay evidential, for example (for a minimal pair) the Cuzco Quechua sentence (7.2)?

(7.2)   Para-sha-n-si
        rain-Prog-3-SI
        'It is raining.' + speaker was told that it is raining

One might well wonder what to do with this information, especially given the somewhat misleading gloss: recall that according to Faller, sentences with semantic content ϕ marked with hearsay evidentials do not assert ϕ, but instead only "proffer" it to the hearer. By reasoning parallel to the above, the hearer might be justified in concluding that the speaker's credence in ϕ is not that high, and so that she should not update with ϕ at all. Something similar happens in languages in which evidentials have a different semantic character, such as Japanese, where they act something like epistemic modals (in the case of inferential evidentials), or simple perception sentences (in the case of hearsay evidentials), as in (7.3), so that both (7.3a) and (7.3b) implicate something about the speaker's credence in the proposition that John will come to the party tonight.

(7.3)   a. Jon-wa   konya-no   paatii ni kuru mitai   (da)
           John-Top tonight-Gen party to come MITAI (Cop.Pres)
           'It seems that John will come to the party tonight.'
        b. Jon-wa   konya-no   paatii ni kuru soo-da
           John-Top tonight-Gen party to come SOO-Cop.pres
           'I heard that John will come to the party tonight.'

Note further that, although one might think that inferences like these will not be warranted in languages where use of evidentials is compulsory, due to the unavailability of evidential-free sentences, such is not the case, for two reasons: first, given the existence of evidential hierarchies (Faller 2002b; Aikhenvald 2004) and the corresponding rankings on the reliability of evidence sources, implicatures will necessarily arise, and, second, there are cases in which speakers have choices about which evidential to employ, for example when a piece of hearsay counts as the "best possible grounds" for a proposition in Faller's (2002b) sense. Consider for instance a situation in which we are wondering whether Mary plans to go to the pool tomorrow and have only her word to go on. Use of a hearsay evidential in such circumstances will presumably induce some implicatures different in kind from what arises when hearsay evidence is not the best available.

The question of "update policies" does not exhaust the issues. What is the status of conflicting information across evidentials and evidence sources? If I learn φ on the basis of source e_1, and $\neg\varphi$ on the basis of e_2, what should I believe? For a specific example, consider an agent who observes utterances of $Dir(\phi)$ and $H(\neg\phi)$; should she believe ϕ or not? And, further, since ordinarily such observations are sequential, supposing that one has observed one or the other utterance, what should she do after observing the second? Formally this amounts to the question of whether the information state σ resulting from this sequence of updates should satisfy $\sigma \models \phi$ or $\sigma \models \neg\phi$. In this general outlook, the issue is how to understand the behavior of evidentials with respect to belief revision, in the sense of e.g. Gärdenfors (1988).

The problem is not, of course, limited purely to evidential sentences, insofar as the truth or felicity conditions of such sentences supervene on the presence of different sorts of evidence. Different evidence already yields different degrees of informational reliability. Consequently, we get a general kind of cognitive conflict, which should admit a general solution, and a linguistic phenomenon whose analysis requires a look at more general issues of cognitive modeling. I will thus take as a starting point the general reliability of evidence of different kinds, and then consider how this reliability is reflected in linguistic facts such as evidential hierarchies and in "update policies" of speakers with respect to evidentially marked content.

These questions are the focus of the present chapter. I will first discuss situations in which this or that evidence source seems to "outrank" another: specifically, I will consider (i) discussion of these issues in epistemology with respect to consistency of belief, (ii) evidential hierarchies (an issue returned to in detail in section 8.3), and (iii) initial considerations about the reliability of testimony, which is addressed in much more detail in the subsequent chapter 9. These observations and background can be found in section 7.2. Section 7.3 then provides a formal system and model of information change which can be used to model the findings of section 7.2. The system is a dynamic logic along the lines of Baltag and Smets (2008, 2009). Their logic is designed to model preferential belief revision and the merge of multiple belief states, as in the aggregation models of the social preference literature. Consequently, section 7.3 first exhibits their models—Kripke frames augmented with preference relations over states—and then shows possible aggregation procedures over such models. The strategy used for modeling evidential update is to take such update as a kind of aggregation: agent information states are taken to consist of multiple submodels, each of which is associated with a different evidence sort or class of such sorts, which are then merged according to a lexicographic ordering over evidence sources. Finally, the last part of the current chapter, section 7.4, presents a number of case studies and shows how the system handles familiar dynamic phenomena such as presupposition.

The model of this chapter suffices for a basic understanding what is going on in update, as I will show, but it has a blind spot: it has nothing to say about the *source* of the preference relation over evidential sources. This question is left temporarily unaddressed until the next chapter, where I show that it can be derived from induction over evidential observations, in more or less the same manner as the way in which I proposed making judgements about speaker reliability in the first part of the book.

7.1 What evidence takes precedence?

7.1.1 Perception, inference, and hearsay: reliability

The question of reliability is a familiar one in epistemology. Here, the question of what we can safely claim to know depends in large part on our means of acquiring the relevant information. Different sources of putative knowledge are associated with different possibilities for error and different requirements for avoiding such errors (Audi 2002). This is something we have already had occasion to consider above: that perceptual evidence is normally more reliable than testimonial evidence (for example) is something reflected in the pragmatics of evidentials in such areas as the nature of the best possible grounds for a speech act and evidential hierarchies (which are discussed in the next section). The reliability of particular sources is not always constant, however. For example, inferential processes such as induction can vary in stability: though things may well usually proceed as they have done in the past, the assumption that they will is at best defeasible, as shown (though somewhat artificially) by Nelson Goodman's well-known *grue* case (Goodman 1955). Here, the meaning of an artificial predicate *grue* corresponds to "blue" before a time *t* and then alters to "green" thereafter, which has the effect that what's been learned about the meaning of this predicate stops being reliable.[1] Consequently, one cannot ascribe total reliability to inferential processes, or to beliefs obtained by inferential means; indeed, this reliability can change from case to case. The case of testimony is doubly problematic, since agents can vary in trustworthiness and in the reliability of their own beliefs, as I will discuss in more detail in subsequent chapters.

One would like these differences in reliability to be reflected somehow in the belief states used for semantic analysis, especially insofar as such belief states are supposed to support reasoning, and, especially, decisions about action (Stanley 2005). These issues are usually left implicit, but occasionally play a direct role in linguistic analysis (e.g. Davis 2009; Condoravdi and Lauer 2011). In the models of belief states familiar from work on information transmission in formal semantics and pragmatics (e.g. Groenendijk and Stokhof 1991; Stalnaker 1999; Veltman 1996 for some classical loci), beliefs are not distinguished with respect to their origins: they are homogeneous, each with exactly the same status. In general, update of an agent information state with a proposition takes place simply by intersecting the set of worlds corresponding to the agent's existing beliefs with the set of worlds denoted by the proposition: $\sigma[\varphi] = \{w | w \in \sigma\} \cap \{w | w \in \varphi\}$, where σ is itself the result of intersecting the propositions corresponding to the various beliefs of the agent.[2] However, one might intuitively want a way to keep (more or less) certain pieces of information from possibly chancy ones. Such systems can be found in the literature on formal epistemology. My aim here is to adapt one such logic to the particular needs of evidential reasoning. Before doing so, however, some additional background on evidentials is essential. In particular, we need to consider how evidential use interacts with reliability.

---

[1] This is not of course the only lesson that can be drawn from this case, but it is one interpretation.

[2] At least this is so for the simplest models; as theoretical aims become more complex, the models do as well. Prominent here is the addition of assignment functions to dynamic states to model anaphoric dependencies. I won't have much to say about these issues in the present book, though, so I will put the formal complications they require aside here. See Muskens et al. (1997) for a nice overview of some theories in this area.

7.1.2 Evidentials and evidential hierarchies

A perennial question in the study of evidentials has been the degree to which their semantics overlaps with that of epistemic modals (de Haan 1999; Matthewson et al. 2007; McCready and Ogata 2007b). At this point, I think it is pretty clear that the two are quite distinct, given what we have seen in chapter 6: evidentials simply mark evidence source, while epistemic modals indicate something about the information possessed by the speaker (or some other individual).[3] However, it is easy to see why one might think that evidentials carry a modal meaning. If we know that a particular evidence source is not fully reliable, and a speaker chooses to mark her basis for performing a particular utterance as dependent on such a source, one naturally might conclude that she feels some uncertainty about the information carried by the sentence. This kind of inference is quite similar to the implicatures induced by the use of hearsay evidentials.

How can we get these inferences to arise? It seems clear that they are, at some level, scale-based, in this case something like a scale of reliability. Just as the use of an epistemic modal implicates a low confidence of the speaker given the availability of a modal-free utterance, the use of an evidential that indicates an evidence source with low reliability implicates lack of confidence, given that an evidential marking a higher-reliability source is also available. In the case of epistemic modals, this implicature falls out from the standard semantics: since assertion of ϕ requires, at least, belief in the truth of ϕ (on the usual norm), but, as discussed in chapter 4, the assertion of $\Diamond \phi$ requires only that ϕ not be ruled out by the beliefs of the speaker, the modal statement is weaker, and the proper structure for a scalar implicature arises (Levinson 2000). However, as things stand, there is no corresponding formal analysis available for evidentials, only the intuition that one evidence source is more reliable than another. The analysis developed in this book fills this gap when taken in conjunction with the history models of the first part of the book, in addition to its primary goal of clarifying the process of evidential update. This issue will be explored in detail in chapter 8.

A third area in which orderings are useful is in the analysis of evidential hierarchies, orderings of evidentials by preference for use. Evidential hierarchies are usually used to talk about speaker preferences

---

[3] Though there are respects in which they behave similarly, for instance in the areas that have prompted some to propose a relativist semantics for modals (e.g. Egan 2006; MacFarlane 2011); see McCready (2014) for details and discussion.

in use of evidentials by defining an external, purely linguistic, hierarchy. In essence, if a speaker has multiple sources of evidence for some proposition, she should use the higher-ranked evidential in uttering that proposition. This might not seem immediately relevant to us here, given that evidential hierarchies are usually defined directly in terms of linguistic entities, the evidentials themselves. However, Faller (2002a) observes that evidential hierarchies are best thought of as ordering evidence sources, not evidentials themselves, contra much of the literature (see also Faller 2002b; Aikhenvald 2004 for extensive discussion).

Faller takes the proper basis for this ordering to be reliability of evidence source (see also Willett 1988), providing the interesting example given below. In the scenario she tested with Quechua informants, a farmer, Pedro, sees a fox's footprints, and hears from his neighbor that there was a fox. If the neighbor is reliable, consultants indicated that they preferred to use the hearsay evidential; if the neighbor is a drunk and consequently untrustworthy, the inferential evidential was preferred. We can conclude that the perceived reliability of the evidence source is the main factor in deciding which evidential to use. This is, of course, also something that the analysis proposed in the next section can be used to model, as we will see in the case studies in section 7.4.1.

(7.4)   Atuq-chá wallpa-yki-ta apa-rqa-n
        fox-CHÁ hen-2p-Acc   take-Pst1-3
        'A fox must have taken the hen.' (based on some inference)

(7.5)   Atuq-si wallpa-ta apa-sqa
        fox-SI hen-Acc   take-Pst2-3
        'A fox took the hen.' (I heard)

Such scenarios can easily be duplicated in other languages: I will use Japanese, simply because it has both inferential and hearsay evidentials and so reproduction of a similar case is straightforward. Suppose we have some leftover rice cakes in the refrigerator which I plan to eat for breakfast, but they are gone in the morning. My oldest son claims his younger brother ate them before he left for school, which I had already inferred; I also know that (like any pair of brothers) each sibling takes any chance to get the other one in trouble. I then have a choice between the following utterances:[4]

---

[4] Some may find *rashii* on its hearsay interpretation more natural in (7.6b). Changing out the hearsay evidentials does not alter the force of the example, and the reader is welcome to make the substitution if desired.

(7.6) a. Jinan-ga   mochi-o   tabeta mitai
         second.son-Nom ricecake-Acc ate   MITAI
         'My second son probably ate the rice cake.' (based on some
         inference)

      b. Jinan-ga   mochi-o   tabeta soo da
         second.son-Nom ricecake-Acc ate   SOO Cop.Pres
         'My second son ate the rice cake.' (I heard)

Given that I judge my son's testimony not to be particularly reliable given
the circumstances, I am more likely to use the first sentence, that with
the inferential evidential; intuitively, here, the testimony itself can form
part of the grounds for the inference, so there is also partial subsumption
of evidential source.

   We can now ask a question more directly related to the topic of this
chapter: what happens in a case like the above where, instead of choosing
between the utterance of $Evid_1\varphi$ and $Evid_2\varphi$, we stand in the position of
making similar choices from the interpreter's perspective? Specifically,
suppose that we are faced with observations of $Evid_1\varphi$ and $Evid_2\neg\varphi$; this
means that we must choose between update with φ and update with
$\neg\varphi$, possibly with some degree of uncertainty (more on this later). How
can such a choice be made? The answer seems to relate very closely
to the perceived general reliability of the evidence type picked out by
$Evid_1$ and $Evid_2$, and also (as in the above scenario) to the reliability
of the particular source instantiating the evidence type, if it is known.
I conclude that evidential hierarchies, in the flexible and contextually
dependent sense under consideration, play a key role in both evidential
choice and interpretation.

   Faller (2002a) draws a similar though not identical conclusion from
these examples. Her concern is to make sense of the traditional notion of
an evidential hierarchy, on which it determines, in an invariant manner,
which evidential should be used in a given situation. But this kind of
picture is incompatible with the example above, where Pedro's evidential
choice was dependent on how reliable he gauged his available evidence
sources to be. A view taking evidentials to be placed in an unchanging
linear order cannot say much about this kind of situation. Consequently,
Faller (2002a) opted to introduce a complex graph, where essentially
hearsay and inferential sources are not ordered with respect to each
other:

$$\begin{array}{ccc} & SECOND & \rightarrow & THIRD & \\ & \nearrow & & & \searrow \\ VIS & & & & ASSU \\ & \searrow & & & \nearrow \\ & AUD \rightarrow O\_SENS \rightarrow INF\_RESULT \rightarrow INF\_REASON \end{array}$$

The conclusion here is that it is not trivial to decide how to order particular information sources for the general case. This seems obviously right: different inferences will not be equally reliable, and neither will the testimony of particular individuals. All in all, we can safely conclude that the evidential hierarchy is nothing more than a guide to the use and interpretation of evidentials, not an absolute dictator.

The lesson from the above I take to be that evidential hierarchies are essentially a baseline metric for judging the reliability of a particular information source in context. Without conflicting information, we can follow what evidential hierarchies dictate about preferences.

7.1.3 Summary and requirements

The upshot of this brief discussion is that a theory of information transmission and preferentiality with evidentials requires the following components (as well as any account of evidential hierarchies and variability in hierarchies to be built on such a theory). First, we need a way to integrate information acquired via different evidence sources (so that speakers can make the proper decisions about which evidentials to use) and so that speakers can learn information together with a proper degree of credence, given the relevant information about the source (e.g. via the presence of an evidential construction). Second, we need a picture of how rankings of evidence sources fall out formally. How can a particular source be taken to be reliable or unreliable, and how can sources be ranked with respect to each other? Finally we need a way to give an initial ranking and to alter that ranking when circumstances make it necessary, for example when a neighbor gives up drinking and becomes a reliable source, or as we learn more about the testimonial habits of a new acquaintance. In the next section, I will give a theory which satisfies the first criterion by adapting a dynamic system due to van Benthem (2007) and Baltag and Smets (2009). Chapter 8 will focus on addressing the other two criteria.

7.2 Dynamics of source-based information change

This section introduces a recent dynamic model of information change that complicates standard dynamic models, on which information states simply consist of sets of worlds updated in a purely eliminative manner (e.g. Stalnaker 1999). This is the theory of Baltag and Smets (2008, 2009). On this theory, models are enriched with orderings of worlds, where a world is privileged over another if it is considered more plausible by the agent (meaning that the models are already perspective-dependent). It is possible, in this system, to define updates which alter the ordering relation while keeping the set of worlds constant. As a result, the definition of multiple kinds of update is possible. As we will see in section 7.3, the flexibility of the new system is necessary; there, I will use it to build a theory of evidential update.

The basic models here are known as *conditional doxastic models*, which are set up over *plausibility frames* ($\mathcal{A}$ the set of agents).

(7.7)   **Plausibility frames.**
   A plausibility frame is a multi-agent Kripke frame $\langle S, R_a \rangle_{a \in \mathcal{A}}$ where the accessibility relations R_a are called "plausibility orders" written $\leq_a$, and assumed to be locally connected preorders.[5]

The idea here is that worlds s, t are only related by $\leq_a$ if they are comparable worlds for agent a, in the sense that they are epistemically indistinguishable in terms of hard information, but a has (epistemically based) preferences as to which she believes more likely to be the actual world. A plausibility model is then defined as:

(7.8)   **Plausibility models.**
   A plausibility model is a structure $S = \langle S, \leq_a, [\![.]\!], s_0 \rangle$, i.e. a plausibility frame together with a valuation function $[\![.]\!]: At \mapsto \wp(S)$ and a designated world s_0, the "actual world."

A useful abbreviation is $s \sim_a t$, which holds if s and t are comparable; another is $s \cong_a t$, which indicates that agent a is indifferent (has no preferences) between s and t. The indifference relations $\sim_a$ are equivalence relations. We can understand the set of worlds t which are $\sim_a$-related to s, $\{t \in S | t \sim_a s\}$, written $s(a)$, as a's epistemic alternatives at s; in general these sets can be taken to be information states. Within a set of such epistemic alternatives, the one the agent takes to be most

---

[5] A locally connected preorder is a reflexive and transitive relation such that if $s \leq t$ and $s \leq w$ then either $t \leq w$ or $w \leq t$, and if $t \leq s$ and $w \leq s$ then either $t \leq w$ or $w \leq t$.

plausible is indicated by $s \rightarrow_a t$, which holds iff $t \in s(a)$ & $t \geq_a t'$ for all $t' \in s(a)$; the set of such elements is denoted by $best_a(s(a))$. So these models are set up to indicate the range of epistemic possibilities that an individual countenances, just as with more standard models of belief, but in addition allow the specification of more fine-grained considerations of epistemic plausibility.

As usual in dynamic models of epistemic states, it is crucial to define an update operation for change in belief. Baltag and Smets (2009) distinguish three types of update, all of which only involve alterations in the parts of plausibility models that correspond to plausibility frames, i.e. $\langle \pi_1(S), \pi_2(S) \rangle$. Since update will never (in the analysis of this book at least) affect the interpretation function or distinguished actual world in S-models, I will define updates only over these submodels, which I will denote by σ, following the usual practice. Looking at the varieties of update available should help clarify the role of the $\leq_a$ relation in the model, and the ways in which it extends versions of dynamic semantics familiar to the linguistics community. The three types of update we will examine here correspond to three possible attitudes toward new information.[6] That information can be completely certain; it can be strongly believed, and hence viewed as highly probable, yet still conceivably false; or it can be believed in a more tentative way. What do these different kinds of belief amount to? They can be viewed as indicating the degree of permanency to which the updating agent is willing to commit when eliminating incompatible possibilities. For example, if upon observing your utterance with content φ and choosing to accept that content, I am willing to completely disregard the possibility of $\neg\varphi$ thereafter, then I am performing an update of the first kind; if I am highly unwilling to discard such possibilities, then my update is of the third sort. Baltag and Smets (2009) use the symbols !, $\Uparrow$, $\uparrow$ for the three sorts of update.

The kind of update associated with ordinary public announcements of certain information is familiar from standard dynamic semantics and is denoted "[.]!". It is defined in the usual way from dynamic semantics.[7]

---

[6] Baltag and Smets (2009) state these notions in terms of public announcements and belief within groups. However, they carry over easily to the single-agent case more familiar in the context of work in linguistics. In any case, the single-agent case is only a special case of group belief (for this application, at least).

[7] I write $\sigma[\varphi]!$ for an update of type $!\varphi$ to indicate that the update is an action performed, or even chosen, by the updating agent. The other standard notation used by Baltag and Smets, $\sigma[!\varphi]$, strikes me as obscuring the difference between semantic content and pragmatic action.

(7.9) $\sigma[\varphi]_! = \sigma'$, where $S' = \{s \in S | s \models \varphi\}$ and $s \leq'_a t$ iff $s \leq_a$ t & $s, t \in S'$.[8]

Thus, $[.]_!$-update with φ eliminates worlds in which φ is false, and otherwise does not alter the preference relation $\leq_a$. As we will see, both these points contrast with the other two kinds of update.

The symbol $[.]_{\Uparrow}$ is used to denote update with information coming from a source which the agent trusts to a large extent, but which is not completely certain. It is a kind of lexicographic upgrade: $[.]_{\Uparrow}$-update with φ promotes all φ-worlds over all $\neg\varphi$-worlds, but leaves the set of worlds constant. It can thus be seen as a more tentative kind of update: since the original set of worlds remains, it is still possible to retract belief in φ without performing any nonmonotonic operations on the sets of worlds themselves.

(7.10) $\sigma[\varphi]_{\Uparrow} = \sigma'$, where $S' = S$ and $s \leq'_a t$ iff either (i) $s \notin \varphi$ and $t \in s(a) \cap \varphi$, or (ii) $s \leq_a t$.

The final operation we consider is what I will call *tentative belief*, denoted by $[.]_{\uparrow}$. Here, the only alteration that accepting φ makes is to upgrade the *best* φ-worlds; everything else is left equal. Consequently, this is a very weak notion of upgrade, as only the worlds already viewed as most plausible are considered.

(7.11) $\sigma[\varphi]_{\uparrow} = \sigma'$, where $S' = S$ and $s \leq'_a t$ iff either (i) $t \in best_a(s(a) \cap \varphi)$ or (ii) $s \leq_a t$.

These three kinds of update obviously have many epistemological applications, but they can also be applied to formal pragmatics, though in the present work the first two will be the primary players.

It may be helpful to consider examples of the three kinds of update here. To this end, consider the following single-agent model, with agent a. Here arrows represent plausibility preferences. I write p, q for propositions; this should be understood as expositional shorthand for those propositions true at a world, so, for instance, $\{p, q\}$ describes a world s where p and q are both true.

$$\{p, q\} \xrightarrow{a} \{\neg p, q\} \xleftrightarrow{a} \{p, \neg q\} \xrightarrow{a} \{\neg p, \neg q\}$$

---

[8] I relax Baltag and Smets's condition that φ must be supported (in Veltman's 1996 sense) by the input state, to allow for failed communicative moves that "crash" the discourse. As far as I can see the two give the same result, if we view disallowing update at all to be the same as allowing update resulting in a null or empty information state.

In this model, then, a has not conclusively ruled out either of p or q, but finds them less plausible than their negations; the case where both p and q are false is the most plausible of all. Call this information state σ. What happens in the case of public announcement update of $p \wedge q$, so the case of $\sigma[p \wedge q]_!$? This case is simple: all $\neg p, \neg q$ worlds are eliminated as inconsistent with the newly introduced "hard" information. The result is just the least preferred state of the model, $\{p, q\}$. Thus, the preference relations actually play no role when new information is certain; when one learns something new and incontrovertible, it doesn't matter any longer what one previously considered, tentatively, plausible. Conversely, consider the original model σ again (as it was before $[.]_!$-update with $(p \wedge q)$). Suppose now that we use update of the second sort, but this time with only p, so we have an update of the form $\sigma[p]_\Uparrow$. In this case, the new information state σ' will be

$$\{\neg p, q\} \xrightarrow{a} \{\neg p, \neg q\} \xrightarrow{a} \{p, q\} \xrightarrow{a} \{p, \neg q\}.$$

Thus, in the new state σ' resulting from update, p-worlds are preferred to not-p-worlds, but the initial preferences between q and $\neg q$ worlds are maintained.

To see the application of the "$\uparrow$" modality, we need a new model. Take this one, so that p-worlds are preferred to $\neg p$-worlds, but a is indifferent between q and $\neg q$.

$$\{\neg p, \neg q\} \xrightarrow{a} \{p, q\} \xleftrightarrow{a} \{p, \neg q\}$$

Suppose this model is $[.]_\uparrow$-updated with q, i.e. that we have $\sigma[q]_\uparrow$. We then get

$$\{\neg p, \neg q\} \xrightarrow{a} \{p, \neg q\} \xrightarrow{a} \{p, q\},$$

because the q-worlds which are $\leq_a$-maximal have been upgraded above the other previously $\leq_a$-maximal worlds which did not verify q.

At this point, we are ready to turn to a model of evidential update proper, in the following section.

7.3 Update with hierarchies

As previously mentioned, the strategy for modeling evidential update will be to store information gained from different evidential sources in distinct belief states. An agent's "global belief state" will then be defined by merging these distinct (sub)states via an operation of belief aggregation like those discussed in the previous section. This section makes the strategy explicit. Doing so requires three main decisions. First, what should the operation of update on each evidence-based belief state look like? Using plausibility models widens the options from the traditional, purely eliminative notion of update most often used in linguistic semantics (and pragmatics). I examine this issue in section 7.3.1. Second, what kind of merge operation should be used to combine the belief states obtained through update? Here, again, the options are various, but all can be defined in terms of the parallel and lexicographic merge operations defined later in this section (7.3.2), where I will also indicate what I take to be the best such operation for the purposes of analyzing evidential update. The third decision is more complex in many senses. How should evidence sources be ranked with respect to each other, and are there sources which should not be so ranked? Here we get into a range of interesting empirical and philosophical questions, which will be deferred to later chapters. Before addressing them, I will provide some case studies in section 7.4 to show how the theory is meant to work for the basic cases.

7.3.1 How to update with evidence

Let me first remind the reader of the standard model of update in dynamic semantics. For the propositional case, the model is essentially an eliminative one.[9] If an utterance carries any information new to the hearer, processing that utterance will lead to a "narrowing" of the hearer's set of possibilities to one which verifies the new information. Concretely, update looks like this, for σ a set of worlds s:

(7.12)   **Standard update.**

$$\sigma[\varphi] = \{s \in \sigma \,|\, s \in \varphi\}.$$

This notion of update leaves non-φ worlds out in the cold: once a world is eliminated from an information state σ, it is gone, and can be recovered only via revision (see Gärdenfors 1988). As a result, this kind of update is relatively drastic. The above, as the reader will note, corresponds closely to the $[.]_!$ operation on plausibility models. For our purposes, a different notion of update is required, because we don't want update to be completely impossible to override; we want information acquired

---

[9] The first-order case is of course more complex: the presence of (for example) an indefinite will lead to an extension (or just change, depending on the specific technical instantiation) in the assignment function. This case is somewhat orthogonal to our discussion here and I will consider only the propositional version.

via more reliable evidence sources to be able to "take back" updates that might have been made on a questionable basis. In the previous section, I gave the definitions of two other commonly used update operations, $[.]_\uparrow$ and $[.]_\Uparrow$. Is either of these appropriate for our purposes here?

Recall that, of the two operations, $[.]_\uparrow$ is the operation which makes the smallest change in the original information state (indeed the minimal possible change that intuitively captures change in information), while $[.]_\Uparrow$ makes a somewhat more extensive change. The difference lies in which worlds are pushed higher in the plausibility ordering: for $\sigma[\varphi]_\uparrow$, only the most plausible worlds in σ verifying φ are upgraded, while for $\sigma[\varphi]_\Uparrow$, all φ-worlds are shifted above the $\neg\varphi$-worlds in the relevant part of σ.

The simplest possible model of evidential update might go as follows. Recall that one aspect of such updates is that information marked by an evidential ranked highly in the evidential hierarchy is privileged above information marked by lower-ranked evidentials. This means that, given two evidentials $Evid_1$ and $Evid_2$ such that $Evid_1 \prec Evid_2$ (where "$\prec$" indicates the ranking between evidentials corresponding to the evidential hierarchy, and supposing higher-ranked sources to be preferred, a position that will be justified shortly), we want $\sigma[Evid_1\varphi \wedge Evid_2\neg\varphi]$ to correspond to $\sigma[\neg\varphi]$ instead of $\sigma[\varphi]$. The most obvious way to handle this in the context of plausibility models is to separate evidentials into categories and associate each category with a different style of update. In particular, we might use the following:

(7.13)   **Evidential update (direct version).**

$$\sigma[Evid\varphi] \quad = \quad \begin{cases} \sigma[\varphi]_! \text{ if } e \text{ is judged reliable} \\ \sigma[\varphi]_\Uparrow \text{ if } e \text{ is judged relatively reliable} \\ \sigma[\varphi]_\uparrow \text{ if } e \text{ is judged relatively unreliable} \end{cases}$$

where e is the source associated with $Evid$.

Thus, the updates associated with different evidential classes correspond to the three sorts of update made available by plausibility models. Those evidentials judged as marking reliable information sources induce what amounts to public announcement; information introduced with evidentials marking sources which are relatively reliable, though not completely certain, are associated with lexicographic updates; and evidentials marking weakly reliable sources induce only weak belief in the proposition they introduce. Of course, this kind of account assumes that we have an independently available theory of how to derive evidential hierarchies in context; providing such a theory will be the topic of the next chapter, where I will show that the same kind of mechanism used to make judgements about speaker reliabilities can be used.

This view is simple; in fact, too simple. It makes three possibilities available for evidential update. This is, of course, two more possibilities than we had before, when we considered only nonpreferential updates "[.]¡",[10] so this is an advance; but there are still only three possibilities available, meaning that we cannot distinguish between more than three evidence classes. This situation is therefore perfectly fine for evidential systems with only three (or fewer) alternatives, but as systems become more complex, something more fine-grained will be needed. There are many such systems. Aikhenvald (2004) cites numerous examples of systems marking four distinct types of evidence, and a few with five choices; further, if one wished to use something like the proposed system to analyze utterances marked with evidence source but outside the category of grammaticalized evidentiality, there are obviously very many more than three options. Further, there are clear issues with using [.]¡ for evidential update at all, given that no evidence source is meant to be fully infallible.

A more complex system therefore seems called for. Such a system would not only be useful for the current application. Consider the obvious possible uses of a system that allows preferential update based on evidence sources. One could immediately analyze update with verbs of perception, various kinds of attitudinal constructions, and even perhaps modals and other kinds of sentences which proffer their prejacent content.[11] I won't pursue these applications in the present book, but one would certainly like to have a system flexible enough to handle them. And, given that only making a three-way distinction available would be insufficient to analyze even certain evidential systems, it seems obvious that something more fine-grained is required. I turn to providing such a system in the next section.

7.3.2 Source-based merge

The main idea of my treatment here will be to use a relatively complex notion of information state. On this view, what I will call *global* infor-

---

[10] Note that the situation is similar also for the theory of Murray (2010), who has something like preferential update in her theory (in the context of inquisitive update in the style of Ciardelli and Roelofsen 2011) but doesn't make use of it in the way the present analysis suggests.

[11] An obvious problem for such a move is modal subordination contexts, because we certainly don't want the prejacents of modals to introduce antecedents for anaphora when there is no counterevidence; I will discuss this case in detail in section 7.4.5.

mation states, written σ as usual, will be thought of as comprising sets of information states indexed by different evidence types. Thus, update with content marked as coming from source e_i will induce an update in the corresponding $\sigma_i \in \sigma$. The beliefs of a given agent will be obtained by aggregating these substates in an appropriate manner, which will be one that privileges information stemming from evidence sources which are highly ranked in terms of reliability. I will now spell out the details of how this is done.

Assume the existence of a collection of evidence sources $\mathsf{Source} = \{sensory, hearsay, \dots\}$; this is precisely the same as the collection of source indices used by McCready and Ogata (2007b) in the analysis of Japanese evidentials, as detailed in the last chapter. However, for this application we wish to assume a more general notion of possible sources in order to allow for variation in what a particular language may make available as linguistically relevant evidence sources. For instance, we might suppose that the content of Source for the case of Quechua is $\{direct, inferential, hearsay\}$, thus making the three-way distinction relevant for the characterization of that language's evidential system as described by Faller (2002b), though this style of analysis is a bit reductive; I will give a more adequate treatment in section 7.4.2. We might also wish to allow for a more general view which would not tie the set of available sources so directly to the precise evidentials available in a language. Doing so would allow the analysis of evidence-based reasoning in a more general sense. I will return to this point below.

Given the set of indices Source, we can define information states as having the form $\sigma = \{\sigma_i | i \in \mathsf{Source}\}$. Thus, global states σ are collections of substates, one for each information source made available in the set Source, where each state is, as usual, a collection of worlds together with a plausibility ordering, i.e. a plausibility frame.[12] Update with evidence can then be defined as follows.

(7.14)   **Evidential update (substate).**

$$\sigma[E_i\varphi] = \sigma' \text{ where, for all } \sigma_j \in \sigma, \begin{cases} \sigma'_j = \sigma_j[\varphi] & \text{if } i = j \\ \sigma'_j = \sigma_j & \text{if } i \neq j \end{cases}$$

Thus, when updating with an evidentially marked sentence, the substate corresponding to the evidence sort the evidential marks is updated, and the other substates are left unmodified. The result is a picture of evidential update on which changes in information track their sources,

---

[12] Or, if the reader prefers, points of evaluation, or any other of the usual interpretations.

so an agent retains information about the source of her beliefs in addition to the content of the new beliefs themselves.

There is a gap in this definition, given the current framework. Update is defined in terms of transitions between states: an initial information state σ was mapped to a new one σ' differing from σ only (possibly) in the contents of the substate corresponding to the evidence source of the new information. However, recall that plausibility models make available three distinct kinds of update: public announcements $[.]_!$, plausibility update $[.]_{\Uparrow}$, and tentative belief update $[.]_{\uparrow}$. Which of these three is the appropriate choice for the present task? For reasons to be made clear below, the appropriate operation turns out to be $[.]_{\Uparrow}$. Therefore, in (7.14) and through the rest of the book, $[.]$ should be understood as $[.]_{\Uparrow}$.

The definition in (7.14) has a consequence that some may deem unwelcome. Since all updates are defined on those substates which have the same evidential index as the evidence sort of the sentence which introduces them, update is undefined for propositions which lack such an index. Simple updates of the form $\sigma[\varphi]$ are therefore absent in this system. The result is that all sentences must be introduced with some evidential parameter. Can this be reasonable?

I do not find this consequence particularly alarming. In considering update of information states by actual agents, it is not clear that there ever *are* updates with information which lacks a source; where would such information have come from? Presumably all newly acquired information comes from some observation or other, whether it be in the context of linguistic communication or via learning something about the world from other means, for instance due to the acquisition of sensory evidence. There is a precedent in the linguistic literature, in fact: McCready and Ogata (2007b) treat all observational sentences as introducing evidence in a source-indexed manner, as described in the last chapter. To my knowledge, this aspect of the theory has not been controversial. The present system simply extends this (Quinean) view to the definition of update itself, as opposed to the syntactic definition of well-formed formulas in the logical language. From the perspective of existing analyses of evidentiality, then, the moves made here are not that worrisome.

However, there is an interesting difference here from the McCready and Ogata (2007b) model. On that theory, observations introduce indices via (essentially) a dynamic existential quantifier, and the use of evidentials introduces variables which must be bound by a previously introduced quantifier. Formally, this operation is parallel to the analysis of discourse-bound pronouns in dynamic theories like dynamic predicate logic (Groenendijk and Stokhof 1991). Evidentials are thus used on the basis of a discrete event of evidence acquisition. This looks reasonable, but raises some strange questions. For instance, suppose there are two observations that ϕ on the basis of distinct pieces of auditory evidence (I hear the ship's horn, and I hear its engine). Which is the basis of my subsequent utterance of $\triangle_a^i \phi$ ("The ship has come-mitai.")?[13] The question does not seem answerable or even useful. But on the current proposal, evidential observations simply update the information state corresponding to their use; evidentials can then be taken to simply check for whether the substates of σ corresponding to the right kind of evidence entail the proposition they modify (perhaps together with some other conditions). A specific proposal for some evidentials is made in section 7.4, and detailed further in the formal Appendix. Evidential use thus depends on the whole evidential basis for the use of a proposition, rather than on a particular event of evidence acquisition, and the question raised above does not arise. I take this to be a positive feature of the analysis.

The above seems satisfactory as an initial model of evidence-based update. We have information states consisting of sets of worlds (subinformation states) and preference relations, each indexed with an evidence type, and updates which sync those substates with evidence types. However, as things stand, there is no coherent notion of belief, which means that one of the initial questions I set out to address, that of contradictory evidence, cannot be answered. Suppose that substate $\sigma_1 \models \varphi$ and $\sigma_2 \models \neg\varphi$ (where both are of course substates of the same information state σ). What should we conclude about the global information state: is it true that $\sigma \models \varphi$ or not? At this point we have no way to answer this question. The reason is that we have not made any provision for the combining of content from distinct evidence sources. This is where we begin to have a need for a merge operation: we need a way to aggregate the substates constructed by the definition of evidential update. As we have seen, trying to define evidential update in terms of the three different update methods made available by preference models is a losing proposition. Consequently, the main focus of our discussion

---

[13] Recall that $\triangle_a^i$ is the operator used in McCready and Ogata (2007b) to model inferential evidentials.

here, and of our model of update with evidence and evidentials as a *semantic* rather than a pragmatic issue, will be belief aggregation.

To see the nature of the belief aggregation issue, consider an interesting problem in epistemology, that of belief formation across groups of agents.[14] What can we say about "group beliefs," or what is known by a group (as opposed to the knowledge of the agents that comprise it)? In the simplest case, the answer is obvious in a standard model: we simply take the intersection of the belief sets of all agents, stated in terms of their epistemically accessible worlds:

$$CBT_G = \bigcap_{a \in \mathcal{G}} \{s | s_0 R_a s\},$$

for $G \subseteq \mathcal{A}$, where s_0 is the actual world as before. So CBT_G just takes the beliefs of all the relevant agents, meaning that the resulting set contains only the commonly held beliefs. In the new setting of plausibility models, the situation is similar, but we define common beliefs in terms of the "best alternative" relation. Given the nature of $[.]_\Uparrow$-update, suboptimal worlds remain in the information states, although they are downgraded by the priority relation, so it is not enough to simply consider the accessible worlds. In this system, standard modal operators can be recovered via the following definition:

$$[R]P := \{s \in S | \forall t[sRt \Rightarrow t \in P]\}.$$

Then knowledge (of agent a) can be viewed as the modality defined by $[\sim_a]$, as $[\sim_a]\phi$ means that ϕ holds in all a's epistemic alternatives, and belief corresponds to the relation defined by the optimal alternative relation $[\to_a]$, as $[\to_a]\phi$ indicates truth in all the most plausible of such alternatives. We thus define a belief operator as follows:

(7.15) $\quad \sigma[B_a\phi] = \sigma$ iff $\{s \in \pi_1(\sigma) | s \in best_a(s(a))\} \subseteq \phi$, where $best_a\phi := \{s \in \phi | t \leq_a s$ for all $t \in \phi\}$

As a result, suboptimal states are left out of the computation of beliefs.[15] The definition of common belief follows the same pattern.

---

[14] This discussion is partly based on Baltag and Smets (2009).

[15] The system is flexible enough to model several other kinds of epistemic attitude with a less idealized character, however, which are perhaps more like the attitudes normally held by epistemic agents, such as safe belief, strong belief, and irrevocable knowledge; details can be found in Baltag and Smets (2009). For present purposes, we will not need to worry about this aspect of the system, though it has obvious epistemological relevance, and most likely would be useful in linguistic pragmatics as well.

$$CB_G\phi = \bigcap_{a\in\mathcal{G}} B_a\phi = \{s \in S|best_a(s(a)) \subseteq \phi\}.$$

CB_G is then more or less the same as CBT_G in the new models. The above definitions work well for cases in which the belief sets of the group members are compatible.

However, the situation is not usually this clean. In general, people believe different and incompatible things: they have different background information, which leads to views that can vary in a myriad of unpredictable ways. If the members of a group have incompatible beliefs, the group will have no collective knowledge, by the definitions above. This is the problem of belief aggregation.

Why should we care about belief aggregation in groups in the context of evidentials? Because the formal situation in evidential update can be viewed in a manner parallel to that of belief aggregation for groups of individuals. My strategy for analyzing evidential update is to consider an agent as having not a single belief set, but several, each associated with a different evidence source or set of such sources. Each such set is updated when a new piece of information coming from a source of the relevant kind is learned, as in (7.14). An agent's *global beliefs* are the result of merging the information in her belief sets, and so will be the combination of the information from all evidence sources. A belief aggregation operation is thus clearly necessary. The interesting part of such operations here is how they work to prioritize this or that kind of information over other kinds; merge operations can prioritize the information of different individuals, or treat all equally. For evidential update, this distinction amounts to giving preference to information from certain evidence sources at the expense of others; clearly, this ought to relate to the reliability of such sources. The details of how these computations of reliability are made will be the focus of the next chapter. For the present, let us consider the range of possible merge operations.

What is a merge operation? In the present context of plausibility frames, it is a way of combining sequences of preference relations $\{R_i\}_{1\leq i\leq n}$ into a single such relation R. In terms of agent-dependent plausibility relations, it takes the plausibility relations of multiple agents and transforms them into a single relation for the group. In the following, I will apply merge relations to evidence-based plausibilities and show how they can yield a single plausibility relation for an agent. But which relation to use?

The basic operations for combining preferences are "parallel merge" and "lexicographic merge." As shown by Andreka et al. (2002), any merge procedure can be defined by composing these two operations. Consequently, for the moment I will restrict myself to defining parallel and lexicographic merge operations, leaving the details of what kind of merge is needed for the evidential application until afterward, where we can consider the empirical details of how a global plausibility relation should follow from the "local" ones resulting from different kinds of evidence. Parallel merge gives equal weight to each merged relation. In terms of group preferences, it is a fully "democratic" system. If any two agents disagree on any pair, that pair is left out of the result of merge. We thus get the following definition, where "$\overline{\wedge}_{a \in G} R_a$" denotes the parallel merge of the belief states of all agents in group G.

(7.16)   **Parallel merge.**

$$\overline{\wedge}_{a \in G} R_a := \bigcap_{a \in G} R_a.$$

Clearly, this operation by itself won't do to define the action of evidentiary reasoning. It leaves only those pairs of worlds on which the plausibility relations of all agents agree. In a setting where agents are construed as corresponding to evidence sources, this operation will obviously not do the required work, for not all evidence is equally reliable, as we have seen, and indeed language makes use of evidential hierarchies, which are precisely a way to privilege some information sources over others. Stated in terms of belief aggregation, we need to give some evidence sources precedence over others in the merging process.[16] Parallel merge lacks this flexibility, given that it treats the "opinions" of all "agents" as having equal weight. But this operation can be useful in combination with the other fundamental merge operation, lexicographic merge.

Lexicographic merge introduces priorities among individuals. Suppose that a group of agents are not all created equal in their epistemic status, and that the hierarchical relations holding between them are clear, as is the case with the model of evidential information to be developed. In this case, use of lexicographic merge is appropriate. This operation assumes the existence of a total ordering on agents called a priority order. The epistemic priorities of agents ranked higher in

---

[16] Aggregation procedures more generally are used in analyzing voting and the preferences of groups. In this setting, the above amounts to saying that the opinions of certain individuals must be given precedence over others, even up to dictatorship (Nitzan 2009).

the ordering always take precedence over those of lower agents. More specifically, given agents a, b such that $a \succ b$, the merge operation gives the following: first a's preferences are adopted, and when two worlds are unranked by a, b's preferences determine the final ordering. Still, if a finds two worlds incomparable (so that they are not epistemically indistinguishable for a, and so already lack the same epistemic status with respect to the whole group), the group leaves them incomparable. We get the following formal definition.

(7.17) **Lexicographic merge.**

$$R_{a \cap b} := R_a^{\prec} \cup (R_a^{\widetilde{=}} \cap R_b) = R_a^{\prec} \cup (R_a \cap R_b) = R_a \cap (R_a^{\prec} \cup R_b)$$

Hereafter I will write $A \cap B$ for the result of applying this operation to information states A and B. In the evidential setting, use of this operation by itself means that information from higher-ranked evidence sources always take precedence, in a pure way, over information from lower-ranked sources. This seems to be much closer to the right view of relations between evidential types, and approaches what we see with evidential hierarchies.

As we've seen, of the two basic merge operations, parallel merge won't do; but clearly, lexicographic merge has the resources needed for a proper analysis of evidential update: it allows certain epistemic sources to take priority above others, but leaves preferences which are undetermined by higher-ranked "agents" to be set by those of lower rank. Thus lexicographic merge appears to be a suitable operation for unifying evidential belief states, at least given certain assumptions. In what follows, I will make use of lexicographic merge defined on substates σ_i of global information states σ in my analysis of evidential update.

The main assumption required, in my view, involves the relation between the various kinds of evidence-based belief and notions of "hard" information, which is non-defeasible and not subject to revision, and "soft" information, which is consistently defeasible given the right counterevidence. The distinction roughly corresponds to the difference between knowledge and belief as it is usually construed. In lexicographic merge, the output of the merge operation depends on the soft information present in the states: the plausibility rankings of higher-rated agents (or, here, evidence sources) always outranks that of other agents. Baltag and Smets (2009) give the example of a professor and student (on the assumption that the topic of discussion is some sort of academic issue). If it can be the case that lower-ranked agents/sources have access to hard information which should not be overruled by the higher-ranked agent, lexicographic merge is inappropriate. Here, one can introduce further options, for instance the relative priority merge discussed by Baltag and Smets. However, for the present application it is not clear that there ever *is* any hard information. Evidence is always defeasible; evidence-based knowledge is always, at some level, fallible. Therefore I will take lexicographic merge to be sufficient for the current application.[17]

Let us first consider public announcements. Suppose that we are interested in understanding how information coming from this or that evidence source can be privileged above information coming from some other. What kind of update must we use? Suppose that we have available only the standard kind of update in dynamic semantics, that in (7.12), denoted in preference models by "[.]!". It is not easy—and perhaps not even possible—to define the kinds of merge relations we are interested in for present applications across sets or sequences of information states obtained only by such models. For instance, we might try something like this: suppose that $\sigma_1 \leq \sigma_2$, and each just consist of a set of states. Then there are three cases to consider. Suppose that $\sigma_1 \supset \sigma_2$. Then, denoting the merge as $\triangledown(\sigma_1, \sigma_2)$, we have $\triangledown(\sigma_1, \sigma_2) = \sigma_2$. The same will of course hold if $\sigma_1 = \sigma_2$. In the third case, we have $\sigma_1 \subset \sigma_2$. What now would we like to say about the relations between the two? Presumably, again, we would like σ_2 to be the output of the merge operation. But then we have a very unsubtle picture of the relations holding between information obtained from different evidence sources, or information marked by different evidentials. Concretely, the lower-ranked source can never play any substantial role in influencing the output of the merge operation. This is similar to the parallel merge operation discussed above. Reasons much like these prompted development of plausibility models in the first place.

Given these considerations, we are left with the update operations $[.]_{\uparrow}$ and $[.]_{\Uparrow}$. These are the only possibilities if we want to make general use of lexicographic merge as a means of unifying the information provided by various evidence sources. But as previously mentioned,

---

[17] If there turns out to be good reason to privilege certain kinds of information provided by certain evidence sources, one can easily alter the picture. For instance, one could use priority merge, where hard information is retained:

$$R_{a \times b} := (R_a^{\lessgtr} \cap R_b^{\frown}) \cup (R_a^{\widetilde{=}} \cap R_b) = R_a \cap R_b^{\frown} \cap (R_a^{\lessgtr} \cup R_b).$$

But for present purposes I will not make use of this operation or any other of the many available possibilities.

$[.]_\uparrow$ is extremely weak: it only reorders those worlds which are already deemed maximally plausible by an agent. For a general analysis of update, we need something stronger. I therefore will make use of $[.]_{\Uparrow}$ as a general update operation, as already mentioned above.

Let us see how this merge operation applies to a few simple cases. First, take a case in which two agents have conflicting information. Suppose that agent a finds p more plausible than its negation, and b feels the opposite, but both agents agree that not-q is more plausible than q. This situation is described by the following model.

$$\{p, q\} \overset{a}{\underset{b}{\rightrightarrows}} \{p, \neg q\} \overset{a}{\underset{b}{\leftrightarrows}} \{\neg p, \neg q\}$$

Now suppose that we wish to merge the information states of these two agents using the operation of lexicographic merge given that $a \succ b$. What will be the result? For this model, $R_a \sqcap R_b$ will be

$$\{p, q\} \rightarrow \{p, \neg q\} \leftarrow \{\neg p, \neg q\}$$

because, since here a takes precedence over b, the plausibility ranking of a is retained when the rankings of the two agents conflict, as they did here for the choice between p and $\neg p$. This is a situation in which the information of one agent overrides that of the other. Of course, the example works in the identical way if we view a and b as evidence sources instead of individuals: here, the higher ranking of a indicates that it is a more reliable source of information, and its information can override that provided by b. Again, the higher ranked of a and b determines which belief will survive in the global state.

Let's now consider a slightly different situation: when one agent has information that determines something the other agent lacks knowledge about. Suppose we have two agents, as follows:

$$\boxed{\{\neg p, \neg q\} \overset{a}{\leftarrow} \{p, \neg q\} \overset{a}{\longleftrightarrow} \{p, q\}} \, , \, \boxed{\{\neg p, \neg q\} \overset{b}{\leftarrow} \{p, \neg q\} \overset{b}{\leftarrow} \{p, q\}}$$

Here a and b agree on the relative plausibility of p and $\neg p$, but a is indifferent between q and $\neg q$, while b prefers the latter. After merging the plausibility relations of these two agents (where again $a \succ b$), we get

$$\{\neg p, \neg q\} \leftarrow \{p, \neg q\} \leftarrow \{p, q\},$$

as, since the higher-ranked agent a was indifferent between q and $\neg q$, b's preferences determined the case. For the evidential interpretation, this is a situation in which the higher-ranked source of information was silent on the issue of whether q holds, so the information derived from source b was allowed to decide the issue.

We are now finally in a position to give a means of understanding what happens when evidence sources conflict in the present system. The first thing to observe is that it must be defined in terms of the global information states derived from all the substates of σ by lexicographic merge, for that is the level at which conflicts in source-based information are resolved. It is therefore necessary first to define what I will call *total* information states, which I will write as σ_T. The basic idea is to recursively merge each pair of substates of the global state, which, given the use of lexicographic merge, will retain the ordering over worlds associated with the highest-ranked source at the end of the process. The formal procedure by which this recursive update takes place is described in the Appendix. This operation derives total information states σ_T from the substates σ_i of the global information state σ. Its intuitive basis will be explained in chapter 9, after I present some additional background about testimonial evidence. Note that σ includes only substates such that the agent has acquired some information from the evidence source associated with that substate. The reason for this is that I will later propose that each testimonial agent is associated with a unique substate, opening the door to a potential proliferation of substates. Restricting σ to substates which the agent has made use of is meant to rule out the necessity of having substates for all possible testimonial agents.

At this point, the theory of evidential update is in place. Information states consist of sets of substates, each associated with an evidence source; these sources are ranked by a priority ordering based on their reliability. The substates can be unified to yield a total information state over which attitudes such as belief can be defined. The next section shows the application of the theory and discusses some of its relationships to more standard dynamic theories.

7.4 Case studies

We are now in a position to consider how the system can be applied to the particular analysis of evidentials. I will begin with a simple case of communication on an evidential basis, and then work through an example of an evidential system, that of Quechua. These two cases together will show how the system will work. I then turn to an instance of an evidential hierarchy. Here, I will introduce a ranking on evidence sources, which will correspond to a priority ranking for evidential merge; I will conclude by showing how this ranking can be used to model how speakers make choices about evidential use, and how interpreters can select between conflicting pieces of information on the basis of their evidential indices.

7.4.1 Communication with evidentials

My analysis of evidential update and choice is intended as a model of the whole process of information acquisition, transmission, and processing. The first part of the process is the acquisition of the relevant information by the speaker. This information comes from a particular information source; we can understand the result of observation of some external phenomenon as inducing update of the speaker's information state with a proposition of the form $E_i\varphi$ (defined as in McCready and Ogata 2007b), where i indicates the source of information. This will result in update of the substate σ_i of the speaker's global information state σ which, in the absence of conflicting information from higher-ranked sources, will induce belief in φ. Let us now suppose that the speaker wishes to communicate φ. Given a language with grammaticalized evidentiality, this requires a choice of evidential; in a language with optional evidential expressions, the speaker may choose to use one of these. The choice of which expression to select will be dictated by which substate of σ was originally updated with φ. Supposing that the source index of $E_i\varphi$ mapped directly to a substate σ_i, the evidential corresponding to i-type evidence should be chosen. This observation further supports the present analysis: without substates corresponding to the various evidence types, it's not clear how a speaker could choose an evidential at all.[18] Then, for the interpreter, the observation of a sentence of the form $Evid_i\varphi$ induces update of the relevant substate again. On my analysis, then, the mapping between speaker evidence source and hearer evidence type is a highly transparent one.[19]

---

[18] There are other analytical possibilities, but it's not clear how distinct they really are from the current one. For instance, one might take each bit of learned information to be indexed with metainformation about how it was acquired. Such metacontent would not play a role in update except to help adjudicate in cases of conflict. But such a system looks somewhat messy and hard to work with; my proposal is, I think, much cleaner.

[19] The directness of this mapping will be relaxed in chapter 9, on the basis of the observation that an evidential sentence does not only indicate evidence of some type, but is also itself a piece of testimonial evidence. So the current analysis is only preliminary. In chapter 9, I will adopt a more complex picture on which each testimonial agent is associated with a distinct substate σ_a which is itself complex; update with evidentially

Let's consider one example in detail. Take the case of agents a and b, speakers of a language with obligatory evidentials, who are interested in what is happening with the weather. Suppose that a, on looking out the window, observes that it is raining; it is cloudy, everything is wet, and there are drops of water falling from the sky. This is visual evidence. Consequently, a's information state is updated with a proposition of the form in (7.18).

(7.18) $E_{visual}rain$

This update results in an update to the substate $\sigma_{visual} \in \sigma^a$, the global information state of agent a, yielding $\sigma_{visual}[rain]_\Uparrow$. The output of this update, σ'_{visual}, contains the same worlds as σ_{visual} but upgrades those worlds at which $rain$ is true above those at which it is not (leaving other aspects of the preference relation unchanged). Supposing that visual evidence is highly ranked in the evidential ordering, which it will be in nearly all normal contexts, this upgrading of $rain$-worlds will carry over to the global information state σ.

Concretely, suppose that σ_{visual} contains three worlds $= \{w_1, w_2, w_3\}$, that $w_1 \prec_a w_2 \prec_a w_3$, and that $[\![rain]\!] = \{w_1, w_2\}$. Then $\sigma'_{visual} = \sigma_{visual}[rain]_\Uparrow \{w_1, w_2, w_3\}$, as before, but the new ordering on these worlds is $w_3 \prec_a w_1 \prec_a w_2$, as the world w_3 where $rain$ is false is downgraded to fall below the $rain$-worlds w_1 and w_2, whose original ordering is retained.

Now suppose that b is in the room, and that a wishes to communicate to b that it is raining outside. Let us assume the existence of the following pragmatic principle.

(7.19)   **Strongest evidence principle.**
When uttering a sentence with propositional content ϕ, use the evidential associated with the highest-ranked evidential source i such that $\sigma_i \models \phi$.

There are two key aspects to this principle. First, it requires use of an evidential associated with a source which is associated with an information substate which entails the evidential prejacent. This already severely limits the possibilities for evidential choice. The options are further restricted by requiring use of the evidential related to the highest-ranked

---

marked sentences of the form $E_i\varphi$ uttered by agent a will then update the substate σ_a^i which is, itself, a substate of σ_a.

such substate.[20] Plainly speakers follow something like this principle and it does no harm to encode it explicitly, though it likely follows from something like Gricean Quantity for evidentials and is thus limited to cooperative speakers. Extensive discussion of this issue can be found in Faller (2012).

Given the **Strongest evidence principle**, a will be required to use the evidential which is associated with the highest-ranked information source which has provided the information that it is raining. Here, by assumption, that source is visual evidence; the result is that a will need to use whatever evidential the language provides for visual evidence. Call this evidential $Evid_{visual}$. So, given the presence of obligatory evidentials and the principle in (7.19), a must utter $Evid_{visual}rain$ in order to communicate that it is raining.

What will b do after observing this utterance? On the supposition that b accepts the proposed update, he will perform the update $\sigma_i[rain]$ for some appropriate σ_i. (Recall that the option of directly updating the global information state is not available in the current system.) What σ_i should be chosen? Presumably the one associated with the sort of evidence the speaker a is indicating herself to have, in this case visual evidence: that means σ_{visual}. The status of this choice seems rather more semantic than that found in the evidential choice process; I therefore find it intuitive to realize it as a semantic criterion for coherent communication. In fact, this criterion nearly follows from the definition of evidential update I provided in (7.14). According to that definition, updating with $E_i\varphi$ induces a change in the substate σ_i corresponding to the evidence type. But, if a speaker is cooperative, then her observation of $E_i\varphi$ should cause her to use $Evid_i\varphi$, given the obvious assumption about sincerity, already codified in (7.19); this means that it is reasonable for an interpreter to use the following update principle:

(7.20) **Evidential to evidence.**
   If a speaker uses $Evid_i\varphi$, assume that she has E_i-type evidence for φ.

This principle provides a bridge from evidential expressions to evidential facts on the basis of considerations of sincerity. Given that principle,

---

[20] What if there is more than one such state—i.e. if ϕ is entailed by mutually unranked substates? Here we have several options. The most obvious is to allow free selection between them. Another is to implement something corresponding to the Limit Assumption for counterfactuals of Lewis (1973), and assume that one source is always ranked more highly. For the present, I will choose the first; we will return to the issue of ranking in the next chapter.

together with the assumption that learning $E_i\varphi$ causes update of σ_i, the agent b will update σ_{visual} with the proposition *rain*; assuming that b's visually acquired information is the same as that of a, the result will be that their visual evidence information substates mirror one another, which is what we want, at least for now; as I mentioned before, the analysis of testimony will be elaborated in chapter 9. Of course, the extent to which the **Evidential to evidence** principle should be acceded to depends on the extent to which the speaker is judged trustworthy. This means that sincerity considerations play a key role in evidential update as well; this issue will be discussed in detail in the next chapter.

7.4.2 Example: a three-evidential system

The above example of a and b of course simplifies the realities of evidential communication in several ways. One obvious one is the assumption that there is an evidential specified exclusively for visual evidence. In general, there will be no such one-to-one mapping between evidence sources and evidentials; in fact, the most complex evidential systems known make only a five-way grammatical distinction (Aikhenvald 2004), which obviously is not enough to distinguish all the possible evidence sources which are actually available. Let's now consider a slightly less schematic example: a case study of an actual evidential system.

The case we will make use of is that of (Cuzco) Quechua as described by Faller (2002b). Recall that Quechua has three evidentials: a direct evidential *-mi*, an inferential evidential *-chá*, and a reportative evidential *-si*. In what follows I will write these *Dir*, *Inf*, and *Rep*. How can this system be modeled in the current framework?[21]

The answer is more or less straightforward, though some complications arise that didn't for the a and b case. First, each evidential must be associated with a source type or set of source types. This requires a more explicit set of source types. I will assume that the following are universally available:

(7.21) **Available source types.**
Source $= \{tact, aud, internal\_sens, vis, other\_sens, hearsay,$
$quot, conc\_inf, inf, gen\_kn\}$

---

[21] I should note again that I will not be paying much attention to the compositional semantics of evidentials in the present work, as my focus is more pragmatic here. For compositional treatments and discussion of meaning types, the reader might consult Faller (2002b); McCready (2008a); Murray (2010); McCready (2010c), among others.

I take it that most of these sources are obvious, but some likely are not. The evidence types listed fall into several classes. The first are those which we generally might consider sensory evidence: *tact* labels evidence acquired through tactile means, *aud* evidence from auditory observations, *internal_sens* evidence stemming from non-tactile internal sensations, *vis* visual evidence, and *other_sens* other kinds of sensory evidence. Several kinds of reportative evidence are distinguished: *hearsay* marks evidence acquired through testimony where no particular source is indicated, while *quot* indicates testimonial evidence with a specified source. Some evidential languages have a grammatical distinction between these two types. Finally, there are several kinds of "other" evidence, a kind of catch-all category: here we find evidence acquired purely through inference *inf*, and inferential knowledge acquired via inference about concrete and observable facts *conc_inf* (also a distinction made by some languages). Lastly, we have *gen_kn*, general world knowledge, understood as those things which are generally believed to be true as a part of social belief. Wittgenstein's (1991) example of the world being more than 100 years old falls into this category. It will be convenient in what follows to codify these informal distinctions. I believe that these source types are sufficient to model what we find in the world's languages; if not, the set of available sources is easily modified.

With this background in place, we can turn to a characterization of the Quechua system. For present purposes, we can take *Dir* to be associated with sensory evidence of all kinds, *Inf* with inferential evidence, and *Rep* with evidence coming from testimony, as in (7.22).

(7.22)   a. $Dir = \{tact, aud, internal\_sens, vis, other\_sens\}$
         b. $Inf = \{conc\_inf, inf, gen\_kn\}$
         c. $Rep = \{hearsay, quot\}$

We then get these appropriateness conditions for use of the Quechua evidentials, as a first approximation:

(7.23)   a. $\textit{-mi}\varphi$: $\sigma_i \models \varphi$, where $i \in Dir$
         b. $\textit{-chá}\varphi$: $\sigma_i \models \varphi$, where $i \in Inf$
         c. $\textit{-si}\varphi$: $\sigma_i \models \varphi$, where $i \in Rep$

The above captures the basic (pragmatic) behavior of the Quechua evidentials. Given observation of their prejacents via the appropriate evidence source, they can appropriately be used. Of course, the above fails to capture some of the complexity of their meanings, especially as regards their interactions with context. For instance, as mentioned previously, the direct evidential can be used when the only available evidence is reportative if such evidence would be the best available; if the prejacent proposition is not verifiable by sensory means, as with futurate propositions, the direct can still be used. If I hear Juan say that he is going to fix his bicycle tire this afternoon, I can report this using the direct, because I could not have had better reason to believe that he is going to fix his tire. This sort of variation in best possible grounds is something that likely can be captured by the notion of reliability; I will have more to say about this in a moment, and much more in the following chapter, especially in section 8.3.

There is an obvious complication that arises from the bundling of information sources into general categories shown in (7.22). It raises a question about what substate is to be updated after observation of a given evidential. For example (taking the simplest case), observation of *Inf φ* leaves it underspecified whether the inference is made on the basis of concrete (sensory) observations, as in *conc_inf*, general nonspecific considerations (*inf*), or general knowledge of people in the relevant social group (*gen_kn*). Each of these sources is associated with a different substate. But since it's not known precisely what kind of evidence is at issue, how is the hearer to update with the content of the evidential sentence?

The simplest way to handle this situation is to allow update of *all* substates associated with the general evidence type. This is the route I will follow. For this purpose, we need to modify the definition of evidential update to account for cases where more than one type of evidence is at issue. Note that application of this clause won't be limited to linguistically introduced evidentials; frequently when observing events one simultaneously acquires evidence of multiple kinds, and it seems superfluous to need to represent each of these individually as an observation sentence with a single index.[22] The required definition follows; here '*I*' is a set of evidential indices.

(7.24) **Evidential update with multiple sources.**

$$\sigma\,[\mathsf{E}_I\varphi] = \sigma' \text{ where, for all } \sigma_j \in \sigma, \begin{cases} \sigma_j' = \sigma_j[\varphi] & \text{if } j \in I \\ \sigma_j' = \sigma_j & \text{if } j \notin I \end{cases}$$

---

[22] While not strictly necessary for non-evidentials, this is certainly useful; lacking this capacity is a shortcoming of the McCready–Ogata system.

Thus, in order to handle cases of underspecification, we require only a clause that distributes over evidence sources when such sources are plural.

7.4.3 Updating with conflicting evidence

Another main goal of the present analysis has been to give a pragmatically reasonable method of deciding between incompatible updates of evidentially marked information. We now have the resources to do so. Here again is our familiar scenario. Suppose that an agent is faced with a sequence of observations $Evid_i\phi$; $Evid_j\neg\phi$ (where ";" is dynamic conjunction as usual). Should the agent believe ϕ or $\neg\phi$?

The first thing to observe is that, here, when we talk about belief, we mean *global* belief. The agent can consistently update with the evidential sentences in the usual way, because they affect only the substates σ_i and σ_j. The problem of incompatible information, when it comes in the form of sentences marked with evidentials, is a problem about aggregation of incompatible information states, not a problem of updating with incompatible information. This observation is the key to my solution.

After sequentially updating with the two propositions just mentioned, we will have $\sigma_i' = \sigma_i[\phi]_\Uparrow$ and $\sigma_j'' = \sigma_j'[\neg\phi]_\Uparrow$, both substates of σ''. What now happens to the global state σ''? We can query as follows: $\sigma''[?\phi]$, which is a test on the global information state for the truth of ϕ. Such a test can be defined in the present system as a check to see whether the set of $\leq_a$-maximal worlds in σ supports φ.

$$(7.25) \quad \sigma[?\varphi] = \begin{cases} \sigma & \text{if } \{s \in \sigma \,|\, best_a s(a)\} \subseteq \varphi \\ \varnothing & \text{else} \end{cases}$$

Note the close resemblance to the definition of global belief in this system. Whether the test $?\phi$ is successful for the present example will depend entirely on the priority ordering. If $i \succ j$, then ϕ-worlds will be upgraded above $\neg\phi$-worlds in the global state, so that the query $?\phi$ will be successful. If $j \succ i$, $\neg\phi$-worlds will be globally upgraded, and the query will fail. In other words, which of the contradictory propositions the agent comes to believe will depend on the priority given to the information sources from which those propositions come, which in turn will (given the analysis in the next chapter) depend on their perceived reliability.

Let us look at a concrete example. Suppose we take a case from Japanese, let us say the inferential *mitai* followed by reportative *soo-da*;

these correspond roughly to the categories *Inf* and *Rep*. Thus suppose that we have an agent who observes a discourse of the form *Inf* ϕ; . . . ; *Rep* $\neg\phi$, so a discourse with a *mitai* sentence with prejacent ϕ followed by a *soo-da* sentence whose prejacent is the negation of ϕ. (Note that this is intuitively consistent; it frequently happens that one sees some event happen but later hears or reads that it has not in fact happened, or encounters a claim that the event took place in a different way than it actually did.) For example, we might have the discourse in (7.26).[23]

(7.26) a. Ame-ga   furu mitai
           rain-Nom fall   MITAI
           'It seems as if it'll rain.'

        b. Demo Taro niyoruto   fur-anai soo-da
           but   Taro according.to rain-Neg SOO-DA
           'But according to Taro it won't rain.'

Let's assume that (like the Quechua case from the previous section) *mitai* is associated with sources in the category *Inf* and *soo-da* with sources in the category *Rep*. This claim is actually a simplification of the case of *mitai*, which has a slightly more limited distribution with respect to possible sources; details will be suppressed here, but can be found in Aoki (1986) and McCready and Ogata (2007b). After update of the input state σ with the first of these two sentences, distributive update over states related to *Inf*-sources will give a new state σ', where $\sigma'_{gen\_kn} = \sigma_{gen\_kn}[rain], \sigma'_{inf} = \sigma_{inf}[rain]$, and $\sigma'_{conc\_inf} = \sigma_{conc\_inf}[rain]$, while all other substates of σ are unaltered in σ'.[24] Correspondingly, update with the second sentence will yield modifications of the states σ_{rpt} and σ_{quot}, yielding $\sigma'_{rpt}[\neg rain]$ and $\sigma'_{quot}[\neg rain]$, respectively. To my knowledge, no discussion of evidential hierarchies in Japanese is to be found in the literature. But it seems reasonable to assume that one's inferences supersede what one has merely heard from others in the general case, though obviously this can be overridden by context in the usual way.

---

[23] I've added the source of the report here to make the discourse sound more natural; without some intervening material it's difficult to construct a coherent example.

[24] This result is slightly counterintuitive; why should σ_{gen_kn} be altered by the observation that it appears likely to rain? If this is indeed problematic (at the moment I cannot see an empirical problem which arises, but there might be some), then the problem is the result of the update mechanism proposed in (7.14), where updates with multiple possible sources were just taken to update all of the corresponding substates. It might be that a more fine-grained mechanism would be desirable here, but I will leave things as they are for the moment.

I thus will take *Inf* $\succ$ *Rep* to hold for the Japanese case. Given this, updates to the states associated with *Inf* will take precedence over updates to *Rep*-states when those states fail to correspond. The result is that the agent observing the discourse in (7.26) will globally believe that it will rain, rather than the opposite.

We have now seen how the analysis applies to update with evidential sentences. The reader will have noted that it has obvious application to other situations as well. The rankings corresponding (at first approximation) to evidential hierarchies allow interpreters to select between incompatible updates when evidentials are used. But, if I am right in following the view of Faller (2002a), that evidential hierarchies simply correspond to perceptions about the reliability of evidence sources, then the proposed system can obviously be used for source-based update in general. Above, we have considered a case from Quechua in which a speaker had to decide between incompatible updates, ϕ and $\neg\phi$, stemming from interpreting evidential sentences with a direct and with an inferential evidential. On the assumption that direct evidence is more reliable than inference, as seems ordinarily plausible, the interpreter comes to globally believe the prejacent of the direct evidential; plainly, the same should happen if the same individual observed ϕ but simultaneously inferred $\neg\phi$ on the basis of some other considerations. In my account, this correspondence is captured by the relationship between $E_i\varphi$-updates and $Evid_i\varphi$-updates imposed by the principles of **Strongest evidence** and **Evidential to evidence** in (7.19) and (7.20).

Of course, my proposal does not represent the only possible analysis; one could, for example, understand evidential choice as dictated by what the speaker's information state entails about how the information was acquired. For instance, one might take an update of the form $E_i\varphi$ to cause belief in φ, but as a side effect to also cause the speaker to believe $E_i\varphi$ itself. One then might take these kind of "dual beliefs" to enter directly into the process of belief revision; externally imposing an ordering on what beliefs an agent might be willing to give up could be made to impact how a consistent belief set is arrived at. There are close connections here with the *epistemic entrenchment* approach to belief revision, where beliefs are ordered in some way which impacts what is given up when revision must take place (see e.g. Gärdenfors 1992; Hansson 2011 for details). On a view like this one, the choice between conflicting information from distinct evidence sources depends on external decisions about the reliability of some source. However, I think that my proposal is cleaner, in two senses. First, for the basic case at least, we don't have to resort to nonmonotonic revision operations, and the representation is, in some sense at least, simpler, in that there is no need for duplication of information. Second, there is no point in the update process at which information must be given up; despite possibly not globally believing in some proposition introduced by low-priority evidence, the fact that it was introduced remains, and can be returned to if the situation warrants. This property might or might not be retained in an entrenchment-style system, depending on the precise implementation. I will not pursue further the details of how such a system could be designed.

7.4.4 Epistemic evidentials

The proposals of the preceding sections have been concerned mostly with the direct observation of evidence. Update with evidentially decorated sentences has been treated on a par with such observations. As the reader may have noted, though, this is sensible only for evidentials whose content is independent of the propositional content of the sentence. When the evidential serves merely to indicate the basis for assertion of a proposition, it makes sense to treat it as an instruction to update the substate of the global state corresponding to the evidence type with that proposition. However, to use the terminology of Murray (2010), only illocutionary evidentials are of this type, and indeed only a subclass of them: the ones which don't make any changes in the content the speech act manipulates. As Faller has shown, evidentials such as the Quechua inferential *chá* alter the propositional content of the assertion in addition to indicating its evidential basis. The Japanese evidentials studied in McCready and Ogata (2007b) are also of this type, as are epistemic evidentials more generally. How should such evidentials be integrated into the current theory?

My discussion here will be focused on the Japanese inferential evidentials. Let us take *mitai* as a characteristic test case. This evidential requires evidence which (together with background assumptions) allows the tentative conclusion of its prejacent. Thus $mitai\varphi$ is appropriate if one can conclude φ on the basis of some piece of evidence ψ. However, such conclusions cannot be definitive; as McCready and Ogata (2007b) show, if ψ allows the conclusion that φ with complete confidence (as for example in a mathematical proof), the inferential evidential cannot be used.

McCready and Ogata model these facts by taking *mitai* to be an epistemic modal with an evidential requirement, as already discussed in the previous chapter. However, their analysis is rather complex. As also mentioned in the previous chapter, part of the reason for this complexity is their goal of simultaneously indicating what evidence is and does. Leaving this part of the model aside allows for a substantial simplification of the analysis. I therefore give *mitai* the semantics in (7.27), while still using their $\triangle_i^a$ notation for the corresponding operator. On this analysis, the inferential evidential indicates the existence of an event of acquiring inferential evidence, as shown by the requirement that φ be supported by a substate of σ of *Inf*-type. Further, the total information state is required to support the proposition that φ is epistemically possible. This replaces the clause requiring that φ be likely but not certain in the original McCready and Ogata semantics. As the reader will note, the possibility statement is substantially weaker. I am allowing the notion of effective inference to do some work here. Inferential processes are not fully reliable, but they are generally reliable, at least defeasibly. Given that reliability, if some piece of inferential evidence is sufficient to cause φ to be supported in the corresponding substate, then, presumably, φ will have a relatively high probability in the total information state, as long as it is not defeated by some higher-ranked substate during the process of merger. And if it is so defeated, then φ-*mitai* should not be assertable in any case.[25]

$$(7.27) \quad \sigma[\triangle_i^a \varphi] = \begin{cases} \sigma \text{ if } \begin{array}{l} \text{i) } \sigma_T \models \Diamond\varphi \text{ and} \\ \text{ii) } \exists i[\sigma_i \models \varphi \ \& \ i \in \mathit{Inf}] \end{array} \\ \varnothing \text{ else} \end{cases}$$

The additional clauses in the definition of McCready and Ogata (2007b) referring to probability increase, lack of total certainty, and probability convexity have been omitted. The first and second I take to follow from the **Evidential to evidence** principle together with Gricean reasoning. The second first: if one is totally certain, then one should not use an inferential evidential at all. As for the first and third conditions (that the evidence source raises the probability of φ, and does not thereafter lower it), this is something that should just follow from the nature of

---

[25] Is it possible to assert sentences of the form "φ-*mitai*, but actually $\neg\varphi$"? It might be possible for some speakers. But if it is indeed possible, there is even more reason to eliminate the requirement that the total information state support a high probability of the truth of φ. Thanks to Chris Davis for discussion here.

evidence. Given a proper definition of evidence (McCready 2014 provides such a definition tailored for natural language evidentials), such a condition should not be needed in the lexical semantics of evidentials themselves.

Hearsay evidentials can be given a weak semantics along similar lines. Such evidentials test for the existence of an event of acquisition of hearsay evidence, according to the semantics of McCready and Ogata for the Japanese case. In the present system, this just amounts to the requirement that some substate of σ associated with reportative evidence supports φ, which will already be guaranteed by the acquisition of a piece of hearsay evidence, given the definition of evidential update in (7.14).

$$(7.28) \quad \sigma[\mathsf{H}_a^i\varphi] = \begin{cases} \sigma & \text{if } \exists i[\sigma_i \models \varphi \ \& \ i \in Rep \cup \mathcal{A}] \\ \varnothing & \text{else} \end{cases}$$

The analysis of epistemic evidentials, then, is straightforward in the present system, though the semantics of each evidential must be stipulated independently and does not fall out directly from the model itself. This is to be expected: the meaning of individual epistemic evidentials is idiosyncratic and not a consequence of any particular theory of evidential semantics or pragmatics.

7.4.5 Relation with standard dynamic theories

The reader might be wondering how all this relates to the set of phenomena that originally motivated the adoption of dynamic semantics in linguistic circles, the core being the analysis of intersentential anaphora and presupposition. There is a great deal of complexity here, as the set of phenomena that have been analyzed using dynamics is by now very large (see e.g. Muskens et al. 1997 for a partial overview). Consequently I won't be able to fully spell out here how the kind of model I have proposed deals with the complete range of data. In particular, since I have been working with propositional models, it is not going to be possible for me to say much about intersentential anaphora at all, much less modal subordination. However, I would like to briefly consider the case of presupposition resolution, something accessible as (in many cases at least) we need only worry about propositional content to understand what is going on.

There are two standard analyses of presupposition in dynamic models. Both assume that presuppositions must be resolved within the model, but the details are quite different. The first assumes a representational level in the style of discourse representation theory (Kamp and Reyle 1993), and uses this level to define a path along which one can travel to find a place where the presupposition can be resolved. The path is determined by an accessibility relation and moves from the possibly embedded level at which the presupposition is introduced to the global level. The other simply checks the local or the global state to see whether the presupposition is satisfied there. In both cases resolution is understood in terms of satisfaction: a presupposition can be resolved at some point if its content is entailed by the content of the information state at that point. Beaver (2001) provides a very clear explication of the details of these analyses.

For my purposes here, to examine how resolution should be understood in the models I am working with, the key thing to note is that presupposition resolution has to happen at the level of the global state, at least in the general case. If it did not, it would become possible to resolve presuppositions that were not entailed at the global level at which belief is defined (cf. 7.15). That means that given a sentence of the form $E_i[\partial\phi]\psi$ (where the ∂ operator indicates a presupposition, following Beaver 2001), despite the fact that σ_i is what gets updated with ψ, nonetheless it is σ_G that must be checked to see whether it verifies ϕ.

The implication of the above is that it is the global state that should be relevant for the familiar dynamic semantic operations, including the analysis of anaphoric dependencies. This should not be a surprise given that belief is already defined at that level. But the extension to the first-order case is not entirely straightforward due to my use of belief aggregation. Concretely, suppose for example that my friend Jim tells a long story about a person he met last weekend while attending a baseball game and subsequently went out for a drink with. Suppose I then learn from a more reliable source that Jim didn't even attend a baseball game on the day in question. This new information is entered into a substate ranked higher than that associated with Jim; when the substates are merged to form a new information state, then, Jim's baseball game anecdote is eliminated in the global state. But then what about the other propositions about going out for a drink? Are they to be eliminated too? After all, nothing has been learned about Jim's activities (let's suppose) except that the baseball game part of the story is not to be relied on. One might want to tentatively retain the rest of the anecdote; but doing so will have bad results, for all sentences containing a variable or discourse referent dependent on that introduced by the initial sentence will no longer be sensible. More generally, the possibility of some propositions failing to survive the transit to the global information state means a possibility of anaphoric catastrophes like those that we find in failed cases of modal subordination. The problems may be partially solvable by the strategy of taking the addition of a discourse referent and predication of it to involve separate clauses (i.e. to have the form $\exists x; P(x)$), which could then be taken to update distinct substates; but it does not look trivial to derive the requisite logical forms or to appropriately constrain them. This is a topic I will leave for later work.

But are the substates good for anything in terms of analyzing the traditional data? The answer depends a bit on how we choose to analyze update with evidential sentences, and with constructions that appear related to evidentials of some kinds, such as epistemic modals. Up to now I have taken evidentials to induce update of their corresponding substates. If so, then the Japanese inferential evidentials (*mitai, rashii*, etc.) should update the family of substates σ_i associated with inferential evidence. Recall from chapter 6 that these evidentials enable modal subordination. How should this work in the present system? Given our current restriction to the propositional case, it's not possible to check the traditional examples, but corresponding cases can easily be constructed where only presupposition is involved, such as this one with *might* (here $r(t)$ indicates that r is true at t and ";" is dynamic conjunction).

(7.29)   a. It might have been raining earlier. It might still be raining now.

   b. $\Diamond \exists t[t < n \wedge r(t)]; \Diamond[\partial \exists t[t < n \wedge r(t)]]r(n)$

It's straightforward to construct corresponding examples with the Japanese inferential evidentials.

(7.30)   a. Saki   ame-ga   futteita   mitai.
            before rain-Nom was.falling MITAI
            'It seems like it was raining before.'

   b. Ima mo futteiru mitai.
            now too falling   MITAI
            'It seems like it's still raining now.'

   c. $\mathsf{E}_{inf}\exists t[t < n \wedge r(t)]; \mathsf{E}_{inf}[\partial \exists t[t < n \wedge r(t)]]r(n)$

What will happen in this latter case is that σ_{inf} will be updated with the content of the first sentence. Then what about the presupposition of the second? It's not so obvious. If it is resolved at the global level, the presuppositional test will fail if there is some conflicting information for the content of the first sentence from a source ranked higher than inference, which is quite plausible. We then have two options: accommodation of the presupposition in the global state or resolution within the substate σ_{inf}. The first option results in an inconsistent global state, so it won't work (cf. discussion of possible locations for accommodation in van der Sandt 1992; Beaver 2001). The second is fine, of course, for no inconsistency results, and indeed the presupposition can be resolved rather than accommodated. This is in effect a new way of viewing what we might call "evidential subordination": instead of updating some context constructed on the fly in order to provide an anaphoric antecedent (in this case for a presupposition), we simply resolve the dependency within an already existing substate. This is fairly attractive, and allows the possibility of modal subordination once the needed first-order machinery is put in place.

Is it going to work across the board? First of all, what about bad sequences where the antecedent in the scope of the evidential in the first sentence is followed by a presupposition trigger in an evidential-free second sentence? The answer depends on what we take the update conditions of evidential-free sentences to be: obviously they must be understood as instances of testimony in the final analysis, but likely as testimony on the basis of something like best possible grounds.[26] Since best possible grounds aren't in general inferential, there is no guarantee of update of the right substate; that means that the dependency isn't expected to be resolvable, so subordination will fail, as desired.

A second case involves hearsay evidentials. McCready and Ogata (2007b) note that hearsay evidentials do not enable modal subordination, considering sequences where an instance of a hearsay evidential is followed by *kamoshirenai* 'might'. This is to be expected on the current analysis, as the substate(s) associated with hearsay are not those associated with epistemic modals (an issue discussed in the next paragraph). However, it does appear to be possible to subordinate with sequences of hearsay evidentials, something not previously discussed in the literature (to my knowledge).

---

[26] The updated analysis of testimonial evidence in chapter 9 will be able to treat this case, though at present this kind of embedding has not been argued for.

(7.31) a. Saki   ame-ga   futteita   soo da   yo.
          before rain-Nom was.falling REP Cop PT
          'I heard it was raining before.'

        b. Ima mo futteiru soo da.
          now too falling   REP Cop
          'I also heard it's still raining now.'

        c. $E_{rep}\exists t[t < n \land r(t)]; E_{rep}[\partial\exists t[t < n \land r(t)]]r(n)$

Again, this is to be expected on the current view, for the same substates are being updated in each case.

For modal subordination proper, the analysis only generalizes if we assume that *might*-sentences also are associated with their own substates in the model. The result is that processing an instance of $\Diamond\varphi$ doesn't update σ with $\Diamond\varphi$, but rather updates $\sigma_\Diamond$ with φ. This means that sequences of sentences modified by epistemic modals will update the same substates, and subordination will be possible. Sequences of epistemic modal sentences followed by "bare" sentences will also be infelicitous, just as with the inferential evidential case. However, one may worry about how this move will impact the global state. I have set things up so that—in the absence of conflicting information—substate content will "percolate up" into the global state. If epistemic modals are associated with distinct substates, it is then predicted that their prejacents will be believed if there is no reason not to do so. Note that this is actually consistent with the analysis of chapter 4, where I said that modals proffer their prejacent content to the hearer; without a reason to reject that content, it might well be that it does indeed become globally believed. I think more examination of these issues is necessary, but it does seem a promising avenue for exploration.

7.5 Additional issues

The above analysis has proposed a solution to the problem of evidential update and belief choice (for this domain, at least). The idea was that information states consist of multiple substates associated with distinct evidence sources, each consisting of a set of worlds or indices of evaluation ranked according to plausibility on the basis of update with particular pieces of information, where the substates are ordered by a priority ranking on information sources that dictates how they are to be combined. I showed that this view gives a satisfactory way to understand some of the puzzles of update with evidentials. Of course, there is still a need to clarify the mechanism by which the priority rankings are induced, which will be done in the next chapter. But before moving to this task, I want to briefly indicate some domains of comparison for the present system, and some areas which still remain problematic for it.

The use of multiple information states invites comparison to the "society of minds" logic of local reasoning given in the sixth section of Fagin and Halpern (1988). This paper has the goal of providing a logic (or logics) for reasoning about knowledge which avoids problems associated with logical omniscience. The foundation of their approach is the following intuition:

> Our key observation is that one reason that people hold inconsistent beliefs is that beliefs tend to come in non-interacting clusters. We can almost view an agent as a society of minds, each with its own set (or cluster) of beliefs, which may contradict each other.   (Fagin and Halpern 1988: 58)

Plainly this idea is close to what I have provided, though their approach aims to model ways in which an agent can, in some sense consistently, *hold* inconsistent beliefs, while the aim of mine is to understand how an agent can *reconcile* inconsistent beliefs acquired on distinct evidential bases. Stalnaker (1984) is a related approach with a more philosophical slant.

Before moving on, let me mention two problems the theory cannot solve. The first is problematic, but entirely in a way which is not specific to the current application. We can ask: What happens if we have two evidence sources i, j, where $i \sim j$ on the priority ranking? Then, given the way the ordering has been set up, there is no way to privilege the information provided by one above the information provided by the other. That being the case, we have no choice but to hope for consistency in the information coming from those sources. But, if consistency is not present (so that we have, for instance, $E_i\phi$ and $E_j\neg\phi$), problems arise; the global belief state will be inconsistent. The upshot is that the present theory does not eliminate the need for a general theory of belief revision. Of course, this is not a surprise; if evidentials eliminated the need for revisions to our beliefs, one would expect that their use would be much more universal than it in fact is. It is even less a surprise given the granularity of the ordering I have indicated. Since there are only finitely many cognitively plausible distinctions between evidence sources, one cannot really expect evidentiary differences to resolve every conflict in belief. I thus do not think that this limitation is very problematic.

The second problem is more severe, and also perhaps more interest-ing. It is well known that there are "voting effects" across ranking sources (cf. e.g. Maynard-Zhang and Lehmann 2003). For example, suppose that I consider my own inference more reliable than the testimony of individuals that I view as non-experts on the topic at issue. Suppose that I infer that $\neg\phi$ and am told by an unreliable individual a that ϕ. Then I will globally believe that $\neg\phi$, disregarding the low-ranked testimony. This situation is modeled by the system I have proposed. However, now suppose that another non-expert also tells me that ϕ. I may continue to believe $\neg\phi$ at this point, but if more people tell me that ϕ, eventually the weight of their testimony will pile up and I will often come to believe ϕ myself. Or, for another sort of case, suppose that one high-ranked source has it that ϕ; this situation is hard to distinguish, in this model, from the intuitively quite different case where every source unanimously gives the information that ϕ. It is not trivial to solve this issue in a system like the one I have presented; I will have to leave the problem for the future.

8

Using priorities

As we have seen, the system given in the previous chapter is able to
model interactions between information coming from different evidential sources. When one source is deemed more reliable than another,
information it provides will trump conflicting information from less
reliable sources. I argued that we need such a system in order to
understand the epistemic behavior of agents faced with the range of
evidential sentences found in natural language, and indeed to model
evidence-based reasoning more generally. However, several issues have
been left underdetermined. Most obviously, the analysis of conflicting
information depends on a ranking based on reliability, but I have not
shown where these rankings come from. As indicated in chapter 6, for
the particular case of evidentials and evidential hierarchies, the rankings
are rather context-dependent. But it would be begging the question to
(for example) simply stipulate the existence of a function from contexts
to hierarchies; without knowing more about how the function works, it
would fail to be a fully meaningful analysis. Consequently my first goal
in this chapter is to derive the required hierarchies.

It is obvious, given the discussion so far, how this should be done. The
method I will use requires unifying the discussion in the two parts of this
book. Faller (2002a) argues that evidential hierarchies are, in part, based
on the perceived reliability of particular information sources. As the first
part of the book showed, the reliability of an agent is one property that
can be derived on the basis of induction from the agent's past behavior.
We therefore can make use of histories here, an option made available
by the treatment of evidentials in terms of source indices. I will spell
out how this is to be done shortly; but, as we will see, it looks more
or less like the way that we enabled judgements about cooperativity in
chapter 3.

However, the picture as currently constituted has a somewhat counterintuitive quality in the context of evidentials. As I have set things up
so far, reliability is computed solely on the basis of past performance,

as it were. But evidential hierarchies clearly do not work like this in every case. In many languages, evidential hierarchies seem to be just brute grammatical facts (Aikhenvald 2004). For this application, therefore, we would like to have a prespecified ranking on sources: in general, perceptual evidence ranks higher than hearsay, for instance, though contextual factors can alter this ranking. Performance is only one contextual factor that contributes to this variation. What's required then is an initial ranking which serves as a default, together with a way to reset the ranking when information about reliability overcomes it. I have already made use of this default ranking in the last chapter.

The need for this structure is not limited to the evidential case. It is well known that human belief about the trustworthiness of agents does not stem entirely from beliefs about how they have behaved in the past, despite the reductive history model of Part 1 of this book. Immediately on encountering other individuals, we form beliefs about them, based on various properties of their appearance and of the setting; one view on testimonial reliability is that judgements based on these factors induce us to trust or not. The view that individuals are trustworthy by default, and their testimony worthy of belief, is only one possibility. I will return to this issue in the next chapter, where we will consider in detail the case of testimony. It will turn out that the analysis of hierarchies developed here is useful (and perhaps even necessary) for the case of trust in testimony as well.

After developing my analysis of shifts in evidential hierarchies, I will turn to one additional application of the theory of reliability. We saw in chapter 6 that direct evidentials in languages like Quechua reference the "best possible grounds" for a particular piece of asserted content. As stated there, it is nontrivial to specify exactly what the best possible grounds are: for externally verifiable facts, the best possible grounds will (in general) be perceptual, but for intentional states and other non-externally verifiable situations, the best possible grounds will not be perceptual (since perceptual evidence is not available), instead consisting of evidence that can be as "weak" as testimony. This variability has not really been addressed in the literature. However, we are now in a position to do so: the best possible grounds for a particular proposition consist of evidence acquired via the most reliable source with respect to information of that particular type. Spelling this out will be the topic of section 8.3.

8.1 Initial judgements and preference relations

The first step toward an analysis of the contextual dependency of evidential hierarchies is to set the initial priorities and to show how they can be reset given the right sorts of information. For a test case, let's suppose we have an information source e and we are interested in placing it in a priority ranking of evidence sources. What can be said about the reliability of e? Where should it be placed in the ranking? I will argue that two kinds of information contribute to this judgement: initial estimations of the reliability of e and further evaluation of e's reliability based on its performance. These two factors, in turn, will induce an evidential hierarchy, and allow it to be updated as estimations of reliability alter. Let us consider them in turn.

Any information source e has a certain degree of reliability. This reliability is, of course, situation-dependent, as can be seen from the standard example of the red-lit room, in which objects that appear red may actually be white; here, perceptual evidence for the color of objects is known to be unreliable (or at least non-normal or biased). Still, in the absence of factors which might work to confound information provided by a particular information source (see Pollock and Cruz 1999), epistemic agents take information coming from those sources to be reliable to a particular degree.[1] We can view this judgement about reliability as the probability that the agent initially assigns to the proposition that the source is reliable. This is the core idea I will work with going forward.

What is meant here by "initial"? One can understand this word in two ways in this context. The first takes initial probabilities to indicate genuinely innate tendencies toward trust, or lack of trust, in particular evidence sources. The second way takes initial probabilities to be formed on the basis of judgements about how likely the source is to be reliable made on some kind of a priori basis, perhaps by considering how probable it is that there are confounding circumstances, or the probability of error in general on the basis of external evidence. In practice it is not easy to distinguish the two views empirically, for by the time judgements of reliability can be made the individual is no longer a blank slate,

---

[1] More precisely, this is so if the agent does not believe confounders to exist. If there are no confounders for a particular source yet the agent falsely believes there to be such, the agent will wrongly give a lower credence to information from that source than she otherwise would; the converse is of course also possible. Thus the reliability of sources in our sense depends on agent beliefs (or knowledge) and perspectives, and so is likely susceptible to the construction of Gettier cases. I will leave these issues aside in the present context.

already having substantial experience in judgement-making in infancy. As a result, the question is controversial; indeed, for the special case of testimonial evidence, the answer to this question represents a major split in philosophical views of reliability, about which I will say more in the next chapter. I think either view is compatible with my purposes here, especially as regards evidentials; we can simply take the initial probability of the reliability of a particular source to be given, and leave it open whether it is given on the basis of experience or otherwise.

The upshot of the preceding discussion is that each evidence source comes with a prior probability of being reliable, where a reliable source is one which provides correct information. Call the property of being reliable Rel. Then the prior probabilities have the form $P(Rel(e))$ for each source e. As in chapter 3, $Rel(e)$ holds if the probability that any event of information acquisition via e tracks truth exceeds a contextually set threshold. As a result, the probability of a particular observation being accurate depends on the probability that the source accurately transmits information, due to the dependence between single observations and the general propensities of agents for communicating the truth, and of sources in general for transmitting it.

Note that since each source is now associated with a probability, an ordering is already induced on the set of evidence sources. The higher the initial probability associated with a particular evidence source, the higher it will be in the ordering; since the order is total, every evidence source will be mutually ranked. This ordering is precisely what is needed as input to the logic introduced in chapter 7. Each evidence source is prioritized to the degree indicated by its initial probability of reliability. Given that evidence acquired via visual perception is deemed more reliable than (say) testimonial evidence, vis will be assigned a higher initial probability than $hearsay$; since $P(Rel(vis)) > P(Rel(hearsay))$, it is the case that $vis \succ hearsay$, and therefore information in σ_{vis} will have a higher priority than information in $\sigma_{hearsay}$ in the aggregation process resulting in the global information state σ.

So far all this is not much more than a stipulation that information of some kinds takes priority over others. The interest of the model comes in the interaction that it allows with additional information coming from experience. This interaction will be detailed in the next section. But first it is necessary to clarify the nature of the probabilities, and thus the priority rankings, in question.

There are two interpretations that appear possible for these priorities, given the intended use of the model. The first is as genuine reliability in an epistemological sense. Particular information sources may just be better at providing accurate information than others. This is essentially the intuition we have been working with up to this point. But the model is also meant to help us to understand the functioning of evidentials and of evidential hierarchies, which are a grammatical phenomenon. How can it do so, given that evidential hierarchies are at least in part grammatically given and need not correspond to "genuine" reliability?

My response to this possible difficulty is to claim that, in fact, evidential hierarchies reflect learned experience. The common feature of evidential hierarchies across languages is that visual evidence takes highest position: this corresponds to the observation that visual evidence is less ambiguous, and hence more reliable, than other evidence sources in the general case. Here preferences made on the basis of genuine reliability dovetail neatly with preferences that are (possibly) grammatically induced. This is to be expected on the assumption that evidential hierarchies track "standard" patterns of evidential reliability. I therefore make the claim that evidential hierarchies are epistemologically significant in that they reflect observations about the reliability of particular kinds of evidence.

The reader might be wondering how to square the view I have just stated with the examples given by Faller (2002a) about variability in the preferred evidential to use in a given context. Consider again her examples (7.4) and (7.5), repeated here. As she observed, speakers will choose to use whichever of (7.4) or (7.5) is related to the more reliable source of evidence, something I have codified as the Strongest evidence principle in the last chapter (7.19). In particular, (8.2) (=(7.5)) will be used if the informant is judged trustworthy, and (8.1) (=(7.4)) otherwise. But how could this be, if evidential choice is made on the basis of epistemological considerations about reliability, supposing that we merely choose between inferential and testimonial evidence?

(8.1)   Atuq-chá wallpa-yki-ta apa-rqa-n
        fox-CHÁ hen-2p-Acc   take-Pst1-3
        'A fox must have taken the hen.' (based on some inference)

(8.2)   Atuq-si wallpa-ta apa-sqa
        fox-SI   hen-Acc take-Pst2-3
        'A fox took the hen.' (I heard)

The answer is obvious once the question is posed. We do not simply rank evidence sources in general, but evidence sources in particular conditions of evidence acquisition, and with respect to particular properties of the evidence acquisition situation. Evidential hierarchies as a grammatical phenomenon thus represent only the least fine-grained view of evidential use and by extension of the reliability of categories of evidence.

But how can this view be implemented? As it turns out, the kind of variation that arises in the use of evidentials as a result of the reordering of evidence sources in particular situations is a direct prediction of the full version of the present system.

Up to now I have treated the system developed for evidential update in the second half of this book as independent of the system proposed for analyzing trust and hedging in the first half. In fact, the two systems are meant to be integrated. Evidential updates have been taken to occur on simplex objects, propositions indexed by an evidence source. But recall that histories of discourse moves, as treated in the first part of the book, have the form of sequences of triples. Here, each triple is of the form $\langle \varphi, v, \mathcal{P} \rangle$ where φ is the action taken by the agent (as before restricted to linguistic moves), v indicates the truth or falsity of the content, and $\mathcal{P}$ indicates relevant properties of the action and its context. As a result, since elements of discourse histories are actually instances of the transmission of information via testimony, we at present have a disconnect between the representation of testimonial evidence (as used for pragmatic purposes) and the representation of all other evidence sorts, including in fact testimonial evidence, within the update system. This is obviously undesirable.

The solution is (relatively) straightforward. Take events of evidence acquisition to have the same form as the elements of the histories of interaction: $\langle \varphi, v, \mathcal{P} \rangle$. In chapter 3, the first elements of each game iteration were of the form φ, the propositional content which was the object of the communicative act. In chapter 7, this was still the case, but I assumed that each information acquisition event was of the form $\mathsf{E}_i \varphi$, because information can be acquired only via some source, i.e. via an evidential basis. There, the evidence sources were used to analyze evidential choice and update. But they can also be used in order to facilitate reasoning about changes in reliability of particular sources, and to provide a base for computing reliabilities in the first place.

Chapter 4 took judgements about agent reliability and cooperativity to depend on examinations of the interactional histories associated with that agent. Elements of those histories were classified into accurate (true) and inaccurate (false) utterances: a high enough proportion of accuracy led to being judged reliable. In the present context, the classification will be into true and false utterances, just as before. The difference will only be that, for each evidence source, there is a distinct history. This enables calculation of the reliability of each evidence source with respect to the present discourse, the whole expanse of memory, or a sequence of whatever length is currently deemed to be useful, just as we saw with interactional histories. Thus, we have $\langle \varphi, \nu, \mathcal{P} \rangle_a$ for conversational agent a, and, similarly, $\langle \varphi, \nu, \mathcal{P} \rangle_i$ for evidence source e_i; the form of the histories is identical. The analogy between conversational agents and evidence sources here is not accidental; in chapter 9 I will argue that each agent should be viewed as a separate evidence source, and the reliability of this source should relate directly to the perceived quality of the information provided by the testimonial agent.

This analytical move requires a slight extension of the analysis of history construction in chapter 3. There, history building was taken to happen via a simple process of concatenation: a new discourse move added a new element to the tail of the history sequence. Some additional complexity is required for the current application. The simple structure of chapter 3 does not make provision for multiple agents, in the sense that only one history is taken into consideration. This corresponds to a view of information states on which they are homogeneous, and new information is added to the global state. The reason is, of course, that in chapter 3 I considered only cases of interaction with a single agent whose cooperativity was to be judged. But, in the more general case currently under consideration, we need a way to separate out the different evidence sources with respect to histories, just as I did in the last chapter with information states.

The required extension is rather straightforward. In chapter 3 I took histories to have the form $H_a^{m,g,n}$, for histories H of games g with m moves at iteration n as played by agent a. The agent index was taken as given; because only the two-player case was under consideration, there was only a single agent whose contributions to the history were relevant for judging reliability (on the assumption that conversational agents don't need to make judgements about their own reliability). For the system to provide histories for evidence sources more generally, we need only allow the "agent" index in histories to be drawn from the set of source indices Source: the result will be that any evidence source can be drawn from in history creation. However, we cannot limit attention to objects in Source, for then we will have no way to analyze histories of the communicative actions of agents. I thus take the available indices to come from either Source (as defined in (7.21) and clause 2.c of the Appendix) or the set of agents $\mathcal{A}$. In addition, rather than having distinct histories for each agent or evidence source, I will assume a "global history" of information acquisition events, within which each "game" iteration is indexed with an evidence source. We thus get the following.

(8.3) **Form of histories.**
       Elements of histories are of the form $\langle \varphi, v, \mathcal{P} \rangle_i$, where $i \in$ Source $\cup \mathcal{A}$.

We are close to having what we need, but one thing is still missing: it is necessary to specify how given information acquisition events are mapped into histories. I will assume the following mechanism for constructing histories of information acquisition. Note that in this definition, and hereafter, the subscript a on histories $H_a^{m,g,n}$ will indicate the agent of the history in the sense of the agent making the observation, rather than the agent whose actions are observed. The latter is now indicated by subscripts on the event of information acquisition itself, i.e. the game iteration.

(8.4) **Making evidential histories.**
       Let history $H_a^{g,n}$ be the current move history and suppose that $E_i\varphi$ is observed, with truth value v' and where the relevant conditions are $\mathcal{P}'$. Then $H_a^{g,n+1} = \langle\langle \psi, v, \mathcal{P} \rangle_j, \ldots, \langle \varphi, v', \mathcal{P}' \rangle_i \rangle$.

This mechanism ensures that i-sourced observations are mapped to i-indexed information acquisition events in histories. Situations where the source is a testimonial agent fall out as a special case. This structure enables easy restriction to a particular agent or evidence source by restricting the global history to that subsequence of elements labeled with the relevant source index.[2]

Let us take stock. We have each evidence source associated with a history of information acquisition events of the form $\langle \varphi, v, \mathcal{P} \rangle_i$ and an initial probability of being reliable. The goal now is to use this theoretical apparatus to model evidential hierarchies. I will first consider "default" hierarchies and then show how the ordering of preferred evidentials may change under special circumstances, such as the cases of reliable and unreliable testimony above.

---

[2] It is worth noting that I have modeled the mechanism associated with information acquisition as an operation on move histories, rather than game histories. There seem to be two ways to think of information acquisition in repeated-game terms: either as an infinitely extensible sequence of single-move games, or as an extremely large single game. It is not so obvious how to choose between these, but I have gone for the first option as I find it more conceptually transparent.

To do so I will need to make one assumption about the setting of initial probabilities. The epistemological literature makes it clear that all information sources are fallible, but that some are less fallible than others. It is easy to make errors in reasoning, especially when the premises which are being used are also fallible, so information acquired via inference is plainly not fully reliable in general.[3] Testimony obviously comes in various degrees of reliability, depending on the speaker and the circumstances of utterance. It is also easy to make mistakes about the content of perception (e.g. Jackson 1977), but these mistakes are less common and arise only in more special circumstances. Consequently, the initial probability that a perceptual source of information is reliable can (more or less) safely be taken to be higher than the reliability of information derived by inference; testimony, with its even wider variance, might generically be taken to be less reliable than either one. We are left with the situation that $P(Rel(Dir)) > P(Rel(Inf)) > P(Rel(Rep))$, where the evidence sources are as in (7.22).[4]

I should note that these rankings hold only for the general case; as we have already seen with Faller's fox example, individual instances of testimony can be judged more or less reliable than inference, or even than perception for cases like teachers transmitting (say) scientific information. My science teacher's statement that the earth is round might trump my visual evidence that it is flat. For the converse case, consider the case of the politician discussed in chapter 3; no matter how many times an individual politician speaks truly, still his reliability might be judged low, for his profession leads us to judge him completely untrustworthy at the initial point. This kind of case provides another argument for treating each individual source of testimony as a separate evidence source, a point which will be elaborated on below and in chapter 9.[5]

---

[3] Issues like these play a role in the extensive literature on the problem of whether or not knowledge is closed under inferential processes; see (for instance) Hawthorne (2004) for discussion.

[4] Here, since the evidence sources are somewhat unspecific, we must allow the ordering to hold over set-valued objects: I will just take, for example, $P(Rel(Dir))$ to be the average probability of reliability of the sources in Dir, and let the ordering hold for those average values. Other possibilities of course exist, for example taking the maximal or minimal probabilities of reliability of the sources in the set, but the ordering based on averages seems to me to be the 'null hypothesis'.

[5] It is interesting to note that this judgement of unreliability is rather difficult to alter on the basis of interactional histories. Within the model this observation could be accommodated in various ways: by setting the initial probability of reliability so low as to be very hard to raise (even say $-\infty$, so that it can never be raised high enough to exceed the threshold for being judged reliable, though allowing this kind of value requires modifying the model a bit), or by restricting histories to unreliable moves for the political case.

I argued above that the ordering of priorities for evidential merge should mirror the ordering imposed by the probability of reliability of the evidence sources to be merged. If this is the case, then we have *Dir* ≻ *Inf* ≻ *Rep*, which seems reasonable. Thus, these relations should be reflected in the relative priority given to information coming from different sources of this kind in case of conflict, which seems to be generally correct.[6]

Now, given the **Strongest evidence principle** in (7.19), it follows that a speaker should use an evidential that indicates the existence of *Dir*-type evidence if such exists, otherwise an evidential indicating *Inf*-type evidence, and, lacking that, resort to a hearsay evidential. But this is just the standard kind of default evidential hierarchy described by authors like Faller (2002a,b) and Aikhenvald (2004). Thus, given the assumption that the preferred evidential to use tracks the reliability of evidence sources, we have derived the existence of evidential hierarchies. It is also clear that the hierarchies reflect more general facts about the (perceived) reliability of different information sources.

But, again, these hierarchies are not set in stone. How can we derive the mutability discussed by authors like Faller (2002a)? The potential to do so is already present in the system; in fact, the system as currently set up predicts that doing so should be possible, in two distinct ways. Each requires the ability to revise estimates of probability based on experience. The required machinery will be introduced and applied in the next section (8.2). After introducing it, I will turn in section 8.3 to an application: an understudied concept in the theory of evidentials, that of *best possible grounds*, and how the present system can help in understanding it.

8.2 Overriding default hierarchies

So far I have assumed that there is an externally imposed hierarchy of evidence sources, corresponding to a default evidential hierarchy. But as we have seen this hierarchy is somewhat mutable. When a

---

[6] There is one problem with this method that I should mention. Since each evidence source is associated with a probability of reliability, they all come with indices in the interval [0, 1]; but all such indices can be compared. This means that all evidence sources should be mutually ranked for reliability. If Faller (2002a) is right in thinking that some evidence sources are not mutually ranked, then the analysis fails to fully capture the behavior of evidential hierarchies. A possible response is to note that, even if sources are not obviously ranked with respect to each other, the update process still must decide what to do when such sources contradict each other, which is something my model will get right. I must leave this issue undecided for the present.

particular source is known to be unreliable—or reliable—in some set of circumstances, the hierarchy can be overridden. This is one of two sorts of context dependence in evidential orderings I will discuss. The second involves changes in the perceived reliability of evidence sources on the basis of experience. In order to model such changes, we need to consider how observations about evidential reliability interact with the general assumptions about reliability encoded as default hierarchies. An analysis of this second kind of context dependence will naturally lead to an analysis of the first.

I have argued that each evidence source is assigned an initial probability of reliability. Subsequently, an agent's acquisition of information from that source is assembled into a history of evidence acquisition events. In this setting, the question of how interaction between default expectation and experience works in the case of evidential sources amounts to asking how the initial probabilities and the information provided by the histories interact.

This question allows a number of different answers. I think the most natural is to begin with the initial probability of reliability associated with the evidence source and let each instance of information acquisition update the probability via conditionalization.[7] The conditional probability of an event A on another event B is the probability of $A \wedge B$ divided by the probability of B:

$$\frac{P(A \cap B)}{P(B)}.$$

Conditionalizing on B yields a new probability for A, namely the conditional probability of A given B. Thus, the probability that an evidence source is reliable is, given $P_I(C)$ the initial probability that a given event of information acquisition via this source yields correct information and $P_I(R)$ the initial probability of general reliability of the source,

$$\frac{P_I(R \cap C)}{P_I(C)}.$$

---

[7] The other obvious possibility is to take the probability of reliability yielded by the history and combine it with the initial probability using some operation. For instance, one could simply take the average of the two probabilities. But this leaves out the important information given by the length of the history: a single interaction would be assigned the same weight as an interaction with length ω. Obviously this is not right. One could try to solve this problem by weighting the probability given by the history, say by using a weight $w \in [0,1]$ corresponding to the length of the interaction, so that $w = 0$ for length 0 and approaches 1 as length approaches ω. One could then give the initial probability a weight of $1 - w$ (followed by a normalization process on the product); but it does not seem trivial to decide w for any given point, since interactional histories are taken to be potentially infinite. How close to 1 should we set an interaction length of 10,000?

After conditionalization, then, the updated probability that a source is reliable is the probability of a reliable source type and an accurate piece of information, divided by the simplex probability that the information is correct.

This seems correct, but it must be admitted that it is rather vague in the absence of concrete probabilities for the correctness of the acquired information. It is also not possible to put accurate numbers to the initial reliability assigned to the sources; we know only what is given by the rankings, so we only have "qualitative" information about how the different information sources relate. Still, the setup makes it clear that, over time, consistently getting accurate information from a source will make $P(R)$ move toward 1, and consistently getting inaccurate information will cause $P(R)$ to move toward 0.[8]

The result of the above is that rerankings of the evidence sources become possible. Suppose that, as a default order, we have $e_1 \succ e_2$, so e_1 has priority. But now suppose that we see a large number of instances of inaccurate content acquired via e_1 and a large number of examples of accurate content acquired via e_2. The conditionalization operation above will cause $P(R(e_1))$ to drop and that of $P(R(e_2))$ to rise. Given sufficient such observations, eventually it will follow that $P(R(e_1)) < P(R(e_2))$. Since source rankings are determined by probabilities, at that point $e_2 \succ e_1$, meaning that information acquired via e_2 is prioritized above e_1-type information. Now, since the operation of evidential hierarchies depends on the priority ordering, the reversal of the ordering implies reversal of the hierarchy, and we come to expect that a speaker will choose to use the evidential $Evid_2$ associated with e_2 rather than the evidential $Evid_1$ used for e_1-type evidence, given the choice. The system is thus able to derive Faller's observation about the context-dependence of evidential hierarchies.

As it turns out, Faller's example of the fox in the henhouse exemplifies this kind of shift in the default order, together with the first kind of context dependency I mentioned above, namely the consideration of a particular set of circumstances. As the reader will recall, the choice of hearsay or inferential evidential in Faller's case depended on the speaker's judgement about the reliability of the informant. If the informant was judged reliable, the hearsay evidential would be preferred; if the opposite, the inferential evidential would be used. How can this be accounted for in the present system? It would seem, at first glance,

---

[8] Over an infinite horizon, indeed, the probabilities will converge to these values.

that doing so is difficult; if different informants are assigned different degrees of reliability, how can we even give a consistent position in the priority ordering to testimonial evidence? This is quite correct. I therefore propose that each individual be thought of as a distinct source of testimonial evidence. Note that making this move is already provided for in the formal system, given the new definition of possible indices for histories in (8.3).[9]

If each individual is (potentially) distinct in the ordering, every source of testimony is associated with her own source index. This already yields the fox case: we can simply assume that the sources associated with unreliable individuals are ranked lower than *inf* (inference), which in turn is lower than the sources of reliable individuals. Why should we end up with such a ranking though? There are two possible reasons: the first involves initial probabilities, so cases where an individual is judged likely (un)reliable on the basis of some external factors, and the second downgrading or upgrading based on histories of the individual's testimony, in just the way discussed in chapter 3. This is all completely analogous to what we saw in the previous discussion of evidence sources, and easily implemented given what has been done before.

The resources we have available call another kind of case to mind, though not one that has to my knowledge been discussed in the literature on evidential hierarchies. Suppose we have two individuals, a and b; a is generally unreliable and b generally reliable, so we have $b \succ inf \succ a$. However, a knows a lot about an obscure subject, say edible fungi; her communications about what mushrooms can be eaten safely have always been completely accurate, which cannot be said for b. Inference is not reliable in this domain either. We would thus like to privilege the information provided by a above *inf* and above b with respect to this domain. How can this be done? Here, we can restrict the histories H_b and H_a to fungi-related utterances, giving $H_b \restriction_{fungi}$ and $H_a \restriction_{fungi}$.[10] Then we can conditionalize over $P_I(R(a))$ and $P_I(R(b))$ on the basis of these restricted histories as before, giving new probabilities of reliability. If the probability of getting the fungi facts right is sufficiently low, it won't take many utterances to push $P(R(b))$ above $P(R(a))$ when mushrooms are concerned. Here we have a prediction about evidential hierarchies

---

[9] The next chapter expands on and provides additional support for this position.

[10] As before, I assume that this can be done, either by examining $\pi_1(i)$ for each element i of H for instances of certain terms or via some kind of "aboutness" function.

which it would be interesting to test for the general case, though my informants confirm it for the case of Japanese.

Summing up, I have shown a way to alter the priority rankings associated with different information sources on the basis of performance. I hope to have demonstrated that the system I constructed for computing the trustworthiness of individuals in the first part of the book is the same system that is needed to understand certain pragmatic aspects of evidentials. The next chapter will deepen this connection by examining in more detail the relationship between testimony and evidence, and by trying to spell out how the present proposal fits into current (philosophical) views of the nature and use of testimony. Before that, though, I want to exhibit one more application of the present system as it applies to evidentials proper: the analysis of the notion of *best possible grounds*.

8.3 Best possible grounds

I have already touched on the concept of best possible grounds in chapters 6 and 7. It concerns the evidence required for use of a direct evidential. Ordinarily, such evidentials are taken to test for the presence of perceptual evidence for the prejacent of the evidential, but in some cases this view cannot be right; as discussed extensively by Faller (2002b), perceptual evidence is not even well defined for certain kinds of claims. What kind of perceptual evidence could there be for the claim that I am going to France tomorrow, or for the claim that John might be coming to the party? There is none, or at least none that does not require an inferential step; one might take one's observation of plane tickets for Paris sitting on my table to be evidence that I am going to France tomorrow, but the tickets themselves qua objects of perception are not evidence, but yield premises in a deduction yielding the conclusion that I will be going to France. But there doesn't seem to be anything that *could* be better evidence for this claim. Perception of the tickets, or hearing me say that I plan to go, seems to be as good as it gets. This is the notion of best possible grounds: the best kind of evidence in principle available for a claim of a particular kind.

Given that this characterization of the notion of best possible grounds is correct, the requirements for an analysis are clear. We need only a way to determine what the best kind of evidence is in a particular situation. Then, given that evidence of that kind is available, it will be possible to use evidentials that require the best possible grounds for a claim.

Clearly a simple analysis can be given in the current system. The key feature of the system is that it involves a ranking over evidence sources. Within this ranking, the notion of best possible grounds can be spelled out as follows, as a first attempt.

(8.5)   **BPG (global; first attempt).**
        $BPG_a(\phi) \longleftrightarrow \exists i[E_i\phi \wedge \forall j[i \succeq_a j]]$

Thus, an agent a has best possible grounds for a claim ϕ just in case the agent has observed that ϕ on the basis of a maximally ranked information source. Abstracting away from this, we can simply say that the best possible grounds for a claim ϕ are those which are maximally ranked in the reliability ordering.

Still, this first attempt fails to account for some aspects of the variability of what the best possible grounds for a claim might be. First, as we have seen, the best possible grounds vary depending on the content of the claim. For the proposition that it is raining, perceptual evidence would be best; for the claim that John is going to town tomorrow, testimonial (or possibly inferential) evidence will be the best grounds available. This must be accounted for in the system. Fortunately, this is straightforward; we need only relativize the ranking over information sources to particular kinds of content. The tools for doing so have already been provided in chapter 3 in the context of making judgements about agent reliability with respect to particular domains, a point also touched on in the last section.

The key suggestion there was that judgements about reliability are made on the basis of observations of how reliable a particular source has been in the past. There I showed that, since histories consist of sequences of tuples of the form $\langle \varphi, v, \mathcal{P} \rangle$, it is possible to restrict attention to tuples in which $\mathcal{P}$ contains a particular property of current interest. A similar operation can be used to find the best possible grounds for a claim of a particular type. Since the first object in the tuples comprising history elements is the propositional content of the claim made in that iteration, it is possible to restrict histories to contents of particular types. Such restrictions can then be examined for reliability, yielding an ordering on sources as usual; such a case has already been seen in the example of discourse about edible fungi in the last section.

More concretely, suppose that we have a history H_a of the evidentially based observations made by agent a. Suppose that we are interested in deciding what counts as best possible grounds for claims about future events. Then we can classify these observations (the history elements) into two types: observations made about external objects in the present or past and observations made about mental states or future events. The assumption here is that there can be no concrete perceptual evidence for the latter which does not involve any kind of inference or testimony, whereas externally oriented claims about occurrences in the past or at the present time can have external correlates and so be the objects of perception.[11] The classification itself can be done on the basis of the presence of certain kinds of operators in the propositional content, such as those corresponding to verbs of perception or attitude, or to the future tense. I will not try to spell out how this might be done, but techniques from automatic event classification seem to be highly useful here.[12] This will give two subsequences of H_a: $H_a \lceil_{concrete}$ and $H_a \lceil_{nonconcrete}$.

With this, it becomes possible to examine each subsequence for evidence type. On the assumption that we are (as before) dealing with Quinean observations, each element i of the sequences will be of the form $\langle \varphi, v, \mathcal{P} \rangle_j$. Now one can sort the elements on the basis of the indices j, which correspond to different evidence types. This will give a collection of subsequences of $H_a \lceil_{concrete}$ and $H_a \lceil_{nonconcrete}$, each corresponding to propositions learned via a different type of evidence. It is easy to check these sequences for reliability by the same procedure as before: starting with the initial probability of reliability of the evidence type $P(R(e_i))$, conditionalize over it with each element of the corresponding sequence, which contains information about content and accuracy of observation. The result will be a probability of accuracy for each evidence type on the basis of all observations made. As usual, a priority ordering can be defined on the basis of these probabilities. At this point, one can examine the collection corresponding to the evidence types found in $H_a \lceil_{nonconcrete}$ to see which type is maximal in the ordering as restricted to those types. Given that propositions in $H_a \lceil_{nonconcrete}$ are not acquired via perceptual sources, no perceptual sources will be found there; the result is that, although perceptual evidence will in most situations be maximal in the priority ordering, it will not be locally maximal in that ordering as restricted to the sources in $H_a \lceil_{nonconcrete}$. Consequently, for the case of communication about mental states, perceptual evidence will not be the best possible grounds

---

[11] The metaphysical status of these claims may be hazy, but for the purposes of the analysis of natural language this distinction seems to be what is needed.

[12] See e.g. Kulkarni and Harman (2011) for some aspects of the general theory of classification, and e.g. Naughton et al. (2010) for the particular case of event classification.

after all, and (for the case of Quechua) the direct evidential will be usable despite no "direct" perceptual evidence being available.

For a specific example, consider an assertion about a future event. Suppose that I want to tell you about a concert that I believe will be held next Saturday night. I believe this on the basis of having seen an advertisement for the concert on the Internet. What kind of evidence is this? It is not direct perceptual evidence of the concert; the concert hasn't happened yet, so it cannot be perceived. Is it inferential evidence? Maybe; but if one accepts the analysis of disclaimers from chapter 3, then advertisements count in some sense as instances of communication, and thus as testimony of a particular kind. Of course such testimony can play into inference, and some sort of inference is required to move from testimony to knowledge, but this kind of inference is more a Wittgensteinian hinge than it is an activity which must be intentionally pursued. I conclude that such an advertisement is indeed a kind of testimony. Now, what are the best possible grounds for this assertion? Since the event cannot be observed, it is nonconcrete, so we must examine $H_a \lceil_{nonconcrete}$ for the maximal kind of source. Here we will find nothing more reliable than testimony in the form of advertisements (by assumption at least), so indeed I have best possible grounds for my assertion, and the direct evidential can be used, should my language have one. Further, given that bare assertions can be interpreted as having best possible grounds (as claimed in the last chapter, and also by Faller 2002b for Quechua), it is possible for the hearer to use the **Strongest evidence principle** and **Evidential to evidence** to conclude that I must have evidence of (something like) this kind for my assertion about the concert.

The upshot of the above discussion is that the notion of best possible grounds does indeed involve maximal reliability, but not in a global sense. Rather, we are interested in a local notion of maximality with respect to the priority ordering in the sense that the source must be maximally reliable with respect to some particular kind of content, a notion which can be modeled in the current system by considering subsequences of evidential histories. The definition in (8.5) must be modified to one that respects this weaker notion, yielding (8.6). The notion of "ϕ-relevant subsequence" used in (8.6) refers to the restriction of $H_i^{m,g,n}$ to ϕ-type elements, in the way described above.

(8.6) **BPG (local; final).**

$BPG_a(\phi) \longleftrightarrow \exists i[E_a^i \phi \land \forall j[j$ occurs in the ϕ-relevant subsequence of the global history $H_a \to i \succeq_a j]$.

The above defines what it is to have best possible grounds for a claim of ϕ; as before, the general notion can be obtained by abstracting away from the agent. I take this to be the right way to spell out the idea of best possible grounds; I think that the ability to do so gives some extra sense of the utility of the framework proposed in this book.

8.4 Conclusion

The aim of this chapter has been to deepen the analysis of the previous chapter and improve its empirical base to yield an understanding of context-dependency in evidential hierarchies and the notion of best possible grounds. To this end, I have incorporated a probabilistic analysis of initial judgements of reliability and shown how they may be altered by experience via a process of probabilistic conditionalization. The conditionalizing itself takes place over agent experiences with particular kinds of evidence acquisition events; the presence of histories of such events parallels the kind of experience of interaction which can lead to judgements about reliability and trustworthiness, as I argued in the first part of the book. Here we see that the judgements conversational agents make about the cooperativity of others are, in some sense, only a special case of a more general phenomenon of judgement about the reliability of information sources.

The analysis in this chapter has an interesting consequence. I have claimed that the choice of one evidential over another is dictated by reliability: the speaker is (normatively) required to pick the evidential corresponding to the maximally ranked source in the ordering of evidence sources. One obvious result of this process is that the choice of one evidential over another shows something about the speaker's beliefs about the reliability of various evidence sources. In particular, choosing a source e means that the speaker judges it more reliable than its alternatives: when more than one source of evidence exists and so multiple evidentials are usable in principle, the preferred evidential must mark the most reliable source. Returning to Faller's fox case, choosing to use a reportative evidential means that the speaker believes the source of the testimony to be extremely reliable, given that other evidentials could have been used. This side effect shows similarities with the use of gradable predicates to indicate what the speaker takes to be the standard for the predicate, discussed by Barker (2002); I may predicate *tall* of an individual even when her height is known to my interlocutor in order to indicate what I take to be the predication conditions of *tall*. A difference between the two is that it is possible for this "side effect" to be the main point of an utterance in the gradable predicate case but apparently not in the evidential case; I am not sure at present why this should be so, but it may have to do with the fact that there are no objective, external correlates of evidential strength, unlike gradable predicates such as *tall*, where one can easily check the height of the individual of which the predication is made. This could mean that coordinating over reliability is impossible, whereas it is possible with externally verifiable phenomena like height, in the way sketched in McCready (2012b).

In chapter 9, I wish to return to conversation, now considered as a species of information acquisition: the case of testimonial evidence and information acquired via testimony. Before this, however, I must note two possibly problematic points with respect to the whole project of this chapter. The first is that, as the reader may have noticed, I have drastically altered the interpretation of the histories. In the first part of the book, histories were histories of interactions between individuals and of discourse moves. I think that the existence of this kind of history should not be too controversial. But in this chapter histories are understood more generally, as histories of information acquisition events, only some of which happen via testimonial sources. This means that the elements of the histories are less discrete and are much harder to enumerate. One might question whether it is even possible to spell them out at all, leading to serious doubts about the whole project. This is of course legitimate.

For me, two main considerations speak in favor of the approach I describe (leaving out general considerations about model construction in the sciences and the relation of models to real-world phenomena). First, I find the empirical payoff to be substantial. The approach I have taken allows an explanation of variability in evidential hierarchies, and consequently of evidential choice; it also allows us a better understanding of the idea of "best possible grounds." In general, the interplay between initial settings of "trust in evidence" and experience about how evidence works is something that plays a major role in language use, and should be explained. But the main reason to accept the view is, I think, the deep parallel between our belief (or lack of belief) in the words of others and how our beliefs arise on the basis of nonlinguistic evidence. The processes described in the first part of the book and those considered in this chapter are so similar that ignoring their close relationship would miss out on a number of interesting generalizations.

This point, again, I will return to in chapter 9; the case of testimony discussed there is one for which the situation is ambiguous in that the evidence just *is* the discourse move, meaning that the worry I have just described arises exclusively for the analyses in the present chapter. But I take it that there are good reasons to accept the view I have proposed (as well as, perhaps, good reasons to deny it).

The second concern is about the feasibility of the procedure I have described. This concern was present in the first part of the book as well, but some might find it more acute here. The way I am computing reliability depends on checking the correctness of claims, in the first part, and of observations, in the case of this chapter. But is it always possible to know whether a particular claim/observation is true? Of course it's not.[13] Isn't this a problem for the account? In some sense, yes; it corresponds quite closely to the problem of assuming complete information in game theory, something already mentioned earlier with respect to the analysis of reliability in the first part of the book. Whether it is genuinely problematic in the present case depends on whether one thinks that the particular kind of abstraction I am employing distorts the data in a pernicious way. I don't think that it does; in particular, I think that it is reasonable just to disregard those cases where truth cannot be verified one way or the other, which corresponds in this framework to leaving them out of the computation of reliability, something already discussed in chapter 3. Formally I implemented a solution by using a third truth value in addition to T and F, namely "?", and allowing it to appear as the second element of the history-element tuples. I then excluded ?-valued tuples from the computation of reliability. I think that the availability of this kind of move should alleviate this particular concern about the model. On the assumption that it does, I will turn to testimony next.

---

[13] It might be impossible in various ways: we could just lack any way to find out, as with claims we don't know how to verify, or it could be literally impossible to learn, as on epistemicist analyses of vagueness.

9

Testimonial evidence

The first part of this book was concerned with cooperation and trust in language use, and especially with the problem of when it is appropriate to believe the utterances of others (together with some linguistic consequences of the proposal). The second part has discussed various pragmatic aspects of evidence and evidentiality, with the dual goals of showing how source reliability influences the use of evidentials and examining how judgements about such reliability are arrived at and changed. As we have seen, the two kinds of phenomena correspond to a surprising degree.

There is an obvious point of overlap between these two topics, one already discussed to a certain extent in the last few chapters: the case of testimonial evidence. Here, we have information acquired via linguistic sources, in particular the testimony of others. Not just any such information qualifies. For instance, we would not want to say that, speaking to you for the first time on the phone, I acquire via your testimony the knowledge that your voice is husky; presumably this information is acquired from my perception of your vocal qualities. In general, information acquired via testimony is limited to the directly communicated content of the utterance comprising the testimony. For our purposes here, this will do well enough as a working definition of what testimony is; a much more substantial discussion can be found in chapter 2 of Lackey (2008).[1]

The nature of testimony, and its role in the acquisition of knowledge, has been getting a good deal of scrutiny in the philosophical literature in recent years. Section 9.1 is devoted to a consideration of some of this literature and its relation to the present work. We will see that the approach I have proposed relates closely to some philosophical views, but is distinct from them in various respects. Here I will also discuss the

---

[1] I do not wish to enter debates about the precise definition of testimony, e.g. the problem of whether the speaker need intend to communicate the testimonial content, or the relation of testimony to "what is said" in the sense of Grice (1975) or Bach (1999).

relation of my analysis to the problem of the acquisition of knowledge from testimony, the focus of most of the recent literature. I will then turn to two problems in the semantics and pragmatics of testimonial evidence. Section 9.2 considers a semantic issue. Suppose that each speaker is associated with an evidential source index, as I proposed in the preceding chapters; suppose also that other evidentials are also associated with such source indices. Each index is associated with a degree of reliability. But what happens when the two combine, i.e. where we observe a testimonial event of the form $Evid\phi$? Should the likelihood of ϕ be upgraded or downgraded on the basis of the dual separation from the initial observation induced by the evidential plus the testimony itself; and should update take place on the substate associated with the speaker, or on that associated with the evidence source the speaker cites as her basis? I will claim that, here, we again encounter a reason to implement priority reasoning at two levels. As it turns out, the pragmatic discussion of the first part of the book proves to be more closely parallel with the assignment of reliability to nonlinguistic sources than to linguistic sources, whereas the assignment of reliability to evidentials simply shadows this within the purely linguistic system. These observations lead to the implementation of a genuinely two-level system of reliability determination and corresponding priority orderings across evidence sources. The result proves to immediately provide a solution to a kind of pragmatic paradox, considered in section 9.3. In the philosophical literature, one can find the normative principle that one ought to trust in testimony in the absence of confounding factors. There are reasons to think that this principle is true. Nonetheless, it conflicts with what we intuitively find with respect to the assertion of evidential content. As we will see, the separation of evidential reasoning into two levels allows a simple way to avoid this problem, and thus solve the "paradox."

The final part of the chapter, section 9.4, is devoted to disclaimed content. Disclaimed content is still asserted on the picture I developed in the first part of this book; this means that it is incorporated in some way into the belief state of the hearer. But how? And what should the hearer do with such content? I will explore several approaches to these issues, concluding that disclaimed testimony should be assigned its own (speaker-relative) index, allowing disclaimed testimony to be assigned a different status than nondisclaimed testimony within the process of evidential update. The result places disclaimers and hedges into the class of evidentials from a formal perspective.

9.1 Philosophical approaches

Before considering philosophical views in more detail, I want to briefly remind the reader of the analysis I have developed in the preceding chapters.

On my story, trust in testimony is based on two distinct factors. The content of testimony is information; information comes from an evidence source. The reliability of information is derived from the reliability of the source of that information, its evidential basis; this basis in turn is given an initial probability of reliability based on external factors. Subsequent experience with that source changes the likelihood that information coming from it is true due to confirmation or discon-firmation of the hypothesis that the source is reliable, a process handled by conditionalization over accurate or inaccurate observations on the basis of the source. This is the basic process of computing how worthy of trust an information source is.

Testimony is just one special case of this process. The reliability of a case of testimony is associated with the reliability of the source of that testimony. Here, the key is to treat each individual who can be the source of testimony as a distinct evidence source, as proposed in the last chapter; this allows for variations in reliability on an individual basis, something which is clearly desirable from both empirical and intuitive standpoints. This treatment implies that each individual can be associated with an initial probability of reliability. I believe that this is correct; some points in favor will be raised in the remainder of this section.

With this outline again in hand, let us turn to consider some philo-sophical analyses of testimony. I will begin in section 9.1.1 with a pair of traditional views in the Western tradition, those of Reid and Hume, on which much of the subsequent literature is based, and then turn, in section 9.1.2, to more recent and complex pictures of testimony. Throughout, my aim will be less careful exegesis than an attempt to place my own account within the landscape of testimonial analysis. I should add a caveat: the literature on testimony is very large, and I will not attempt anything like an exhaustive overview here.[2] My aim is mainly to try to achieve a clearer understanding of the picture developed in this book.

---

[2] See Adler (2013) for a very useful survey, as well as Lackey (2008) for something a bit more opinionated.

9.1.1 Two classical views

The starting points for the present revival in work on testimony in philosophy are the views of David Hume (1977) and Thomas Reid (1997), which are often now referred to as reductionist and anti-reductionist views about belief in testimony. The views are stated relatively briefly and admit a variety of interpretations.[3] In outline they are clear, though; the basic conflict is over whether justifying belief in testimony requires appeal to factors external to our linguistic practice. Hume thinks it does; Reid thinks it doesn't.

What kind of external factors need we appeal to, according to Hume? On this picture, we need to find independent evidence for trustworthiness. We might check a person's appearance for cues that we associate with being worthy of trust; we might check a person's previous history of testimonial interaction for reliability. Generalizing, the source of external evidence will be something acquired (for instance) through perceptual sources, and which will not require any kind of principle specific to testimony. There is empirical support for this view: to take only one instance, even young children consider the previous reliability of informants, as well as information concerning their relation to social norms, in deciding whether to believe testimony in the case of conflict (Harris and Corriveau 2011). It thus seems very likely that adults, who are generally far less credulous, make use of similar though presumably more complex mechanisms. Still, contemporary proponents seem to ignore work on cooperation in evolutionary theory, as well as the work of Grice (1975): the lesson from, for example, the results of Nowak and collaborators (Nowak 2006; Ohtsuki and Iwasa 2004) is that an initial cooperative move tends to lead to the most advantageous scenario, and so (given that most of our communication is cooperative at some level) humans have likely evolved in such a way as to make presumptive moves about interlocutor cooperativity (see also Tomasello 2008). It seems hard to reconcile these results with pure reductionism.

Anti-reductionist views originate with Thomas Reid (1997), who discusses "a propensity to seek truth" and "a disposition to . . . believe what [others] tell us." Taking these principles together, we find a kind of social contract between speaker and hearer: the hearer believes the speaker, and (given a shared goal of truth-seeking) the speaker is inclined to present the facts in an accurate way. This kind of view,

---

[3] See, for example, van Cleve (2006) and Graham (2006a) for some possible ways to spell them out more fully.

as Adler (2013) notes, relates closely to Gricean cooperation and so is familiar to linguistic pragmatics (as usually practiced). It also seems well supported by the results about cooperative behavior in game theory and theoretical biology discussed in chapter 2. But we should not accept the testimony of others willy-nilly. Doing so would be evolutionary suicide, given that individuals ordinarily do not have fully aligned interests: when communicating, one's incentive to lie might be quite large in many cases. Ignoring these facts would violate the "Epistemic Vigilance" principles of Sperber et al. (2010). Thus there is a reason to take into account the relative trustworthiness of others when considering how to treat the information they give us. Although we might begin by trusting others, we will stop if they violate that trust enough times.

It therefore seems that there are arguments on both sides of the reductionist–anti-reductionist debate. But in fact, the views are not incompatible, as also pointed out by Graham (2006b). It is plainly possible that people might have a predisposition to cooperation which is expressed in part as an inclination to trust others (and to be Gricean cooperators in general), yet also "vet" other agents for reliability based on various external factors. In fact it seems pretty clear that this is exactly what people do. The communicative norm on this picture, then, is to trust as a default, but allow that default to be easily overridden by specific information about the communicating agent. This kind of synthesis appears to be a highly attractive view; in fact even philosophical views explicitly self-describing as reductionist or anti-reductionist in character often import portions of the opposing picture to handle various empirical contingencies.

In this sense, my own analysis is typical. I have argued on the basis of game-theoretical considerations that a move of initial trust is optimal, and that this is a kind of implementation of the Gricean picture;[4] this is a kind of anti-reductionist element in the theory. But I have also argued that agents make use of relatively strict mechanisms for evaluating the trustworthiness of other agents, implementing them as histories of actions and inductive calculations over such histories about future behavior. Plainly such histories provide a source of data external to the current act of testimonial transmission. External factors are in play even more obviously after the extension of the theory developed in the previous chapter, on which each agent is associated with an initial

---

[4] I further showed that when Gricean norms are violated, language makes available a means of compensating for those violations.

probability of trustworthiness via the source index assigned to her. These probabilities are, necessarily, set on the basis of external factors, for they are initial and thus present before any linguistic interaction takes place. Thus the theory incorporates a reductionist element as well.

One question that might arise is whether the assumption of initial probabilities is really compatible with the notion of initial trust. How can a speaker be said to make an initial cooperative move with respect to another's testimony if she is simultaneously evaluating that agent for the likelihood of trustworthiness? The two are compatible, I think, but it's likely that there is a threshold beyond which initial trust does not apply. Let's consider how probabilities might interact with initial trust. Consider first a case where the initial probability is very high. For this, we can take a classical example from the literature on games of coordination. Suppose that you are arranging a business meeting and are deciding where to meet. The other party would like to sell you a product; negotiations are complete, and all that remains is to sign the contract. But it must be signed today. If you cannot meet, the sale cannot be made, and the salesperson cannot get her commission. Thus she has every incentive to meet you. She tells you the name of a coffee shop where you will meet to sign the contract and says that she will be there at 3 pm. Should you trust her? Of course. She has every reason not to lie. Here the initial trust move dovetails with the prescription made by the initial, high probability of reliability, and trust is dictated.

Now imagine you are a policeman who has just pulled over a person who has been driving erratically, weaving all over the road and shouting incoherently. After you flashed your lights at them for several minutes, they finally came to a stop, but only when they hit a trash can. The person cannot stand straight and looks extremely drunk. You ask if he has been drinking and he denies it. Here the probability of reliability is minimal. The driver knows he is in trouble and he has every incentive to lie; in addition, all environmental clues make it clear that he is not to be trusted on this issue. Thus the initial trust move is overruled; the probability is just too low.

The interesting case is the intermediate one, where the probabilities are not overwhelmingly high or low. Suppose that we encounter someone who is, most likely, trustworthy, given the setting: for instance, imagine having a discussion about driver license registration procedures with an employee at the municipal office. The employee looks normal and has no reason to lie; we have no reason to disbelieve, but no particular reason to believe either, for what do we ultimately know about this person's motivations? Here is where initial trust comes into play; for cases like these, the account has an anti-reductionist component. This view can easily be spelled out formally using the threshold-based system of Kennedy (1999, 2007) used in chapter 3 to make judgements about cooperativity. We simply need to say that there is a threshold for initial probability below which trust is *disallowed*, and one above which it is *dictated*; between those thresholds, in the reliability "penumbra" in the sense of Fine (1975), initial trust will indeed apply.

9.1.2 Testimony and knowledge

An important thing to note is that the recent philosophical literature is almost entirely concerned with when testimony yields knowledge. But for the purposes of asking what should be done about update with evidentials—and, more generally, with testimony—we need not concern ourselves with the question of knowledge proper, but only with when it is justified to believe some testimonial (decorated with an evidential, or not, as the case may be). Work on belief acquisition and common ground within linguistics in general, and dynamic semantics in particular, has never seriously (to my knowledge) taken into account any distinction between knowledge and belief; indeed, to the extent that such a distinction can be supported, it does not seem to be relevant for the analysis of linguistic communication and information transfer.

Still, this epistemological literature on testimony must answer questions closely related to what I have developed in the preceding chapters. If the main question about testimony is the circumstances under which an instance of testimony can result in knowledge, then it becomes possible to isolate factors which can play a role in determining whether an instance of testimony counts as knowledge. As it turns out, there are a great number of such factors, including the testimonial agent, the circumstances of the testimony, its content, and so on, many of which we have seen earlier. It is impossible to survey all this work here; instead, I will just pick up some representative work and try to compare it to my own, and also show how my system addresses some criticisms of testimonial views and criteria for accounts of testimony proposed in that work.

We may begin with Coady (1992), whose work started off the resurgence of interest in testimony. Coady offers an anti-reductionist account, presenting various arguments against reductionist approaches. One such argument (in his chapter 4) is leveled against the original reductionist, Hume. Hume seems to assume that we have access to a general set of observations about testimony: the observations made by a group of individuals. Such a set is necessary to make judgements about the general reliability of testimony, because obviously every individual doesn't have a way to compute the reliability of all kinds of testimony or the testimony of any given agent. But this assumption seems unmotivated; speakers actually only have access to the observations they themselves have made. Thus, according to Coady, the reductionist view does not have access to everything needed for a general account. This is one motivation for an anti-reductionist view which takes testimony to be worth trusting by default; in my account, this is realized as the introduction of the "Gricean step" at the beginning of an interaction, when, as I argued, considerations of future utility motivate a move of initial trust.

Elizabeth Fricker (1995: 397) makes an interesting criticism of Coady's approach. Fricker's reading of Coady has him leaving a pair of key issues open: (i) the relationship between the authority of the speaker and the reliability or epistemic status of that speaker's testimonial, and (ii) whether the hearer must be *aware* of that reliability. Clearly, the ultimate reliability of a testimonial will depend on the speaker's epistemic authority, and so, without a way to judge that authority, it is difficult to make judgements about reliability. Fricker herself takes the view that one can and should judge *on a given occasion* whether the informant is sincere and knowledgeable; if so, one should trust the informant, and if not, not. She calls this view *local reduction*. This view is attractive but it comes with a difficulty: one must develop a mechanism on which such judgements can be based without resorting to prior instances of behavior (together with an initial trust move).

On my own view, the judgement is built into the pragmatic representation: since judgements about reliability depend on past observations, inductive reasoning directly gives a way to judge a speaker's epistemic authority.[5] But in initial interactions, judgements of epistemic authority are not available, requiring that we begin with an initial move of trust (which amounts to the assumption of reliability), as required by Grice. These judgements are not local in the sense that they depend only on the current discourse move, but they are local in the sense that judgement itself is made locally rather than generally. Still, the view I develop is very close in many respects to that advocated for by

---

[5] Of course, prior probabilities also come into play. See also Olsson (2005) on this issue.

Fricker: she wishes testimony (contra Coady) to be a "disaggregated" or nonuniform category. My theory achieves just this: each individual is treated as a distinct information source, to be judged trustworthy or not-trustworthy on an individual basis. Implicit in my categorization, though, is that other information sources be aggregated to some extent, since generalization over source types is, to some degree, necessary. We cannot simply distinguish each instance of sense perception, but instead have to deal with sense perception of a particular kind, possibly under some circumstances or range of objects, or even with sources of sensory evidence as a general class.

Let us turn to another source that will shed some light on my view: Graham (2000). Graham provides three assumptions that he takes to be crucial for accounts of testimony (on p. 699), in particular for accounts which take it that trust in testimony should track epistemic authority and, in general, reliability. The first is his *discovery assumption*: in cases of "bad testimony," hearers will learn that speakers are unreliable and speakers will learn that hearers are unreceptive. The second is the *rationality assumption*: if hearers have evidence that speakers are unreliable, they will not believe them anymore, and if speakers have evidence that hearers will not believe them they will stop reporting. Last is the *veracity assumption*: roughly, speakers are experts in their domains of discourse. Without these three assumptions, testimony will be unable to effectively transmit information, according to Graham.

As might be clear to the reader already, each of these assumptions corresponds to an aspect of my model. In terms of my account, the discovery assumption amounts to assuming that agents have sufficient information about histories to make proper judgements. If they do not, they may fail to properly use the information provided by histories to track reliability in the desired way. I have assumed, in fact, that agents have perfect information about histories, but it seems likely that some weakening of this assumption would still deliver (much of) the desired results. The second assumption, about rationality, is the key assumption of the game model: game players must be rational and behave in accordance with their best interests. I make this assumption together with the whole literature on cooperation in games, I believe. Finally, the veracity assumption is key to all Gricean accounts of communication: agents must be assumed to have at least some degree of expertise, or we have no reason to believe anything they say, for they would have no way to respect Quality. A detailed discussion of this point can be found in

Geurts (2010) and also in Schulz and van Rooij (2006), in the context of discussions of the derivation of conversational implicatures.[6]

Let me now turn to a final instance of philosophical analysis of testimony, the work of Jennifer Lackey. Lackey provides an attractive account of how knowledge is acquired from testimony: its key feature is that knowledge comes from the testimony itself and is not parasitic on the beliefs or knowledge of the testifier. I believe that such a theory will not be very surprising for researchers in formal pragmatics. For linguists, it seems to be a normal assumption that we learn information from utterances, not from speakers, so speaker mental states are not directly relevant to the evaluation of what is learned, because what is learned from an utterance is independent of whether or not the speaker is right in believing what she says. My model, on which any utterance induces the update of an epistemic substate of some kind, is in this tradition and makes the same assumption. Thus the problems Lackey outlines in her chapters 2 and 3 do not arise for me at all.

Ultimately, Lackey arrives at a theory on which speakers learn information from utterances, and whether that information counts as knowledge depends jointly on properties of speakers—whether they are reliable, and whether the information they have is reliable—and properties of hearers—whether they have information that serves as a defeater for the utterance content. This kind of view seems highly reasonable, and it is at least partly carried over in my account. For me, reliability is something that hearers judge on the basis of their experience with individual speakers (the histories), and on properties of such speakers that may influence whether they appear reliable (the initial probabilities). This is the speaker side of Lackey's view. Regardless

---

[6] Graham gives an example which points up problematic issues for a wide range of formal approaches to pragmatics. His scenario involves a community where speakers communicate at long distances about trivial matters. They have no reason to care whether each other's utterances are true or not; as he says, for them, reports may all just be small talk. Presumably communication can take place regardless, and trust. What is the moral of this story?

Based on my analysis, I would say that the story indicates that our mechanisms of self-protection with regard to testimony are put in place for purposes that don't involve small talk, so that standard cases of communication in general reflect more directly on utilities. I find this view to be in line with ideas of the genesis of animal signaling in biology. We may then say that speech in Graham's community, and also other instances of small talk in human society, are parasitic on utility-directed (or relevant) communication. Formal pragmatics in general is directed at communication whose aim is information transmission; this is so even in related work in fields like economics (Farrell and Rabin 1996). The lesson, I take it, is that we should carefully consider the relationship between small talk and "contentful" communication; the prevalence of small talk means that our models are missing out on a large amount of human communicative practice.

of such judgements, the hearer will acquire the information transmitted by the speaker, but it may be downgraded heavily in the process of information aggregation, on the basis of these judgements of reliability. Still, in the information aggregation process, the downgrade will only matter if there is conflicting information, i.e. a defeater that the speaker has in some belief state on the basis of a more reliable source. This represents the hearer's contribution. What is left out is whether one *actually* has knowledge. But this property is an extralinguistic one and so has no natural place in my project; further, it's not one that language users are in a position to judge in general, given that they are likely to lack crucial information.[7] Still, reputation-based judgements are likely to track knowledge in at least some cases.

It is interesting here to speculate on the near silence on Grice in the philosophical literature on testimony.[8] It seems to me that Gricean cooperation is a reasonable starting point for a theory of testimony (and its epistemology for that matter); indeed this is what I have tried to provide, in terms of a game-theoretic stance on cooperation. Beginning with Gricean cooperation seems to bring us close to what Lackey wants: no reductionist focus on the hearer, and no nonreductionist focus on the speaker,[9] but instead speakers who, normatively, cooperate by following Quality, and hearers who, lacking information to the contrary, assume that they do and proceed to cooperate themselves by trusting. This is what I have given, and it seems to be roughly in the Gricean tradition.

Of course, one problem with this kind of view is that it doesn't intrinsically have any way to distinguish knowledge from belief. Some means of doing so must be provided independently. The concentration of recent work on testimony on the acquisition of knowledge thus might explain why Grice is not prominent in the epistemological literature. But I think that there is a sense in which this lack of an automatic distinction between testimonially derived knowledge and belief is not particularly problematic: the normative question of when one should take testimony

---

[7] This property is one that most of Lackey's scenarios have: for instance, in her INSULAR COMMUNITY scenario (pp. 164–165), Marvin crucially lacks the information that he is speaking to the only reliably communicative individual in the town.

[8] In (the 2013 version of) the *Stanford Encyclopedia of Philosophy* entry on the epistemology of testimony (Adler 2013), Grice shows up as a reference on "what is said" and its relation to testimony, and as a comparison point for Burge's (1993) Acceptance Principle (on which more below). It does not seem that anyone has seriously adopted a straightforwardly Gricean view.

[9] I am here using Lackey's viewpoint and terminology from her chapter 6.

to provide knowledge is distinct from the epistemological question of when testimony actually does provide knowledge. There seems no special reason to treat them together. What I have done here is to take the two questions to be separate, and treat testimony as just analogous to other kinds of evidence sources. None of this has any implications about knowledge, only about when one is justified in coming to believe some proposition. The only differences between testimony and other information sources, for me, are that testimony comes with an initial disposition to trust that other evidence sources lack, and the complexity of the information states associated with testimonial agents; the former, of course, comes from cooperativity in the Gricean sense, which itself arguably is the result of evolutionary considerations, and the latter from the variety of the information which testimony can provide.

We now have a sense of where my account lies in the landscape of work on testimony. Ultimately there are two components that have to be considered to situate my account: the notion of initial trust, and the effect of histories. Claiming that initial trust is a feature of human communication makes me an anti-reductionist of some species—in particular, a Gricean one, for I take this trust to follow from Gricean considerations.[10] Using histories, in particular, puts me in the company of Goldberg and Henderson (2006), who require hearers to "monitor" testimonial agents for reliability, and withdraw trust in its absence. This is very much what I have proposed here. But my use of initial probabilities is reductionist in character, and makes my theory a mixed one.

9.2 Evidential testimony

I now want to return to linguistic issues and address what might look like a problematic case for my system. What happens in the case of utterances which themselves contain evidentials? It might seem that my system leaves it unclear what should be done with such utterances, for here we have two different information sources: the information source associated with the evidential, and the agent of the testimony. In this section I will show that this worry is unfounded and that there is a straightforward means of updating with utterances like these, once it

---

[10] Note that the prediction is that children will trust in testimony in general, as Reid has it, because they won't have the resources to check for falsity, though this could also be taken to follow from other sources.

is recognized that the two evidence sources are operating at different levels. This way of thinking about these issues will be the key to my treatment of the "paradox" discussed in the next section (9.3).

Concretely, suppose we have a proposition φ learned on the basis of evidence source e. I have argued that adding this proposition to a stock of beliefs induces update in the information state indexed with e, and that the global information state reflects the relative reliability the agent assigns to this and other information sources. Suppose now that the evidence source is the testimony of some agent a. Then the state updated will be that associated with a. If the testimony itself is a sentence of the form $Evid_i\phi$, a sentence marked with an evidential E, then there would appear to be a question about whether we should update the state σ_a or the state σ_i. One might even conclude that we need to jointly update both σ_a and σ_i, for both sources are represented in the observation of the utterance: a as the source of the utterance, and $Evid_i$ as the source of the information a provides.

Resolving these questions is quite simple. We need only observe that in the case under discussion we have an instance of testimony, but of testimony *about* information believed on some evidential basis. The testimony thus incorporates two elements: the information itself, and, secondarily, information about the source as well.

The upshot is that these cases don't need to be treated differently, in any important way, from cases of "pure" testimony: in both, we have update with a proposition φ on the basis of the testimony of a, resulting in the update $\sigma_a[\varphi]$. In the case of update with an evidentially marked sentence, φ merely happens to be of the form $Evid_i\psi$. The testimonial agent presumably chooses to use that sentence, $Evid_i\psi$, because E_i-type evidence is the most reliable sort on the basis of which she believes ψ, but this should not in itself force the hearer to update σ_i with ψ, for σ_i should be reserved for direct updates with i-type evidence. Rather, we simply get the update $\sigma_a[Evid_i\psi]$, as we expect from the basic system. This section will provide the technical extension required for this analysis.

Still, in some cases of observation of $Evid_i\psi$ update with ψ will be warranted. Indeed, we should expect that this will happen quite often. Consider languages with mandatory use of evidentials, so (virtually) all sentences are evidentially marked. It would be odd for conversational agents processing these sentences to learn from them only that the agents of the testimony have this or that kind of evidence for the claims that they are making, but never to learn the content of the actual claims.

We would like our theory of update not to predict this situation: that, from evidential testimony, one can only learn the evidential basis of the testimonial agent. At the moment, this is what we have, which is undesirable.

Fortunately, the theory makes several options available here for a fix. There seem to be two straightforward ways to allow removal of the evidential basis from evidentially marked content in order to update with that content directly. The first follows directly from a natural elaboration of the current system. The second invokes pragmatic mediation between evidence and update. I will explore each in turn, but ultimately show that the second possibility is effectively subsumed in the first, at least within my theory.

The first method starts with the observation that the evidentially marked content will also be part of a hierarchy. Suppose that we have evidence sources e_1 and e_2, where $e_1 \prec e_2$ in the priority ordering. If a acquires φ on the basis of e_1 and ψ on the basis of e_2, then, assuming that φ and ψ are compatible, we will have $\sigma \models \varphi$ and $\sigma \models \psi$ for a's global information state σ; nonetheless, given the Strongest evidence principle, a will communicate φ and ψ with utterances of evidentially marked sentences interpreted as $Evid_1\varphi$ and $Evid_2\psi$ respectively. Suppose now that a's interlocutor updates σ_i with the content of these utterances, the expected result given that update is taking place on the basis of a's testimony; this is possible due to the assumption that each testimonial agent is a distinct evidence source and so associated with a distinct substate. We will then have $\sigma_a[Evid_1\varphi; Evid_2\psi]$, as the part of the interlocutor's information state corresponding to the testimony of a will be updated sequentially with these two pieces of content.

What then is the form of σ_a? This is the key question, and it is one that does not arise in the context of non-testimonial information sources. Up to now all σ_i have had the form of simple sets of worlds together with an ordering on them. But, as noted by authors like Lackey (2008), the content of testimony is extremely heterogeneous. From the utterances of others, we can learn facts about external objects in the world, people's mental states, or even their speculations. All of these things are presumably not equally reliable, and the testimonial agents themselves presumably don't treat them as equally reliable; this is essentially the claim made by the aggregation model I have proposed, to the extent that the presence of substates keyed to different kinds of evidence sources are present in all agents. This observation implies that σ_a should *itself* be the kind of highly articulated information state I have proposed. This is not the case for other kinds of evidence sources, which lack this kind of heterogeneity. Explicitly, then, we want the following to be the case.

(9.1) **Form of information substates.**
  a. $\sigma_i = \langle X, \leq_a \rangle$ for $i \in$ Source, where $X \subseteq W$
  b. $\sigma_i = \{\sigma^j | \exists j E_j^a \varphi\}$ for $i \in \mathcal{A}$

Thus substates associated with non-testimonial information sources are simplex and consist of plausibility frames in the sense of Baltag and Smets (2008, 2009), while substates associated with testimonial agents are collections of simplex states, including a substate for each information source from which the agent has acquired information.

Suppose then that σ_a is articulated in this way; because each evidence source that a has acquired information from is represented as a substate of σ_a, there is guaranteed to be some substate of σ_a corresponding to e_1 and some other corresponding to e_2.[11] I will write σ_a^1 for the first and σ_a^2 for the second. Given this, after the update with $Evid_1 \varphi; Evid_2 \psi$, we will have $\sigma_a^1[\varphi]$ and $\sigma_a^2[\psi]$. This articulation allows us to perform aggregation on these information states before integrating σ_a with the other substates of the agent's global state, to arrive at the global beliefs of the updating agent. Given that there are no conflicts, the global belief state of the agent will verify both φ and ψ, which is what we needed, since the evidential decorations have been removed; even if there are conflicts, the content associated with the more reliable source will be retained minus its evidential decoration.[12] Still, the information about evidence sources remains, buried deeply within the layers of sub-information states corresponding to the testimony of a.

It seems that this natural extension of the theory I have proposed is enough to account for the possibility of what we might call non-evidential update on the basis of evidential sentences, with the added bonus that the evidential information remains for speakers to reason about if such should be required. For example, they might need it in order to evaluate the reliability of a particular testimonial agent with respect to some particular kind of evidence source, as with the cases presented in chapters 3, 7, and 8. I take the availability of this kind of inference to be another argument for articulating the states

---

[11] I assume here that e_1 and e_2 are sufficiently distinct to warrant having separate substates.

[12] Note that the reliability ranking at issue should be that of the updating individual, not that of the speaker.

associated with testimonial agents in the way I have proposed. I believe that all substates corresponding to testimonial agents should be taken to be articulated in this way. This case should be distinguished from the substates corresponding to more monolithic information sources; it's not at all clear to me that the state corresponding to information acquired via visual sources needs to be further articulated, for example, especially given that much of the information we might wish to use such articulation for is already present in the history of acquisition of visual evidence.

I mentioned another, pragmatic, possibility. The idea would be to allow orderings of reliability to mediate introduction of content into information states. In particular, suppose that agent a utters ϕ on the basis of maximally ranked evidence source e_1, as we know from her use of evidential $Evid_1$, which requires e_1-type evidence for its use. Then we might think that there is an implication of maximal reliability, to the extent that we trust the speaker's judgement and honesty. I think that this process is much like what Faller (2012) has in mind with her notion of evidential implicature. I find this kind of view quite reasonable, but something like it is already built into my model: since e_1 is ranked highly, the information it provides will persist in σ_a, and given that the speaker is sufficiently reliable or worthy of trust on the basis of her past history of speech, then presumably information she transmits to us will also be relatively highly ranked. In this situation, that information will be preserved in the aggregation process. I thus think that my system succeeds in spelling out some Gricean aspects of evidential use, just as one would hope, given the spirit of my project.

This is the place to reconsider the process of deriving total information states introduced in chapter 7. Recall that such states are derived by merging all elements of the global information state σ. This is quite straightforward: one need only order those elements according to the priority ranking, and, starting with the lowest-ranked pair of elements, recursively merge each adjacent pair until only a single element is left, which can be identified with the total information state. A complication arises, however, once we allow complex information states for testimonial agents as proposed above. Such states are not of the proper form to enter a merge operation, because instead of being plausibility frames of the form $\langle X, \leq_a \rangle$ (for set of states X and plausibility ordering $\leq_a$), they may contain sets of plausibility frames corresponding to other testimonial agents in addition to "ordinary" plausibility frames. Therefore, in order to ensure that a merge operation can be performed, it is necessary to first merge all complex states until each element in σ has the form of a plausibility frame.

This is straightforward enough (see Appendix, clause 5.b), but requires the assumption that at some depth of embedding all elements of the testimonial state are plausibility frames and not sets of such frames. In other words, there must be a point at which the testimony is grounded in non-testimonial evidence. From an epistemological perspective, this might look worrisome (for some), as it appears to commit us to a foundationalist view of justification. However, note that the model presented here is not primarily epistemological, but is intended to allow us to understand how update proceeds with respect to communicative acts. This is especially so for the case of testimony: substates of the state associated with a testimonial agent are only updated when the agent's utterance includes an evidential. The embeddings here therefore correspond to updates with evidentials, rather than with updates on the basis of particular kinds of justification. Since sequences of evidentials cannot be extended indefinitely, it is clear that the embeddings must terminate at some point. It is therefore guaranteed that the construction will work as intended, without any worry about undesirable epistemological commitments.

9.3 Testimonial update: a paradox and a solution

This section is concerned with an application of the proposal from the previous section. The combination of nonreductionist views about testimony and an idea of evidential implicature gives rise to something superficially paradoxical in the context of utterances including hearsay evidentials, namely that one should, normatively speaking, simultaneously both believe and not believe the prejacent of an utterance marked with a hearsay evidential. After setting up the relevant assumptions, I will describe how the paradox arises, and then close by showing how it evaporates when placed into the framework of the previous section.

For a starting point, consider the anti-reductionist position of Burge (1993). Burge proposes an "Acceptance Principle," which says that one is entitled to accept a piece of testimony in the absence of compelling reasons not to do so. So if there are no defeaters, we normatively ought to believe what is said. Burge takes this to be an innate tendency. Let's suppose that a principle something like this is in effect; in the present setting, it amounts to the move of initial trust, as both low initial probabilities (stemming from observational factors) and past bad experiences with the testifier will count as defeaters for the purposes of the Acceptance Principle.

Now consider the implicatures that arise from the use of evidentials. As Faller (2012) observes, use of an evidential which requires best possible grounds such as the Quechua direct evidential implicates a high degree of confidence, as the speaker is indicating that she has the most reliable kind of evidence available. Other evidentials can implicate lower levels of confidence. Consider the example in (9.2), which contains a hearsay evidential.

(9.2)   Para-sha-n-si
        rain-Prog-3-SI
        'It is raining.' + speaker was told that it is raining (Faller 2002b)

Recall that hearsay evidentials (on Faller's analysis at least) do not genuinely assert their prejacents, but only "proffer" them to the hearer to do with as she will. If this is correct, then the prejacent is taken up for information update via some kind of inferential process, which will not always apply. In general, the sort of reasoning immediately above seems to lead to this process not applying very often, because testimonial evidence varies in quality so widely. Further, it seems that, given that evidentials can induce implicatures, we may get an implicature that the prejacent is not very likely to be true.

Suppose that the speaker has a choice between asserting $Dir\phi$ and asserting $Rep\phi$ (for some direct evidential Dir and hearsay evidential Rep). $Rep\phi$ requires a weaker justification than $Dir\phi$ and is likely to be less reliable. Thus, given that the speaker asserted $Rep\phi$ rather than $Dir\phi$, we can conclude on the usual Gricean grounds that she was not sufficiently confident in her justification to assert $Dir\phi$, though here the notion of Gricean Quantity needs to be modified slightly to refer to justificational strength, not entailment; this notion of strength is essentially that deployed by Faller (2012). But then the justificational basis is, arguably, not very strong, and, on Gricean grounds, it does not appear to be reasonable for the hearer to add ϕ to her stock of beliefs.

But now consider the following alternate pattern of reasoning. Take a hearer who observes an utterance of ϕ and uses the Acceptance Principle. The Acceptance Principle tells us that ϕ should be accepted, given that there are no confounders. Thus the fact that the speaker proffers ϕ will be enough to justify the hearer coming to believe that

ϕ. But now suppose that ϕ is of the form *Repψ* for some hearsay evidential *Rep*.[13] Then should the hearer just come to believe *Repψ*? She should; but perhaps she should do more, given the Acceptance Principle. This principle instructs us to believe the content of testimony; since hearsay evidentials by definition indicate that the information in their prejacents was acquired via the means of testimony, the prejacent should be believed as well.

We now have two inferential chains which lead to contradictory conclusions. This is the 'paradox of testimony' mentioned earlier. It can be resolved in various ways (even if one grants the assumptions which cause it to arise in the first place). In earlier work on the topic I took the right way to think about this case to be to limit the application of the Acceptance Principle to instances of direct testimony (McCready forthcoming, a). The result is that one ought to trust the testimony one is given, but there is no predisposition to trust in testimony which is not given directly. This limitation makes a good deal of sense when one considers Acceptance from a Gricean standpoint: cooperation is a relationship between individuals engaged in certain kinds of interactions, but there is no cooperative relationship between a conversational participant and the anonymous agents of the kind of testimony referenced by hearsay evidentials.

The result of limiting the Acceptance Principle in this way is that there is no predisposition to accept the prejacents of hearsay evidentials at all. This is certainly one way to solve the paradox. But the elaboration of our system in the previous section opens up another option, on which no paradox ever arises at all.

Consider the treatment I have proposed of update with evidential testimony. The basic idea was that each testimonial agent is associated with a complex information state, which itself is subject to the processes of belief aggregation which yield a global information state for the updating agent. The result is something like a two-level system with respect to testimonial update: first the content of instances of testimony which are labeled with evidential sources is added to the relevant substates of the state associated with the testimonial agent, and then, after these substates are combined via aggregation, the resulting information is added, again via aggregation, to the global stock of beliefs of the updating agent.

---

[13] I don't think it matters much for this chain of reasoning whether the evidential is part of the asserted content, modifies the speech act, or whatever other options are available (cf. chapter 6).

On this picture, there is no place for the Acceptance Principle to apply to third-hand reports at all. Content of the form $Rep\phi$, when uttered by an agent a, will be added to the substate associated with general hearsay evidence, but this substate itself, since it results from a's testimony, is included in σ_a, the substate associated with the testimonial agent a, and thus is in fact σ_a^h. The Acceptance Principle, as a pragmatic phenomenon, will apply only to the testimony of a, not to the embedded testimony; further, Acceptance will only militate for update of σ_a, which is not necessarily something which carries over to the global state σ. This means that Gricean reliability inferences can be carried out as usual—in the present framework, though, they will result in beliefs by default, because of the way aggregation has been defined.

We see, then, that within the system of this book nothing special has to be said at all in order to handle the testimonial paradox. This is a nice result, and further demonstrates the usefulness of the system I have proposed. It allows us to make the fine distinctions needed for a proper analysis of the interaction of testimony, evidence, and evidentials, and the way that all three relate to trust and the new beliefs that result from trust.

9.4 Disclaimed testimony and update

Another question with respect to testimony and its reliability involves testimony which has been disclaimed. Recall the analysis of disclaimers from chapters 3 and 5. The presence of a parenthetical which bears content inducing a pragmatic violation when coupled with assertion triggered a disclamation of that assertion; disclaimed discourse moves were assembled into a separate history from nondisclaimed moves. The nondisclaimed moves (at least) were used to compute speaker reliability. But what should a hearer do with the content of the disclaimed moves? Should they be incorporated into her belief state in some way? Or should they simply be ignored? If they are to be incorporated, how should they be? And what level of reliability should they be assigned? I put these issues aside in chapters 3 and 4, but now is the time to return to them. In answering these questions, I will focus on the case of Quality hedges, as they seem to be the ones that are relevant in worrying about update—whether something is (for example) appropriately uttered in a particular context will not affect whether or not we are right in adding it to our stocks of information, only whether or not it will be worthwhile to do so.

Our answer to the question of whether to update will condition all the others. And the answer quite clearly should be positive. Just because a move is disclaimed doesn't mean it should be completely disregarded. The hedge indicates a lessened degree of speaker confidence in the asserted content, but the speaker still deemed making the assertion to be worthwhile. Given the assumption of cooperativity, it could be worthwhile for two reasons: even though the speaker's confidence is relatively low, it is still high enough that the asserted content was judged sufficiently likely to be true, or the usefulness of the information, if true, is high enough that it ought to be taken into account even if it might turn out to be wrong. In short, the speaker must have judged the utility of gaining the information to be high enough—given its probability of correctness—that the assertion would be of value to the hearer, even though the speaker might find herself in pragmatic trouble as a result of the assertion. All this is easily enough spelled out using utility-theoretic notions of Relevance (Merin 1997; van Rooij 2003b). But if the information is that valuable, it would be foolish for the hearer to ignore it. The result is that, in some form, the disclaimed content should figure in the updates to hearer information states induced by the conversation.

But how? Pretty clearly, the idea of adding them directly to the sub-state associated with the testimony of the speaker doing the disclaiming isn't going to do. Suppose that a is the disclaiming agent, and σ_a is the information state associated with a (which is of course one of the states to be aggregated to yield the global state of the hearer). Let ϕ be the content of the disclaimed move. If we take $\sigma_a[\phi]$, we will treat ϕ on a par with content of a's nondisclaimed utterances; but the whole point of a disclaiming ϕ is to lessen her responsibility for errors about ϕ, which she will only need to worry about if her confidence in ϕ is lower than it would be for "regular" assertions. But given this discrepancy in confidence, it would not serve the hearer well to treat the two kinds of utterance in the same way, which would be the result of adding them to σ_a, given the way that the aggregation process is set up.

So we need a different substate to use for disclaimed utterances. In fact, we need at least two substates for each testimonial agent: one for nondisclaimed content, and one for disclaimed content. I will write these σ_a as before, for nondisclaimed content, and $\sigma_{d(a)}$, for disclaimed content. These two states are updated as usual following the procedure in section 9.2. The place these states take in the preference ordering will depend on the reliability index that is assigned to a, by computing reliability over the history of her prior utterances (plus initial probabilities), and to $d(a)$, by computing reliability over the history of her disclaimed utterances (again, with initial probabilities). Should we take the initial probability of reliability to be the same for each case? It might seem that we should, for we might think that there is no a priori reason to assume that a given speaker is less reliable in disclaimed utterances than otherwise. Still, in general, observation of speaker behavior will likely lead to a lower probability of correctness for disclaimed utterances, given the reasoning in the previous paragraphs. That means that we can expect eventually to end up with a lower probability of truth for disclaimed utterances than nondisclaimed ones, which is what we seem to need. However, the generality of this observation means that experience will lead to a lower setting of probability for disclaimed utterances in general: if observing multiple speakers *always* gives a lower position in the priority hierarchy for $d(a)$ than a, it seems clear that, eventually, the initial priority setting for $d(x)$ should be placed lower than that for x, for newly encountered testimonial agent x. I will therefore take $P(R(d(x)))$ to be $cP(R(x))$ for some constant $0 < c < 1$. Exactly how large c should be is an empirical question which I will not attempt to answer here, and in any case the answer likely differs for each speaker or even class of utterances.

Now we are in a position to say a bit more about how update with disclaimed sentences works, though it is really all implicit in what has been said before. The first step in explicating the update process is to add complexity to information states, which are now to be understood as tuples of sets of worlds and histories, of the form $\Sigma = \langle \sigma, H \rangle$, where σ is an information state of the kind proposed in chapter 7 and elaborated on here, and H is a history of information acquisition events, as defined previously. Update can now be defined in terms of two operations. First, the update proper, which consists of the addition of the content of a sentence to the first element of the information state in the manner specified by (7.14) and (7.24). This operation takes place in conjunction with a second operation of history construction in which the current interaction is appended to the interactional history. The result is of the following form:

(9.3)   Let $\Sigma = \langle \sigma, H_a^{m,g,n} \rangle$. Then $\Sigma[E_i\varphi] = \Sigma' = \langle \sigma[E_i\varphi], H_a^{m,g,n+1} \rangle$.

The result of all this is that it is possible to update σ with disclaimed content, in a way distinct from updating with ordinary testimony. Further, since in general $P(R(d(x))) < P(R(x))$, disclaimed utterances will be given less weight than standard testimony in the process of determining global beliefs, and so will not often override information acquired from other sources. The whole system is thus able to model the complex way in which disclaimers interact with assertion: disclaimed content is asserted in a way which is (in some sense) identical to nondisclaimed content, but the two "kinds" of assertions are processed in different ways and make potentially different contributions to the information states of interpreters. I take it that this is in accord with intuitions.

It is interesting to note that on this view, formally, asserted content and disclaimed assertions *update completely different substates of the information state*. Sentences made with different evidential bases, or marked with distinct evidentials, do precisely the same thing. The result is that, on the theory I have proposed, disclaimers have a function completely parallel to that of evidentials. This might seem counterintuitive, but I think it's actually right: evidentials serve to indicate the basis for an assertion, but they also indirectly indicate the speaker's confidence in that assertion, in the way I described at the end of the last chapter. Disclaimers don't make claims about evidence source, but they also allow conclusions about the speaker's confidence. At the pragmatic level, the result is the same. Thus, at a pragmatic level, disclaimers are in a sense a form of evidential.[14]

Turning back to empirical aspects of the model, it's possible to further articulate this process. Disclamations come in different types, which seem to index different levels of confidence.[15]

(9.4) a. I'm not 100% sure about this, but ...
       b. This might not be quite right, but ...
       c. I only heard this from Jerry and I kind of doubt it's true, but ...

The kind of disclaimer used is going to be indexed in the history tuple. Such tuples, recall, are of the form $i = \langle \varphi, v, \mathcal{P} \rangle$, where $\pi_3(i)$ provides various properties of the utterance and its context. One such property is the kind of disclaimer used.[16] With this observation it becomes possible to classify the disclaimers into different "confidence classes" if desired; for instance, "hard disclaimers" like (9.4c), down to "soft disclaimers" like (9.4a). Each of these can be assigned different levels of confidence, meaning they'll act differently in update.

---

[14] This generalization arises because of the way I have allowed semantics and pragmatics to blur in my analysis; to the extent that the generalization is right and interesting, it supports the direction the analysis has taken.

[15] I thank an anonymous reviewer for pressing this point.

[16] I take this to be part of $\pi_3(i)$ rather than $\pi_1(i)$, the content itself, since on my analysis the disclaimer is not part of what's asserted by a given utterance.

Concretely, suppose that we associate the different disclaimer types with distinct substates and let hard disclaimers update information state $\sigma_{hd(x)}$ and soft disclaimers $\sigma_{sd(x)}$, retaining $\sigma_{d(x)}$ for less specific styles of disclamation. Presumably, the harder the disclaimer, the lower the confidence. This can be modeled by setting the initial probabilities via distinct constants: for hard disclaimers, we let $P(R(hd(x))) = hP(R(x))$ and for soft disclaimers, $P(R(sd(x))) = sP(R(x))$, letting $P(R(d(x))) = cP(R(x))$ as before and imposing the condition that $o < h < c < s < 1$. This probability setting will derive the required initial orderings, and, consequently, the relative strength of the beliefs resulting from update with disclaimed content. If it turns out that further gradations are necessary, they can easily be added. In effect, within this analysis, they are distinct evidentials.

With this analysis, we see the flexibility of this system: the use of priority orderings introduces a means of analyzing what look like continuous phenomena, despite the binary way I've modeled the disclamation process. In chapter 3, hedges were taken to disclaim utterances via introduction of a predicate D: the result was that utterances are either disclaimed or not, a binary distinction. But it does seem that different kinds of disclamations might be available, as shown in (9.4), which might influence global information states in different ways, something which I have shown can be modeled in the full system.

9.5 Conclusion

This chapter has closed the circle on this book. Our discussion began with cooperation and trustworthiness in communication, together with disclaimers, and moved on to consider the reliability of information in general, in the context of evidence and evidentiality. This chapter returned to the special case of communication via testimony and considered it in light of the view of reliability developed in the latter half of the book. As I have shown, the combination of the cooperation model and the reliability model yields a rather specific view of the nature of testimony and how it is used in information update, which allows it to be located in the spectrum of philosophical views on testimony. We saw that the model also succeeds in allowing understanding of three distinct, complex phenomena: evidential testimony, the paradox of belief in testimony including hearsay evidentials, and the function of disclaimed utterances in belief acquisition.

10

Conclusion

In this book I have tried to make a case for the importance of one specific kind of world knowledge for pragmatics. The content of past experience, and of expectations about the future that can be derived from that experience, have not really been looked at in detail in previous work in formal pragmatics. My contention here was that such "historical knowledge" plays a key role in at least two distinct areas.

I started the book with an examination of cooperation, in a Gricean sense. We saw that desire for good outcomes in the future interacts with knowledge of how people behave on the basis of what is known about the past to yield cooperation in the best case. The resulting concerns about one's reputation led, I claimed, to the presence of linguistic mechanisms for protecting reputations, namely various kinds of hedging. After proposing an analysis of the function of truth-oriented hedging within a reputation model, I turned to hedging of other kinds of content that might lead to a speaker being viewed as noncooperative: biscuit conditionals and related phenomena. To the extent that my discussion there was convincing (not to say correct), a pretty strong case has been made for the usefulness of reputational data in pragmatics. I then closed the first part by showing how the nonstandard interpretations of certain clauses required for hedging could be derived through other, relatively standard, pragmatic mechanisms.

The first part of the book, then, concerned itself with one means for assessing the reliability of particular speakers: reputation. The second part applied the same sort of mechanism to general processes of information acquisition through evidence, and how these processes interact with interpretation and utterance choice in the domain of evidentiality. We saw that reliability concerns dictate, to a certain extent, whether a speaker ends up believing the content of a particular utterance; my claim was that the result of an update on global beliefs depends on the presence of conflicting information and the historical reliability of the source from which the information was acquired. After providing a dynamic semantic model of this process, I applied it to a number of outstanding (or at least partly outstanding) questions from the pragmatic theory of evidentiality.

The end of the book, finally, returned to questions of testimony, asking what is really required for a speaker to trust a hearer. Situating my account within the philosophical literature, I showed that it is powerful enough to address many of the questions and puzzles discussed there; though it should be said that my proposal is only one possibility that could be framed within the theoretical framework I have set up in this book. For example, by eliminating initial probabilities of reliability—thus causing all information about reliability to arise from induction over past behavior—we would arrive at a quite different class of defeaters; or by eliminating the move of initial trust, we would come to a purely reductionist theory. But my proposal seems to me the one most in accord with the linguistic facts. We also saw there that the two sets of phenomena I have treated—cooperativity and evidentiality—come together in disclaimers and hedges, which, despite their pragmatic function as reputation protectors, in my analysis ultimately turn out to be a kind of evidential themselves.

The two sets of phenomena I have treated are, from most perspectives, quite dissimilar, but in the sense of dependence on histories they share many features, as I hope the reader has been convinced. To some extent, the mysteries surrounding this foundational issue in pragmatic theory have now, I think, been dissipated.

Still, many such foundational issues remain. Let me here briefly discuss one other, which I take to be close to the topic of this book, and yet which this book has left completely untouched.

In the first part of this book, I discussed a metric for deciding whether an interlocutor is cooperative, given in (3.15): examining their past behavior with respect to whether their utterances track truth in the proper way sufficiently often to exceed some threshold. I used this metric to enable judgements about the reliability of particular speakers and of particular utterances of those speakers. I believe (and have argued through much of this book) that this application is well motivated. But does this concept genuinely model *cooperativity*?

It doesn't seem to. Here are two cases showing that it does not. First, consider an agent who always speaks on topic and says things relevant to the current discussion, but whose utterances are made at random. She is quite willing to say things that are false: indeed, for her, considerations of truth and falsity don't arise at all. But she happens to be correct in what she says a high percentage of the time (say 85%). She would count as reliable, but is she cooperative? Intuitively, I think not. For a second, worse case, imagine an individual who also speaks on topic, but is a compulsive liar and never says what he takes to be the truth. But although he's a compulsive liar, he is terrible at executing the task of lying, and what he means to be lies almost always turn out to be the truth. This agent also counts as reliable in the sense of truth-tracking, but he would not count as cooperative. These are essentially Gettier cases for the truth-tracking view of cooperativity (cf. Gettier 1963).[1]

What these cases point up is the essentially intentional nature of cooperativity. An agent can consistently speak truth, but without the intent to do so she cannot be considered a genuine cooperator. On this basis, it could be argued that the account I have provided here is too reductive due to its purely extensional quality. Since my aim here is to account for judgements about reliability and how it figures into linguistic behavior, I don't think this worry is well founded: my model is intended to give an understanding of how computations of reliability work, and how they play a role in linguistic meaning and practice. But it cannot be denied that there is more to the notion of cooperativity than what I have provided here, or indeed what is really available within the extensional models of game-theoretic pragmatics. There remain many deep questions about cooperativity. The aim of this book has been to show the correspondence of some of these questions to more general issues about the reliability of information, and, in general, to show the usefulness of reasoning about reliability in pragmatics.

---

[1] I don't mean these cases to focus on issues of reliability at all: presumably one wouldn't want to count on the truth of this agent's future utterances either, on the basis of what's come before. These problems about induction I take to be orthogonal to the issue I am raising here.

Appendix
Formal system

This appendix collects the formal apparatus from the book and integrates it into a more explicitly defined dynamic semantic theory. The basic system I am assuming for the dynamic theory in this book is a variant of the propositional model of Veltman (1996), combined with aspects of the dynamic system used for the analysis of evidentiality in McCready and Ogata (2007b) (i.e. the language $L_{E,\triangle,F}$). I call the resulting system *reliability dynamic logic* (RDL) for convenience.

1. **Language.** The set of well-formed formulae (WFF) $\varphi \in RDL$ is defined by the following Backus–Naur Form grammar:

$$\varphi ::= \psi \,|\, E^i_a \varphi \,|\, \triangle^i_a \, \varphi \,|\, H^i_a \varphi \,|\, \neg \varphi \,|\, \varphi_1 \wedge \varphi_2 \,|\, \varphi_1 \Rightarrow \varphi_2$$

where $i \in$ Source $\cup\, \mathcal{A}$ as defined in clause 2.

2. **Models for RDL.** Models for *RDL* are of the form $\mathfrak{M} = \langle W, \mathcal{A}, \text{Source},$ $\preceq_a, \{\preceq_a\}_i, I, T, P\rangle$, where
   (a) W is a set of worlds (individuals),
   (b) $\mathcal{A}$ is a set of agents (individuals), such that W and $\mathcal{A}$ are disjoint,
   (c) Source is a set of source sorts such that

$$\text{Source} = \{tact, aud, internal\_sens, vis, other\_sens, hearsay,$$
$$quot, conc\_inf, inf, gen\_kn, a\}$$

   for $a \in \mathcal{A}$,[1]
   (d) $\preceq_a$ is an ordering on Source $\cup\, \mathcal{A}$,
   (e) $\{\preceq_a\}_i$ is a family of plausibility orderings (for agent $a \in \mathcal{A}$), one for each $i \in$ Source,
   (f) I is the interpretation function $I : WFF \longmapsto \wp(W)$,
   (g) T is a dense totally ordered set of times (points), and
   (h) P is a probability function satisfying the conditions in (2.1).[2]
   See chapters 6 and 7 for details.

3. **Global information states.** Global information states σ in *RDL* are subsets of $\wp(\{X|X \in ES \cup EST\})$ as defined in clauses 3.a and 3.b below, where each element of σ is indexed with $i \in$ Source $\cup\,\mathcal{A}$. These information states

---

[1] The set of sources given in (7.21) is here augmented with agents, following the discussion in chapter 9.
[2] See Appendix A of McCready and Ogata (2007b) for details of the structures required to interpret this function (i.e. probability spaces and σ-algebras), which I redact here.

form the first element $\pi_1(\Sigma)$ of the objects of update Σ defined in clause 10 below (see chapter 8).

(a) Evidential substates $(ES) : \sigma_i = \langle X, \leq_a \rangle$ for $i \notin Rep$, where $X \subseteq W$.

Evidential substates ES are plausibility frames in the sense of Baltag and Smets (2008, 2009): multi-agent Kripke frames $\langle X, R_a \rangle_{a \in \mathcal{A}}$ where the accessibility relations R_a are called "plausibility orders," written $\leq_a$, and assumed to be locally connected preorders. See chapter 7.

(b) Evidential substates for testimonial agents $(EST) : \sigma_a = \{\sigma^j | \exists j E_j^a \varphi\}$ for $a \in \mathcal{A}$.

Evidential substates for testimonial agents EST are sets of those substates associated with an evidence source from which the testimonial agent has acquired information (see chapters 8 and 9).

Note that global information states σ are themselves of EST type.

4. **Priority ordering.** The set of indices $\{i | i \in \mathsf{Source} \cup \mathcal{A} \wedge \exists t < n[E_i^a \varphi(t)]\}$ is ordered by a total ordering $\preceq_a$, where $i \prec j$ iff $P(Rel(i)) < P(Rel(j))$.

5. **Total information states.** Total information states are written σ_T, are of the form $\langle X, \leq_a \rangle$ for $X \in \wp(W)$, and are derived by recursively merging all plausibility relations found in $\sigma_i \in \sigma$ via the lexicographic merge operation defined in 5.a, (see chapter 8). See chapter 7 for the basic idea of total information states, and chapter 9 for a discussion of the operation defined in 5.b.

(a) Lexicographic merge: $R_{a \text{\scriptsize ⋒} b} := R_a^< \cup (R_a^{\cong} \cap R_b) = R_a^< \cup (R_a \cap R_b) = R_a \cap (R_a^< \cup R_b)$.

(b) Total information states: Each information state σ is of the form $\{\sigma_i | i \in \mathsf{Source} \text{ and } \exists t < n[E_i \varphi(t)]\}$. Thus the elements of σ can be ordered according to $\preceq_a$, yielding a sequence $\Pi = \langle \sigma_i, \sigma_j, \ldots, \sigma_n \rangle$ such that $card(\sigma) = n$ and $i \succ_a j$.[3] Call this construction *sequencing*. Let the result of sequencing σ be Π^n of length n. For a recursive step, define $\Pi^{n-1} = \langle \sigma_i, \sigma_j, \ldots, \sigma_{n-1} \text{\scriptsize ⋒} \sigma_n \rangle$. Denote the only element of Π^1 by σ_T; this is the total information state. Call this process *incremental merge*.

Let $\sigma^i \sqsubseteq \sigma$ indicate that σ^i is embedded within σ to a depth of i, where $depth(\sigma) = 0$ and $depth(\sigma_i) = n + 1$ if $depth(\sigma_j) = n$ and $\sigma_i \in \sigma_j$. To ensure that σ contains no elements of EST type, the following procedure is used. Examine σ for states of type EST. If there are no such states, incrementally merge the states in σ. If there are states of EST type, they have depth $n + 1$ if the depth of σ is n. For all states of depth $n + 1$ (call them σ^{n+1} in σ^n of depth n), merge them if they contain no EST states, and if they do, continue to σ^{n+2}. Continue until a state σ^i in which no EST-type elements exist. Let the most deeply embedded σ^i be of depth k with respect to σ and

---

[3] Recall that I assume that all information sources are mutually ordered (see footnote 20, chapter 7).

call it σ_k. Sequence σ_k and call the result of sequencing Π_k^n of length n. Incrementally merge Π_k^n and let $\langle \sigma_K \rangle = \Pi_k^1$. Replace σ_k with σ_K. If there is more than one element of depth k, perform the same operation on each such element. Incrementally merge the elements of σ_{k-1} (which is guaranteed possible since all elements σ_k have been replaced with the corresponding σ_K) and continue until $k = 0$. Since this process applies to all sequences of length $j \geq 0$, σ^0 is guaranteed to contain only objects of ES type, which can then be incrementally merged to form σ_T.

6. **Update.** A definition of RDL update is obtained via a function $[.]$ which for each sentence of the language yields an operation on information states. In the following, $[.]$ is to be understood as the $[.]_\Uparrow$ of Baltag and Smets (2008, 2009), defined as follows.

   (a) $\sigma[\varphi]_\Uparrow = \sigma'$, where $S' = S$ and $s \leq'_a t$ iff either (i) $s \notin \varphi$ and $t \in s(a) \cap \varphi$, or (ii) $s \leq_a t$.

7. **Support and entailment.**

   (a) A total information state $\langle X, \leq_a \rangle$ is said to *support* a proposition φ, $\sigma \models \varphi$, iff $\{s \in X | s \in best_a(s(a))\} \subseteq \phi$, where $best_a\phi := \{s \in \phi | t \leq_a s$ for all $t \in \phi\}$.[4]

   (b) The definition of entailment is the standard fixed-point dynamic one modulo the use of $[.]_\Uparrow$, as defined above (assuming left-association for update):

$$\phi_1, \ldots, \phi_n \models_\sigma \psi \text{ iff } \sigma[\phi_1]\ldots[\phi_n] = \sigma[\phi_1]\ldots[\phi_n][\psi].$$

8. **Dynamic interpretation.** The language defined in clause (1) is interpreted dynamically as follows (note that clause 8.a is identical to the definition of update given in clause 6, because update $[.]$ is generally equated with $[.]_\Uparrow$, as discussed in chapter 7).

   (a) $\sigma[\varphi] = \sigma'$, where $S' = S$ and $s \leq'_a t$ iff either (i) $s \notin \varphi$ and $t \in s(a) \cap \varphi$, or (ii) $s \leq_a t$.

   (b) $\sigma[\neg\varphi] = \sigma - \sigma[\varphi]$

   (c) $\sigma[\varphi \wedge \psi] = (\sigma[\varphi])[\psi]$

   (d) $\sigma[\varphi \Rightarrow \psi] = \begin{cases} \sigma \text{ if } \forall \sigma_i \in \sigma[\text{ if } \sigma_i \models \varphi \text{ then } \sigma_i \models \psi] \\ \varnothing \text{ else} \end{cases}$

   (e) $\sigma[\Diamond\varphi] = \begin{cases} \sigma \text{ if } \varphi \cap best_a(\pi_1(\sigma_T)) \neq \varnothing \\ \varnothing \text{ else} \end{cases}$

   (f) $\sigma[\triangle_i^a \varphi] = \begin{cases} \sigma \text{ if } \begin{array}{l} \text{i) } \sigma \models \Diamond\varphi \text{ and} \\ \text{ii) } \exists i [\sigma_i \models \varphi \, \& \, i \in Inf] \end{array} \\ \varnothing \text{ else} \end{cases}$

---

[4] Note that this is essentially identical to the definition of belief in (7.15).

(g) $\sigma[H_a^i\varphi] = \begin{cases} \sigma \text{ if } \exists i[\sigma_i \models \varphi \ \& \ i \in Rep \cup \mathcal{A}] \\ \varnothing \text{ else} \end{cases}$

Since these definitions are not all given in the main text, some comments are warranted. They follow the discussion in chapters 6 and 7, though they are more formal. The clause for the conditional I include for completeness, not because it has played a substantial role in this book; it is essentially a Ramsey test conditional for multistates. It should also be noted that there is no clause for $E_i^a\psi$; unlike the logic of McCready and Ogata (2007b), the evidential predicate is not interpreted semantically, but only plays a role in the way in which information states are updated.

9. **Evidential update.** Evidential update is defined via the following two clauses (cf. chapter 7).

(a) $\sigma[E_i\varphi] = \sigma'$ where, for all $\sigma_j \in \sigma$, $\begin{cases} \sigma'_j = \sigma_j[\varphi] & \text{if } i = j \\ \sigma'_j = \sigma_j & \text{if } i \neq j \end{cases}$

(b) $\sigma[E_I\varphi] = \sigma'$ where, for all $\sigma_j \in \sigma$, $\begin{cases} \sigma'_j = \sigma_j[\varphi] & \text{if } j \in I \\ \sigma'_j = \sigma_j & \text{if } j \notin I \end{cases}$

In this book, only evidential updates are used, since all observations come indexed with an information source.

10. **Histories.** Histories of moves for a choice point are sequences of the moves made at that choice point; histories of games are sequences of histories of moves. Clause 10.a defines the content of the objects comprising histories (chapter 8), clause 10.b defines how moves are added to histories (chapter 3), clause 10.c defines the role of evidential indices in history construction for the particular case of information-acquiring situations (chapter 8), and clause 10.d defines the function of disclaimers: 10.d.i for nondisclaimed games, and 10.d.ii for disclaimed games (cf. chapter 3).

(a) Form of histories: Elements of histories are of the form $\langle \varphi, v, \mathcal{P} \rangle_i$, where $i \in \mathsf{Source} \cup \mathcal{A}, v \in \{T, F, ?\}$, and $\mathcal{P} \supseteq \{P : P(g_i)\}$ for g_i the instance of information acquisition causing the update.

(b) Given $H_a^{g,n}, H_a^{g,n+1} = \langle act_a^1, \ldots, act_a^n, act_a^{n+1} \rangle$.

(c) Extending histories: Let history $H_a^{g,n}$ be the current move history and have the form $\langle \langle \psi, v, \mathcal{P} \rangle_1, \ldots, \langle \psi, v, \mathcal{P} \rangle_n \rangle$ and suppose that $E_i\varphi$ is observed, with truth value v' and where the relevant conditions are $\mathcal{P}'$. Then $H_a^{g,n+1} = \langle \langle \psi, v, \mathcal{P} \rangle_j, \ldots, \langle \varphi, v', \mathcal{P}' \rangle_i \rangle$.

(d) Disclaimed histories.

   i. If $H_a^{m,g,n} = \langle Hn_a^{m,g,n}, Hd_a^{m,g,n} \rangle$, then $H_a^{m,g,n+1} = \langle Hn_a^{m,g,n+1}, Hd_a^{m,g,n} \rangle$, if $D(g_{n+1})$ does not hold.

   ii. If $H_a^{m,g,n} = \langle Hn_a^{m,g,n}, Hd_a^{m,g,n} \rangle$, then $H_a^{m,g,n+1} = \langle Hn_a^{m,g,n}, Hd_a^{m,g,n+1} \rangle$, if $D(g_{n+1})$.

Note that the definitions of histories are separate from the dynamic logic *RDL* itself.

11. **Update with histories.** The above is brought together into the following definition of update, with corresponding additional complexity of information states (cf. chapter 9).

- Let $\Sigma = \langle \sigma, H_a^{m,g,n} \rangle$. Then $\Sigma[\varphi] = \Sigma' = \langle \sigma[\varphi], H_a^{m,g,n+1} \rangle$.

References

Adler, Jonathan. 2013. Epistemological problems of testimony. In E. N. Zalta, ed., *The Stanford Encyclopedia of Philosophy*. <plato.stanford.edu>. Spring 2013 edn.

Aikhenvald, Alexandra. 2003. Evidentiality in typological perspective. In A. Aikhenvald and R. Dixon, eds., *Studies in Evidentiality*, pages 1–31. Amsterdam: Johns Benjamins.

Aikhenvald, Alexandra. 2004. *Evidentiality*. Oxford: Oxford University Press.

Amaral, Patricia, Craige Roberts, and E. Allyn Smith. 2008. Review of *The Logic of Conventional Implicatures* by Christopher Potts. *Linguistics and Philosophy* 30:707–749.

AnderBois, Scott, Adrian Brasoveanu, and Robert Henderson. 2012. At-issue proposals and appositive impositions in discourse. Manuscript, UCSC and McGill University.

Andreka, H., M. Ryan, and P.-Y. Schobbens. 2002. Operators and laws for combining preference relations. *Journal of Logic and Computation* 12:13–53.

Aoki, Haruo. 1986. Evidentials in Japanese. In W. Chafe and J. Nichols, eds., *Evidentiality: The Linguistic Coding of Epistemology*, pages 223–238. Norwood, NJ: Ablex Publishing Co.

Ariel, Mira. 1990. *Accessing Noun-Phrase Antecedents*. New York: Routledge.

Asher, Nicholas. 1993. *Reference to Abstract Objects in Discourse*. Dordrecht, Reidel: Kluwer.

Asher, Nicholas. 2000. Events, facts, propositions, and evolutive anaphora. In J. Higginbotham, F. Pianesi, and A. Varzi, eds., *Speaking of Events*, pages 123–150. New York: Oxford University Press.

Asher, Nicholas and Alex Lascarides. 2003. *Logics of Conversation*. Cambridge: Cambridge University Press.

Asher, Nicholas and Alex Lascarides. 2013. Strategic conversation. *Semantics and Pragmatics* 6(2):1–62.

Asher, Nicholas and Eric McCready. 2007. Were, would, must and a compositional account of counterfactuals. *Journal of Semantics* 24(2):93–129.

Asher, Nicholas and Eric McCready. 2012. Discourse-Level Politeness and Implicature. In New Frontiers in Artificial Intelligence, no. 8417 in Lecture Notes in Computer Science, Y. Nakano, K. Satoh, and D. Bekki, eds., pages 69–81, Springer.

Asher, Nicholas and Michael Morreau. 1991. Commonsense entailment: a modal theory of nonmonotonic reasoning. In J. Mylopoulos and R. Reiter, eds., *Proceedings of the Twelfth International Joint Conference on Artificial Intelligence*, pages 387–392. Los Altos, CA: Morgan Kaufman.

Audi, Robert. 2002. The sources of knowledge. In Paul K. Moser, ed., *The Oxford Handbook of Epistemology*, pages 71–95. Oxford: Oxford University Press.

Austin, J. L. 1970. Ifs and cans. In *Philosophical Papers*, pages 205–232. Oxford: Clarendon.

Austin, J. L. 1975. *How to Do Things with Words*. Cambridge, MA: Harvard University Press.

Bach, Kent. 1999. The myth of conventional implicature. *Linguistics and Philosophy* 22:327–366.

Bach, Kent. 2006. Review of Christopher Potts, *The Logic of Conventional Implicatures*. *Journal of Linguistics* 42:490–495.

Baltag, Alexandru and Sonja Smets. 2008. A qualitative theory of dynamic belief revision. In G. Bonanno, W. van der Hoek, and M. Wooldridge, eds., *Logic and the Foundations of Game and Decision Theory*. Texts in Logic and Games no. 3, pages 13–60. Amsterdam: Amsterdam University Press.

Baltag, Alexandru and Sonja Smets. 2009. Talking your way into agreement: Belief merge by persuasive communication. In M. Baldoni, C. Baroglio, J. Bentahar et al., eds., *Proceedings of the Second Multi-Agent Logics, Languages, and Organisations Federated Workshops*, volume 494 of *CEUR Workshop Proceedings*, pages 129–141. CEUR-WS.org.

Barker, Chris. 2002. The dynamics of vagueness. *Linguistics and Philosophy* 25(1):1–36.

Beaver, David. 2001. *Presupposition and Assertion in Dynamic Semantics*. Studies in Logic, Language and Information no. 16. Stanford, CA: CSLI/FoLLI.

Beaver, David. 2004. The optimization of discourse anaphora. *Linguistics and Philosophy* 27:3–56.

Belnap, Nuel. 1970. Conditional assertion and restricted quantification. *Noûs* 1:1–12.

Benz, Anton, Gerhard Jäger, and Robert van Rooij, eds. 2006a. *Game Theory and Pragmatics*. Basingstoke: Palgrave.

Benz, Anton, Gerhard Jäger, and Robert van Rooij. 2006b. An introduction to game theory for linguists. In A. Benz, G. Jäger, and R. van Rooij, eds., *Game Theory and Pragmatics*, pages 1–82. Basingstoke: Palgrave.

Binmore, Ken. 1992. *Fun and Games: a Text on Game Theory*. Lexington, MA: D. C. Heath.

Binmore, Ken. 2009. *Rational Decisions*. Princeton: Princeton University Press.

Bittner, Maria. 2011. Time and modality without tenses or modals. In R. Musan and M. Rathert, eds., *Tense across Languages*, pages 147–188. Tübingen: Niemeyer.

Borg, Emma. 2007. *Minimal Semantics*. Oxford: Oxford University Press.

Bowles, Samuel and Herbert Gintis. 2011. *A Cooperative Species: Human Reciprocity and Its Evolution*. Princeton, NJ: Princeton University Press.

Brasoveanu, Adrian. 2007. *Structured Nominal and Modal Reference*. Ph.D. thesis, Rutgers University.

Brown, Jessica and Herman Cappelen, eds. 2011. *Assertion*. Oxford: Oxford University Press.

Brown, Penelope and Stephen Levinson. 1987. *Politeness: Some Universals in Language Usage*. Cambridge: Cambridge University Press.

Burge, Tyler. 1993. Content preservation. *The Philosophical Review* 102(4): 457–488.

Camerer, Colin. 2003. *Behavioral Game Theory*. Princeton, NJ: Princeton University Press.

Cappelen, Herman and Ernest Lepore. 2005. *Insensitive Semantics*. Oxford: Blackwell.

Carlson, Greg and Beverly Spejewski. 1997. Generic passages. *Natural Language Semantics* 5:101–165.

Chafe, Wallace and Johanna Nichols. 1986. Introduction. In W. Chafe and J. Nichols, eds., *Evidentiality: The Linguistic Coding of Epistemology*, pages vii–xi. Norwood: Ablex Publishing Co.

Chellas, Brian. 1980. *Modal Logic*. Cambridge: Cambridge University Press.

Cheney, D. L. and R. M. Seyfarth. 1990. *How Monkeys See the World*. Chicago: University of Chicago Press.

Chierchia, Gennaro. 2004. Scalar implicatures, polarity phenomena, and the syntax/pragmatics interface. In A. Belletti, ed., *Structure and Beyond*, pages 39–103. Oxford: Oxford University Press.

Ciardelli, Ivano and Floris Roelofsen. 2011. Inquisitive logic. *Journal of Philosophical Logic* 40:55–94.

Coady, C. A. J. 1992. *Testimony: A Philosophical Study*. Oxford: Oxford University Press.

Condoravdi, Cleo. 2002. Temporal interpretation of modals. In D. Beaver, L. Casillas Martinez, B. Clark, and S. Kaufmann, eds., *The Construction of Meaning*, pages 59–88. Stanford, CA: CSLI Publications.

Condoravdi, Cleo and Sven Lauer. 2011. Performative verbs and performative acts. In I. Reich, E. Horch, and D. Pauly, eds., *Proceedings of Sinn und Bedeutung 15*, pages 149–164. Saarbrücken: Saarland University Press.

Crawford, Vincent and Joel Sobel. 1982. Strategic information transmission. *Econometrica* 50(6):1431–1451.

Davis, Christopher. 2009. Decisions, dynamics and the Japanese particle *yo*. *Journal of Semantics* 26:329–366.

Davis, Christopher, Christopher Potts, and Peggy Speas. 2007. The pragmatic values of evidential sentences. In M. Gibson and T. Friedman, eds., *Proceedings of SALT 17*, pages 71–88. Fort Washington, PA: CLC Publications.

de Haan, Ferdinand. 1999. Evidentiality and epistemic modality: Setting boundaries. *Southwest Journal of Linguistics* 18:83–101.

del Gobbo, Francesca. 2003. *Appositives at the Interface*. Ph.D. thesis, University of California, Irvine.

Denis, Pascal, Jonas Kuhn, and Stephen Wechsler. 2003. V-PP goal motion complexes in English: an HPSG account. In *Proceedings of the ACL-SIGSEM Workshop: The Linguistic Dimensions of Prepositions...*, pages 121–132. Toulouse, France.

DeRose, Keith. 1991. Epistemic possibilities. *The Philosophical Review* 100(4):581–605.

DeRose, Keith and Richard Grandy. 1999. Conditional assertions and "biscuit" conditionals. *Noûs* 33:405–420.

Egan, Andy. 2006. Epistemic modals, relativism and assertion. *Philosophical Studies* 133:1–22.

Fagin, Ronald and Joseph Halpern. 1988. Belief, awareness, and limited reasoning. *Artificial Intelligence* 34:39–76.

Faller, Martina. 2002a. Remarks on evidential hierarchies. In D. Beaver, L. Casillas Martínez, B. Clark, and S. Kaufmann, eds., *The Construction of Meaning*, pages 89–111. Stanford: CSLI Publications.

Faller, Martina. 2002b. *Semantics and Pragmatics of Evidentials in Cuzco Quechua*. Ph.D. thesis, Stanford University.

Faller, Martina. 2012. Evidential scalar implicatures. *Linguistics and Philosophy* 35:285–312.

Fantl, Jeremy and Matthew McGrath. 2009. *Knowledge in an Uncertain World*. Oxford: Oxford University Press.

Farrell, Joseph. 1993. Meaning and credibility in cheap-talk games. *Games and Economic Behavior* 5(4):514–531.

Farrell, Joseph and Matthew Rabin. 1996. Cheap talk. *Journal of Economic Perspectives* 10:103–118.

Fine, Kit. 1975. Vagueness, truth, and logic. *Synthese* 30:265–300.

Fodor, Jerry. 2000. *The Mind Doesn't Work That Way*. Cambridge, MA: MIT Press.

Francez, Itamar. 2010. Implicit content and chimeric conditionals. Talk given at 6th International Symposium of Cognition, Logic and Communication.

Frank, Annette. 1997. *Context Dependence in Modal Constructions*. Ph.D. thesis, University of Stuttgart.

Franke, Michael. 2007. The pragmatics of biscuit conditionals. In M. Aloni, P. Dekker, and F. Roelofsen, eds., *Proceedings of the 16th Amsterdam Colloquium*, pages 91–96. Amsterdam: Universiteit van Amsterdam.

Franke, Michael. 2009. *Signal to Act: Game Theory in Pragmatics*. Ph.D. thesis, ILLC/University of Amsterdam.

Franke, Michael. 2011. Quantity implicatures, exhaustive interpretation, and rational conversation. *Semantics & Pragmatics* 4(1):1–82.

Fricker, Elizabeth. 1995. Telling and trusting: Reductionism and anti-reductionism in the epistemology of testimony. *Mind* 104:393–411.

Fullam, Karen, Jordi Sabater-Mir, and K. Suzanne Barber. 2004. A design foundation for a trust-modeling experimental testbed. In R. Falcone, S. Barber, J. Sabater-Mir, and M. Singh, eds., *Trusting Agents for Trusting Electronic Societies*, pages 95–109. Berlin: Springer.

Gajewski, Jon. 2002. L-analyticity and natural language. Manuscript, MIT.

Gärdenfors, Peter. 1988. *Knowledge in Flux*. Cambridge, MA: MIT Press.

Gärdenfors, Peter, ed. 1992. *Belief Revision*. Cambridge: Cambridge University Press.

Garrett, Edward. 2001. *Evidentiality and Assertion in Tibetan*. Ph.D. thesis, UCLA.

Gettier, Edmund. 1963. Is justified true belief knowledge? *Analysis* 23:121–123.

Geurts, Bart. 1999. *Presupposition and Pronouns*. Oxford: Elsevier.

Geurts, Bart. 2010. *Quantity Implicatures*. Cambridge: Cambridge University Press.

Gibbard, Allan. 2003. *Thinking How to Live*. Cambridge, MA: Harvard University Press.

Gintis, Herbert. 2000a. *Game Theory Evolving*. Princeton: Princeton University Press.

Gintis, Herbert. 2000b. Strong reciprocity and human society. *Journal of Theoretical Biology* 206:169–179.

Gintis, Herbert. 2009. *The Bounds of Reason: Game Theory and the Unification of the Behavioral Sciences*. Princeton, NJ: Princeton University Press.

Glazer, Jacob and Ariel Rubenstein. 2004. On optimal rules of persuasion. *Econometrica* 72:1715–1736.

Goldberg, Sanford and David Henderson. 2006. Monitoring and anti-reductionism in the epistemology of testimony. *Philosophy and Phenomenological Research* 72:576–593.

Goodman, Nelson. 1955. *Fact, Fiction, and Forecast*. Cambridge, MA: Harvard University Press.

Graham, Peter. 2000. The reliability of testimony. *Philosophy and Phenomenological Research* 61:695–709.

Graham, Peter. 2006a. Liberal fundamentalism and its rivals. In J. Lackey and E. Sosa, eds., *The Epistemology of Testimony*, pages 93–115. Oxford: Oxford University Press.

Graham, Peter J. 2006b. Testimonial justification: Inferential or non-inferential? *The Philosophical Quarterly* 56(222):84–95.

Grice, H. Paul. 1975. Logic and conversation. In P. Cole and J. Morgan, eds., *Syntax and Semantics III: Speech Acts*, pages 41–58. New York: Academic Press.

Groenendijk, Jeroen and Martin Stokhof. 1991. Dynamic predicate logic. *Linguistics and Philosophy* 14:39–100.

Grosu, Alexandru and Manfred Krifka. 2007. *The Gifted Mathematician that You Claim to Be*: equational intensional "reconstruction" relatives. *Linguistics and Philosophy* 30:445–485.

Gunlogson, Christine. 2003. *True to Form: Rising and Falling Declaratives as Questions in English*. Outstanding Dissertations in Linguistics. New York: Routledge.

Gutzmann, Daniel. 2008. *On the Interaction of Modal Particles and Sentence Mood in German*. MA Thesis, University of Mainz.

Gutzmann, Daniel. 2012. *Use-Conditional Meaning: Studies in Multidimensional Semantics*. Ph.D. thesis, Universität Frankfurt.

Gutzmann, Daniel and Eric McCready. 2013. Using descriptions. In press for *Empirical Issues in Syntax and Semantics* 16.

Halpern, Joseph Y. 2003. *Reasoning about Uncertainty*. Cambridge, MA: MIT Press.

Hamilton, W. D. 1963. The evolution of altruistic behavior. *American Naturalist* 97:354–356.

Hamilton, W. D. 1964. The genetical evolution of social behavior. *Journal of Theoretical Biology* 7:1–16.

Hammes, David L. 2008. Pareto efficiency. In R. W. Kolb, ed., *Encyclopedia of Business Ethics and Society*, pages 1563–1566. London: SAGE Publications, Inc.

Hansson, Sven Ove. 2011. Logic of belief revision. In E. N. Zalta, ed., *The Stanford Encyclopedia of Philosophy*. <http://plato.stanford.edu>. Fall 2011 edn.

Harris, Paul L. and Kathleen H. Corriveau. 2011. Young children's selective trust in informants. *Philosophical Transactions of the Royal Society B: Biological Sciences* 366(1567):1179–1187.

Hawthorne, John. 2004. *Knowledge and Lotteries*. Oxford: Oxford University Press.

Heim, Irene. 1983. On the projection problem for presuppositions. In M. Barlow, D. Flickinger, and M. Westcoat, eds., *Second Annual Proceedings of the West Coast Conference on Formal Linguistics*, pages 114–126. Stanford, CA: Stanford University.

Heim, Irene. 1988. *The Semantics of Definite and Indefinite Noun Phrases*. Outstanding Dissertations in Linguistics. New York: Garland. [1982 doctoral dissertation.]

Heim, Irene. 1992. Presupposition projection and the semantics of attitude verbs. *Journal of Semantics* 9:183–221.

Heringa, Herman. 2012. *Appositional Constructions*. Ph.D. thesis, Utrecht.

Holliday, Wesley H. 2010. Trust and the dynamics of testimony. In D. Grossi, L. Kurzen, and F. Velázquez-Quesada, eds., *Logic and Interactive Rationality*, pages 147–178. Amsterdam: ILLC, Universiteit van Amsterdam.

Hume, David. 1977. *An Enquiry Concerning Human Understanding*. Cambridge, MA: Hackett. [First published 1748.]

Iatridou, Sabine. 1991. *Topics in Conditionals*. Ph.D. thesis, MIT.

Isaacs, James and Kyle Rawlins. 2008. Conditional questions. *Journal of Semantics* 25:269–319.

Jackson, Frank. 1977. *Perception: A Representative Theory*. Cambridge: Cambridge University Press.

Jeffrey, Richard. 1983. *The Logic of Decision*. Chicago: University of Chicago Press.

Kalenbock, Gunther, Wiltrud Mitasch, and Stefan Schneider, eds. 2010. *New Approaches to Hedging*. Studies in Pragmatics. Bingley, UK: Emerald Group Publishing.

Kamp, H. 1981. A theory of truth and semantic representation. In J. A. G. Groenendijk, T. M. V. Janssen, and M. B. J. Stokhof, eds., *Formal Methods in Study of Languages*, pages 277–322. Amsterdam: Mathematical Centre Tracts.

Kamp, Hans and Uwe Reyle. 1993. *From Discourse to Logic*. Dordrecht, Reidel: Kluwer.

Kaplan, David. 1989. Demonstratives. In J. Almog, J. Perry, and H. Wettstein, eds., *Themes from Kaplan*, pages 481–566. Oxford: Oxford University Press. [Manuscript version from 1977.]

Kaplan, David. 1999. The meaning of ouch and oops: Explorations in the theory of *meaning as use*. Manuscript, UCLA.

Karttunen, Lauri. 1976. Discourse referents. In J. McCawley, ed., *Syntax and Semantics 7*, pages 363–386. New York: Academic Press. [Previously distributed by Indiana University Linguistics Club, 1971.]

Kaufmann, Magdalena and Eric McCready. 2008. Intensifiers. Paper presented at Deutsche Gesellschaft für Sprachwissenschaft.

Kehler, Andrew. 2001. *Coherence, Reference and the Theory of Grammar*. Stanford, CA: CSLI Publications.

Kennedy, Chris. 1999. *Projecting the Adjective*. New York: Garland. [1997 UCSC dissertation.]

Kennedy, Chris. 2007. Vagueness and gradability: The semantics of relative and absolute gradable predicates. *Linguistics and Philosophy* 30(1):1–45.

Klein, Ewan. 1980. A semantics for positive and comparative adjectives. *Linguistics and Philosophy* 4:1–45.

Kratzer, Angelika. 1981. The notional category of Modality. In H.-J. Eikmeyer and H. Rieser, eds., *Words, Worlds, and Contexts: New Approaches in Word Semantics*. Research in Text Theory no. 6, pages 38–74. Berlin: de Gruyter.

Krebs, J. R. and N. B. Davies. 1993. *An Introduction to Behavioral Ecology*, 3rd edition. Oxford: Blackwell.

Kreps, David. 1990. *Game Theory and Economic Modelling*. Clarendon Lectures in Economics. Oxford: Clarendon.

Krifka, Manfred. 2001. Quantifying into question acts. *Natural Language Semantics* 9:1–40.

Krifka, Manfred. 2011. Embedding speech acts. Manuscript, Humboldt University.

Kulkarni, Sanjeev and Gilbert Harman. 2011. *An Elementary Introduction to Statistical Learning Theory*. Hoboken, NJ: Wiley.

Lackey, Jennifer. 2008. *Learning from Words: Testimony as a Source of Knowledge*. Oxford: Oxford University Press.

Lakoff, George. 1973. Hedges: A study in meaning criteria and the logic of fuzzy concepts. *Journal of Philosophical Logic* 2:458–508.

Le, Stephen and Robert Boyd. 2007. Evolutionary dynamics of the continuous iterated prisoner's dilemma. *Journal of Theoretical Biology* 245:258–267.

Levinson, Stephen. 2000. *Presumptive Meanings*. Cambridge, MA: MIT Press.

Lewis, David. 1969. *Convention*. Cambridge, MA: Harvard University Press.

Lewis, David. 1973. *Counterfactuals*. Oxford: Basil Blackwell.

Lewis, David. 1976. Probabilities of conditionals and conditional probabilities. *Philosophical Review* 85:297–315.

Lewis, David. 1979. Scorekeeping in a language game. In R. Bäuerle, U. Egli, and A. von Stechow, eds., *Semantics from Different Points of View*, pages 172–187. Berlin: Springer.

McCready, Eric. 2004. Two Japanese adverbials and expressive content. In R. Young, ed., *Proceedings of SALT XIV*, pages 163–178. Fort Washington, PA: CLC Publications.

McCready, Eric. 2005. *The Dynamics of Particles*. Ph.D. thesis, University of Texas at Austin.

McCready, Eric. 2007. Context shifting in questions and elsewhere. In E. Puig-Waldmüller, ed., *Proceedings of Sinn und Bedeutung 11*, pages 433–447. Barcelona: Universitat Pompeu Fabra.

McCready, Eric. 2008a. Evidentials, knowledge and belief. In Y. Nakayama, ed., *Proceedings of LENLS 5*. Tokyo: JSAI.

McCready, Eric. 2008b. Particles, modality and coherence. In A. Grønn, ed., *Proceedings of Sinn und Bedeutung 12*, pages 430–441. Oslo: ILOS Publications.

McCready, Eric. 2008c. Semantic heterogeneity in evidentials. In K. Satoh, A. Inokuchi, K. Nagao, and T. Kawamura, eds., *New Frontiers in Artificial Intelligence: JSAI 2007 Conference and Workshops Revised Selected Papers*. Lecture Notes in Computer Science no. 4914, pages 81–94. Berlin: Springer.

McCready, Eric. 2008d. Unnatural kinds. *Journal of Pragmatics* 40(10): 1817–1822.

McCready, Eric. 2010a. Evidential universals. In T. Peterson and U. Sauerland, eds., *Evidentials and Evidence*, volume 28 of *UBC Working Papers in Linguistics*, pages 105–128. Vancouver: University of British Columbia.

McCready, Eric. 2010b. Interest-relative pragmatics. Manuscript, Aoyama Gakuin University.

McCready, Eric. 2010c. Varieties of conventional implicature. *Semantics and Pragmatics* 3:1–57.

McCready, Eric. 2012a. Emotive equilibria. *Linguistics and Philosophy* 35: 243–283.

McCready, Eric. 2012b. How to coordinate on pragmatic content. *Sprache und Datenverarbeitung* 2/1:137–149.

McCready, Eric. 2014. *Formal Semantics and Pragmatics: Japanese and Beyond*. E. McCready, K. Yabushita, K. Yoshimoto, eds., pages 155–180, Springer.

McCready, Eric. Forthcoming, a. Testimony, trust, and evidentials. In Chung-Min Lee and Jinho Park, eds., *Evidentials and Modals*. Leiden: Brill.

McCready, Eric. Forthcoming, b. Determining questions. In *Proceedings of Texas Linguistics Society 13*.

McCready, Eric and Nicholas Asher. 2006. Modal subordination in Japanese: Dynamics and evidentiality. In A. Eilam, T. Scheffler, and J. Tauberer, eds., *Penn Working Papers in Linguistics 12.1*, pages 237–249. Philadelphia: Department of Linguistics, University of Pennsylvania.

McCready, Eric and Norry Ogata. 2007a. Adjectives, comparison and stereotypicality. *Natural Language Semantics* 15(1):35–63.

McCready, Eric and Norry Ogata. 2007b. Evidentiality, modality, and probability. *Linguistics and Philosophy* 30(2):147–206.

McElreath, Richard and Robert Boyd. 2007. *Mathematical Models of Social Evolution*. University of Chicago Press.

MacFarlane, John. 2011. Epistemic modals are assessment-sensitive. In B. Weatherson and A. Egan, eds., *Epistemic Modality*, pages 144–178. Oxford: Oxford University Press.

Mailath, George and Larry Samuelson. 2006. *Repeated Games and Reputations: Long-Run Relationships*. Oxford: Oxford University Press.

Masuoka, Takashi and Yukinori Takubo. 1989. *Kisoo Nihongo Bunpoo* [Essential Japanese Grammar]. Tokyo: Kuroshio Shuppan.

Matthewson, Lisa. Forthcoming. Evidence type, evidence location, evidence strength. In Chungmin Lee and Jinho Park, eds., *Evidentials and Modals*. Leiden: Brill.

Matthewson, Lisa, Hotze Rullmann, and Henry Davis. 2007. Evidentials as epistemic modals: Evidence from St'át'imcets. In J. van Craenenbroeck, ed., *Linguistic Variation Yearbook 2007*, pages 201–254. Amsterdam: John Benjamins.

Maynard Smith, John. 1964. Group selection and kin selection. *Nature* 201:1145–1147.

Maynard Smith, John and David Harper. 2003. *Animal Signals*. Oxford: Oxford University Press.

Maynard-Zhang, Pedrito and Daniel Lehmann. 2003. Representing and aggregating conflicting beliefs. *Journal of Artificial Intelligence Research* 19: 155–203.

Merin, Arthur. 1997. If all our arguments had to be conclusive, there would be few of them. Arbeitspapiere SFB 340 101, Universität Stuttgart.

Mitchell, Jonathan. 1986. *The Formal Semantics of Point of View*. Ph.D. thesis, University of Massachusetts at Amherst.

Mithun, Marianne. 1986. Evidential diachrony in Northern Iroquoian. In W. Chafe and J. Nichols, eds., *Evidentiality: The Linguistic Coding of Epistemology*, pages 89–112. New Jersey: Ablex.

Miyara, Shinsho. 2002. Okinawa chuubu hoogen no modariti. *Gengo Kenkyu* 122:79–112.

Moore, G. E. 1952. Reply to my critics. In P. Schilpp, ed., *The Philosophy of G. E. Moore*, pages 533–687. New York: Tudor.

Murray, Sarah. 2010. *Evidentiality and the Structure of Speech Acts*. Ph.D. thesis, Rutgers.

Muskens, Reinhard, Johan van Benthem, and Albert Visser. 1997. Dynamics. In J. van Benthem and A. ter Meulen, eds., *Handbook of Logic and Language*, pages 587–648. Amsterdam: Elsevier.

Myerson, Roger. 1991. *Game Theory: Analysis of Conflict*. Cambridge, MA: Harvard University Press.

Naughton, Martina, Nicola Stokes, and Joe Carthy. 2010. Sentence-level event classification in unstructured texts. *Information Retrieval* 13(2):132–156.

Nitzan, Shmuel. 2009. *Collective Preference and Choice*. Cambridge: Cambridge University Press.

Nouwen, Rick. 2007. On appositives and dynamic binding. *Research on Language and Computation* 5:87–102.

Nowak, Martin. 2006. *Evolutionary Dynamics*. Cambridge, MA: Belknap Press.

Nowak, Martin and Karl Sigmund. 1998a. The dynamics of indirect reciprocity. *Journal of Theoretical Biology* 194:561–574.

Nowak, Martin and Karl Sigmund. 1998b. Evolution of indirect reciprocity by image scoring. *Nature* 393:573–577.

Nute, Donald. 1994. Defeasible logic. In D. Gabbay and C. Hogger, eds., *Handbook of Logic for Artificial Intelligence and Logic Programming*, volume 3, pages 353–395. Oxford: Oxford University Press.

Ochs (Keenan), Elinor. 1976. The universality of conversational postulates. *Language in Society* 5:67–80.

Ohtsuki, Hisashi and Yoh Iwasa. 2004. How should we define goodness?— Reputation dynamics in indirect reciprocity. *Journal of Theoretical Biology* 231:107–120.

Okasha, Samir. 2006. *Evolution and the Levels of Selection*. Oxford: Oxford University Press.

Olsson, Erik. 2005. *Against Coherence: Truth, Probability, and Justification*. Oxford: Oxford University Press.

Parikh, P. 2001. *The Use of Language*. Stanford, CA: CSLI Publications.

Parikh, Prashant. 2010. *Language and Equilibrium*. Cambridge, MA: MIT Press.

Perry, John. 1979. The problem of the essential indexical. *Noûs* 13:3–21.

Pollock, John and Joseph Cruz. 1999. *Contemporary Theories of Knowledge*. Lanham, MD: Rowman Littlefield.

Portner, Paul. 2009. *Modality*. Oxford: Oxford University Press.

Potts, Christopher. 2005. *The Logic of Conventional Implicatures*. Oxford: Oxford University Press. [Revised version of 2003 UCSC dissertation.]

Potts, Christopher. 2006. Clausal implicatures via general pragmatic pressures. In T. Washio, A. Sakurai, K. Nakajima, H. Takeda, S. Tojo, and M. Yokoo, eds., *Japanese Society for Artificial Intelligence 2006*, pages 205–218. Berlin: Springer.

Potts, Christopher. 2007. The expressive dimension. *Theoretical Linguistics* 33:165–198.

Potts, Christopher, Luis Alonso-Ovalle, Ash Asudeh, Rajesh Bhatt, Seth Cable, Christopher Davis, Yurie Hara, Angelika Kratzer, Eric McCready, Tom Roeper, and Martin Walkow. 2009. Expressives and identity conditions. *Linguistic Inquiry* 40:356–366.

Predelli, Stefano. 2003. *Contexts*. Oxford: Oxford University Press.

Predelli, Stefano. 2009. Towards a semantics for biscuit conditionals. *Philosophical Studies* 142:293–305.

Predelli, Stefano. 2013. *Meaning Without Truth*. Oxford: Oxford University Press.

Prince, Ellen F. 1982. Grice and universality: a reappraisal. Manuscript, University of Pennsylvania.

Prince, Ellen, C. Bosk, and J. Frader. 1982. Hedging in physician–physician discourse. In J. di Pietro, ed., *Linguistics and the Professions*, pages 83–97. New York: Ablex.

Quine, Willard Van Orman. 1960. *Word and Object*. Cambridge: The MIT Press.

Rabin, M. 1990. Communication between rational agents. *Journal of Economic Theory* 51:144–170.

Reid, Thomas. 1997. *An Inquiry into the Human Mind on the Principles of Common Sense*. Edinburgh: Edinburgh University Press. [Originally published 1764.]

Reiter, Raymond and Giovanni Criscuolo. 1981. On interacting defaults. In *Proceedings of the 7th International Joint Conference on Artificial Intelligence*, volume 1, pages 270–276. San Francisco, CA: Morgan Kaufmann Publishers Inc.

Rett, Jessica. 2008. *Degree Modification in Natural Language*. Ph.D. thesis, Rutgers.

Richard, Mark. 2008. *When Truth Gives Out*. Oxford: Oxford University Press.

Roberts, Craige. 1989. Modal subordination and pronominal anaphora in discourse. *Linguistics and Philosophy* 12:683–721.

Roberts, Craige. 2012. Information structure: Towards an integrated formal theory of pragmatics. *Semantics and Pragmatics* 5(6):1–69.

Saul, J. 2012. *Lying, Misleading, and What is Said: An Exploration in Philosophy of Language and in Ethics*. Oxford: Oxford University Press.

Schlenker, Philippe. 2007. Expressive presuppositions. *Theoretical Linguistics* 33:237–246.

Schlenker, Philippe. 2009. Local contexts. *Semantics and Pragmatics* 2(3):1–78.

Schulz, Katrin and Robert van Rooij. 2006. Pragmatic meaning and non-monotonic reasoning: The case of exhaustive interpretation. *Linguistics and Philosophy* 29:205–250.

Searle, John. 1969. *Speech Acts*. Cambridge: Cambridge University Press.

Selten, Reinhard and Rolf Stoecker. 1986. End behavior in sequences of finite prisoner's dilemma supergames. *Journal of Economic Behavior and Organization* 7:47–70.

Shan, Chung-Chieh. 2005. *Linguistic Side Effects*. Ph.D. thesis, Harvard.

Shinmura, Izuru, ed. 2008. *Kojien*. 6th edition. Tokyo: Iwanami.

Siegel, Muffy E. A. 2006. Biscuit conditionals: Quantification over potential literal acts. *Linguistics and Philosophy* 29(2):167–203.

Simons, Mandy, Judith Tonhauser, David Beaver, and Craige Roberts. 2011. What projects and why. In Nan Li and David Lutz, eds., *Proceedings of SALT 20*, pages 309–327. Fort Washington, PA: CLC Publications.

Skyrms, Brian. 1996. *The Evolution of the Social Contract*. Cambridge: Cambridge University Press.

Skyrms, B. 2004. *The Stag Hunt and the Evolution of Social Structure*. Cambridge: Cambridge University Press.

Sobel, Joel. 2012. Signaling games. In M. Sotomayor, ed., *Computational Complexity*, pages 2830–2844. New York: Springer.

Sober, Elliot and David Sloan Wilson. 1999. *Unto Others: The Evolution and Psychology of Unselfish Behavior*. Cambridge, MA: Harvard University Press.

Sorensen, Roy. 2006. Sharp edges from hedges: Fatalism, vagueness and epistemic possibility. *Philosophical Studies* 131:607–626.

Sperber, Dan, Fabrice Clémeant, Christophe Heintz, Olivier Mascaro, Hugo Mercier, Gloria Origgi, and Deirdre Wilson. 2010. Epistemic vigilance. *Mind & Language* 25:359–393.

Sperber, D. and D. Wilson. 1986. *Relevance*. Oxford: Blackwells.

Stalnaker, Robert. 1984. *Inquiry*. Cambridge, MA: MIT Press.

Stalnaker, Robert. 1999. Assertion. In *Context and Content*, pages 78–95. Oxford: Oxford University Press. (Orig. pub. 1979.)

Stalnaker, Robert. 2008. *Our Knowledge of the Internal World*. Oxford: Oxford University Press.

Stanley, Jason. 2005. *Knowledge and Practical Interests*. Oxford: Oxford University Press.

Stanley, Jason and Zoltan Szabo. 2000. On quantifier domain restriction. *Mind and Language* 15:219–261.

Stephenson, Tamina. 2007. Judge dependence, epistemic modals, and predicates of personal taste. *Linguistics and Philosophy* 30(4):487–525.

Street, John. 1963. *Khalkha Structure*. Bloomington: Indiana University Press.

Swanson, Eric. 2010. Lessons from the context sensitivity of causal talk. *Journal of Philosophy* 107(5):221–242.

Swanson, Eric. 2013. Subjunctive biscuit and stand-off conditionals. *Philosophical Studies* 163(3):637–648.

Szabo Gendler, Tamar. 2008a. Alief and belief. *Journal of Philosophy* 105(10): 634–663.

Szabo Gendler, Tamar. 2008b. Alief in action (and reaction). *Mind and Language* 23:552–585.

Tomasello, Michael. 2008. *The Origins of Linguistic Communication*. Cambridge, MA: MIT Press.

Umbach, Carla. 2004. On the notion of contrast in information structure and discourse structure. *Journal of Semantics* 21(2):155–175.

van Benthem, Johan. 2007. Dynamic logic for belief revision. *Journal of Applied Non-Classical Logics* 17(2):129–155.

van Benthem, Johan and Eric Pacuit. 2011. Dynamic logics of evidence-based beliefs. *Studia Logica* 99:61–92.

van Cleve, James. 2006. Reid on the credit of human testimony. In J. Lackey and E. Sosa, eds., *The Epistemology of Testimony*, pages 50–74. Oxford: Oxford University Press.

van der Sandt, Rob. 1992. Presupposition projection as anaphora resolution. *Journal of Semantics* 9:333–377.

van Leusen, Noor. 2004. Incompatibility in context: A diagnosis of correction. *Journal of Semantics* 21:415–441.

van Rooij, Robert. 2003a. Being polite is a handicap: Towards a game theoretic analysis of polite linguistic behavior. In M. Tenneholz, ed., *Proceedings of Theoretical Aspects of Rationality and Knowledge 9*. Bloomington: Indiana University.

van Rooij, Robert. 2003b. Quality and quantity of information exchange. *Journal of Logic, Language and Information* 12:423–451.

van Rooij, Robert. 2003c. Questioning to resolve decision problems. *Linguistics and Philosophy* 26:727–763.

van Rooij, Robert. 2004. Signalling games select Horn strategies. *Linguistics and Philosophy* 27:493–527.

van Rooij, Robert. 2005. A modal analysis of presupposition and modal subordination. *Journal of Semantics*, 22(3):281–305.

van Rooij, Robert. 2008. Game theory and quantity implicatures. *Journal of Economic Methodology* 15(3):261–274.

van Rooij, Robert and Katrin Schulz. 2010. Nonmonotonic reasoning in interpretation. In J. van Benthem and A. ter Meulen, eds., *Handbook of Logic and Language*, pages 839–853. Amsterdam: Elsevier. Second edition.

Vanderveken, Daniel. 1990. *Meaning and Speech Acts*. Cambridge: Cambridge University Press. In 2 volumes.

Veltman, Frank. 1996. Defaults in update semantics. *Journal of Philosophical Logic* 25:221–261.

von Fintel, Kai and Thony Gillies. 2008a. CIA leaks. *The Philosophical Review* 117:77–98.

von Fintel, Kai and Thony Gillies. 2008b. Must . . . stay . . . strong. Manuscript, MIT and University of Michigan.

von Fintel, Kai, Irene Heim, and Angelika Kratzer. 2004. Notes on intensional semantics. Manuscript, MIT and University of Massachusetts at Amherst.

Wang, Linton, Richard Hou, and Eric McCready. 2012. Epistemic modality. Manuscript, University of Texas at Austin/Aoyama Gakuin University/National Chung Cheng University.

Wang, Linton, Eric McCready, and Brian Reese. 2006. Nominal appositives in context. In M. Temkin Martínez, A. Alcázar, and R. Mayoral Hernández, eds., *Proceedings of WECOL 33*, pages 411–423. Fresno: Department of Linguistics, California State University.

Wang, Linton, Brian Reese, and Eric McCready. 2005. The projection problem of nominal appositives. *Snippets* 11:13–14.

Weatherson, Brian and Andy Egan, eds. 2011a. *Epistemic Modality*. Oxford: Oxford University Press.

Weatherson, Brian and Andy Egan. 2011b. Epistemic modals and epistemic modality. In B. Weatherson and A. Egan, eds., *Epistemic Modality*. Oxford University Press.

Wechsler, Stephen and Eric McCready. 2011. Why you and I are so special. Paper presented at University of Texas at Austin.

Willett, Thomas. 1988. A cross-linguistic survey of the grammaticalization of evidentiality. *Studies in Language* 12:51–97.

Williamson, Timothy. 2000. *Knowledge and its Limits*. Oxford: Oxford University Press.

Williamson, Timothy. 2009. Reference, inference and the semantics of pejoratives. In J. Almog and P. Leonardi, eds., *The Philosophy of David Kaplan*, pages 137–159. Oxford: Oxford University Press.

Winterstein, Gregoire. 2012. What *but*-sentences argue for: a modern argumentative analysis of *but*. *Lingua* 122:1787–1800.

Wittgenstein, Ludwig. 1991. *On Certainty*. Oxford: Blackwell.

Yalcin, Seth. 2007. Epistemic modals. *Mind* 116:983–1026.

Yalcin, Seth. 2012. Bayesian expressivism. *Proceedings of the Aristotelian Society* 112:123–160.

Zanuttini, Raffaella and Paul Portner. 2003. Exclamative clauses at the syntax-semantics interface. *Language* 79(1):39–81.

Index